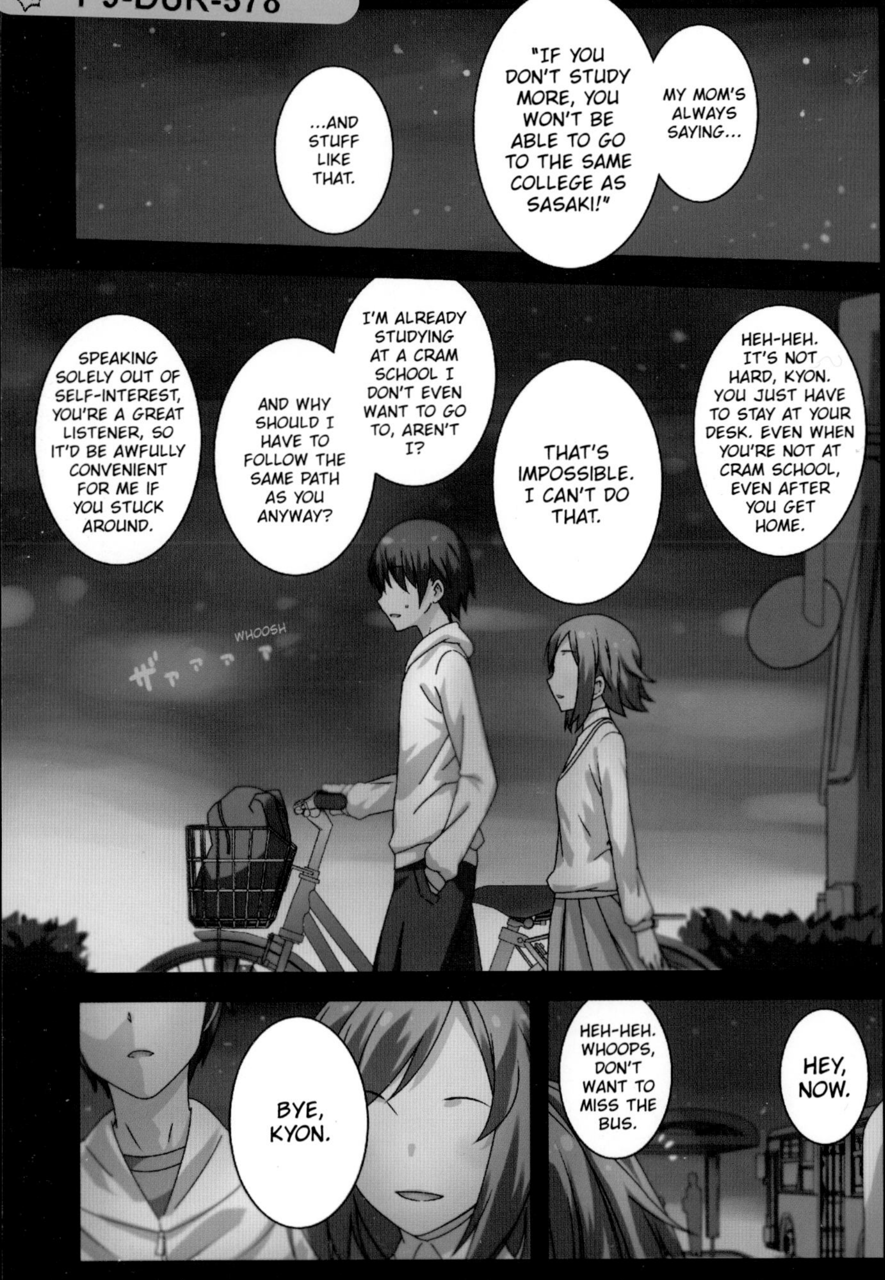
MY MOM'S ALWAYS SAYING...
"IF YOU DON'T STUDY MORE, YOU WON'T BE ABLE TO GO TO THE SAME COLLEGE AS SASAKI!"
...AND STUFF LIKE THAT.
HEH-HEH. IT'S NOT HARD, KYON. YOU JUST HAVE TO STAY AT YOUR DESK. EVEN WHEN YOU'RE NOT AT CRAM SCHOOL, EVEN AFTER YOU GET HOME.
THAT'S IMPOSSIBLE. I CAN'T DO THAT.
I'M ALREADY STUDYING AT A CRAM SCHOOL I DON'T EVEN WANT TO GO TO, AREN'T I?
AND WHY SHOULD I HAVE TO FOLLOW THE SAME PATH AS YOU ANYWAY?
SPEAKING SOLELY OUT OF SELF-INTEREST, YOU'RE A GREAT LISTENER, SO IT'D BE AWFULLY CONVENIENT FOR ME IF YOU STUCK AROUND.
WHOOSH
HEY, NOW.
HEH-HEH. WHOOPS, DON'T WANT TO MISS THE BUS.
BYE, KYON.

Epilogue 40>>

Self-Introduction

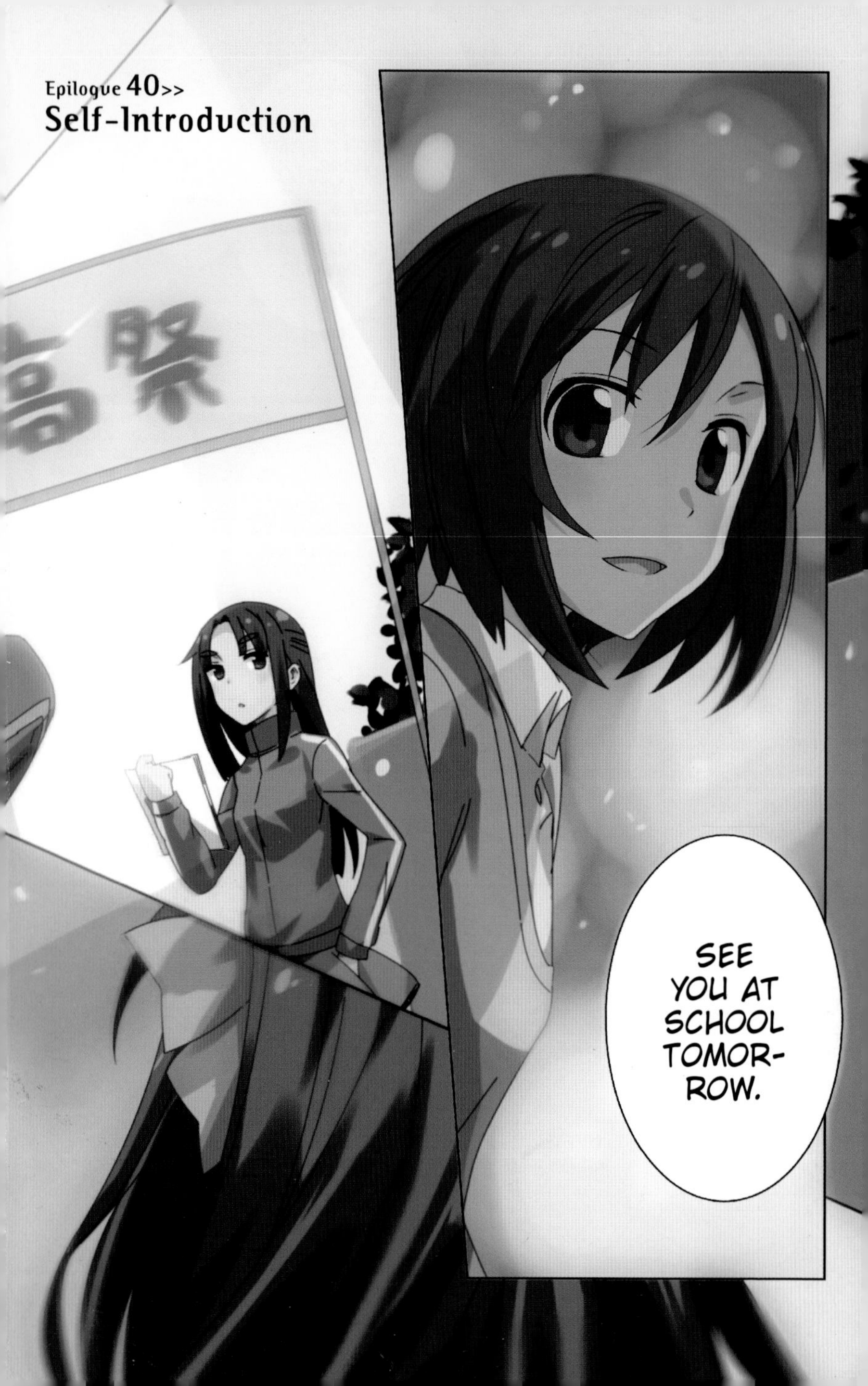
SEE YOU AT SCHOOL TOMOR-ROW.

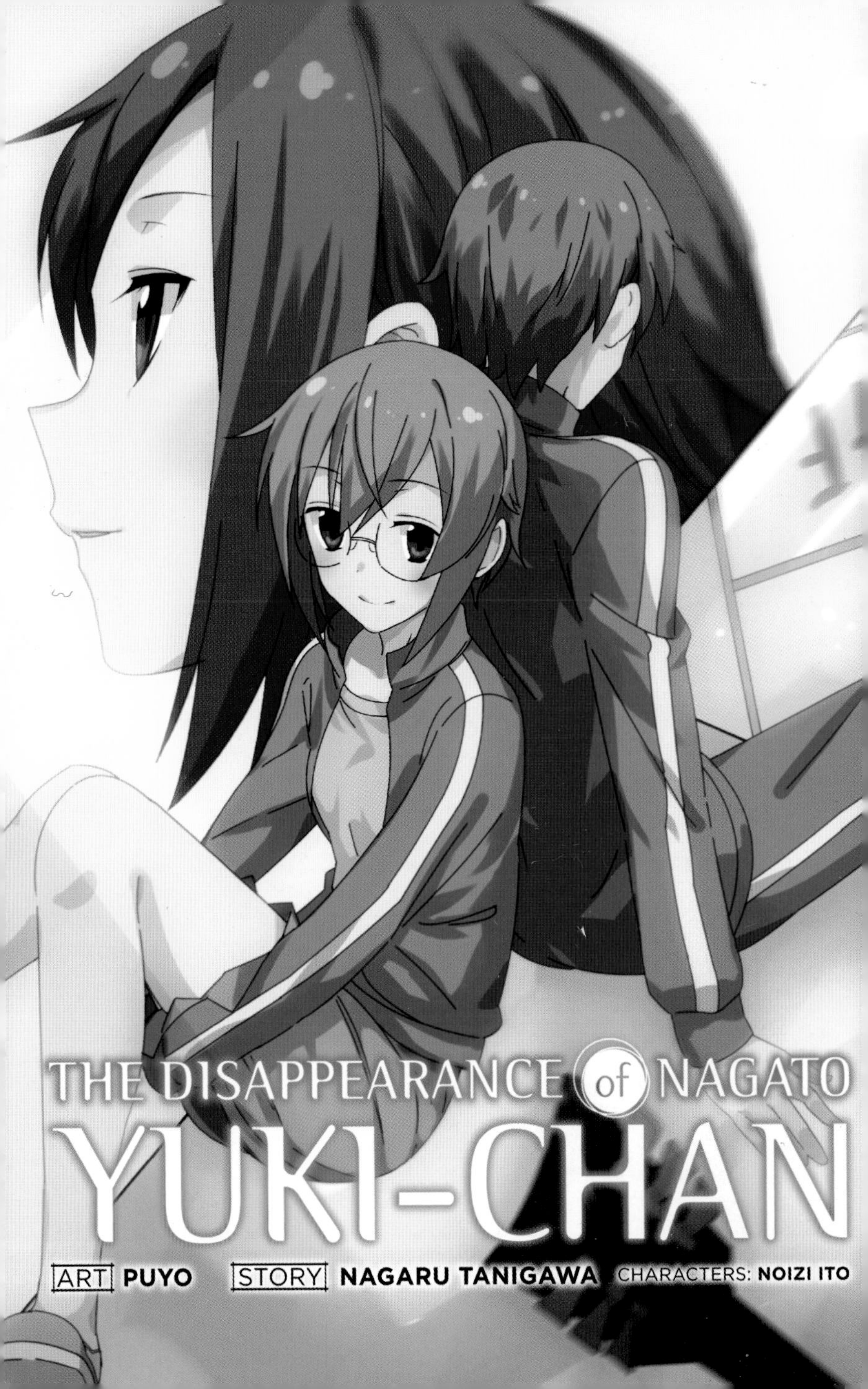
THE DISAPPEARANCE of NAGATO
YUKI-CHAN
ART PUYO
STORY NAGARU TANIGAWA
CHARACTERS: NOIZI ITO

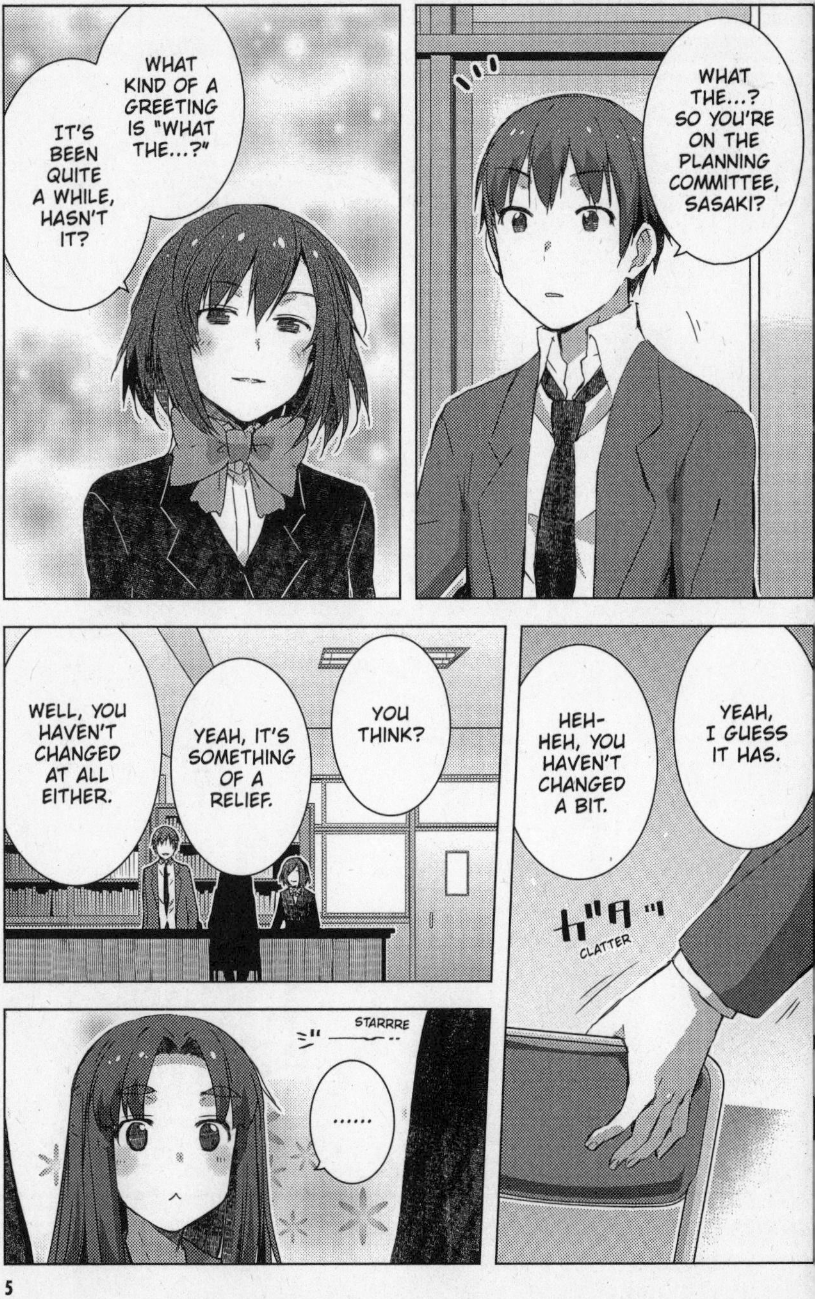
WHAT THE...? SO YOU'RE ON THE PLANNING COMMITTEE, SASAKI?
WHAT KIND OF A GREETING IS "WHAT THE...?"
IT'S BEEN QUITE A WHILE, HASN'T IT?
YEAH, I GUESS IT HAS.
HEH-HEH, YOU HAVEN'T CHANGED A BIT.
ガタッ
CLATTER
YOU THINK?
YEAH, IT'S SOMETHING OF A RELIEF.
WELL, YOU HAVEN'T CHANGED AT ALL EITHER.
ジー
STARRRE
......

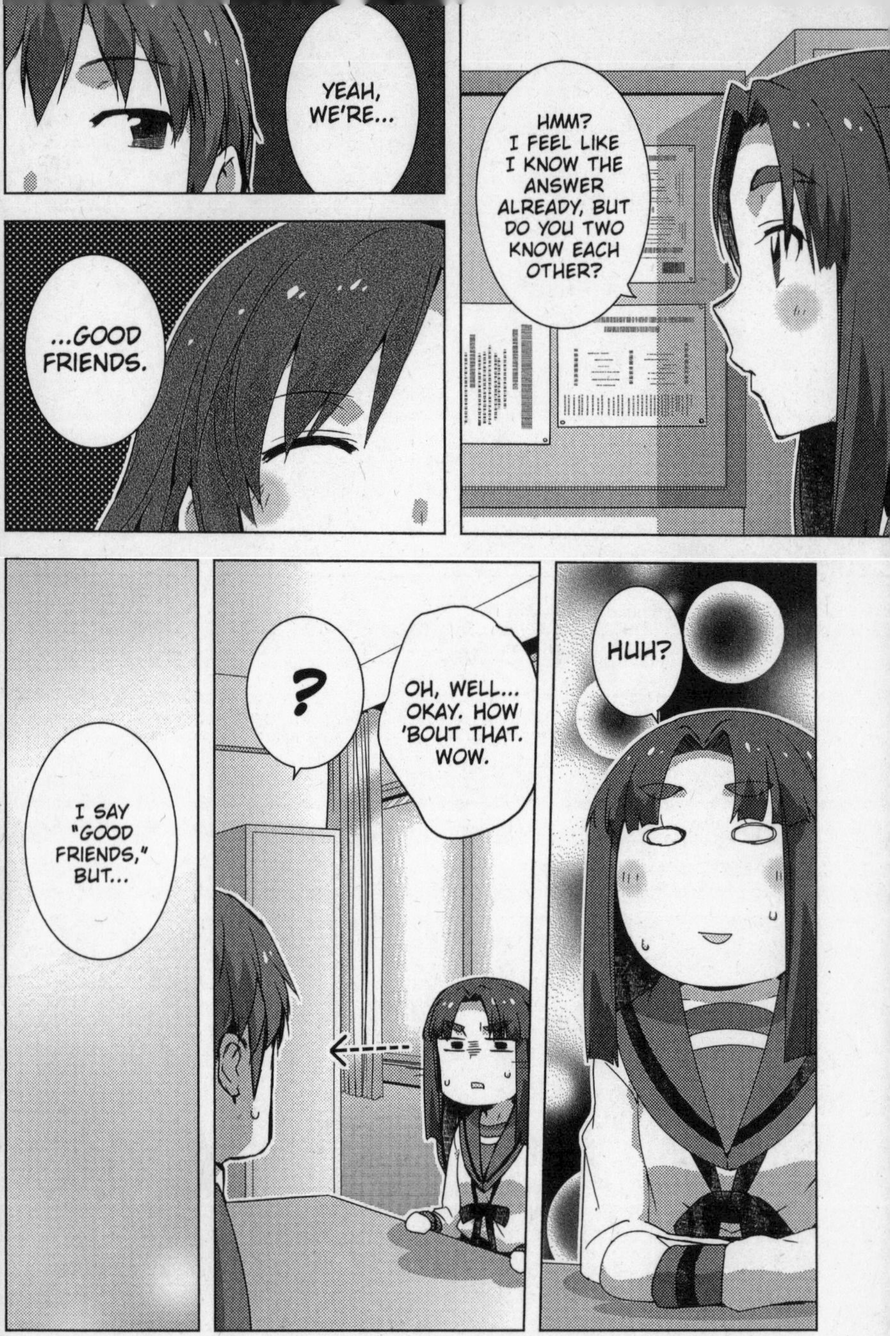
HMM? I FEEL LIKE I KNOW THE ANSWER ALREADY, BUT DO YOU TWO KNOW EACH OTHER?
YEAH, WE'RE...
...GOOD FRIENDS.
HUH?
OH, WELL... OKAY. HOW 'BOUT THAT. WOW.
?
I SAY "GOOD FRIENDS," BUT...

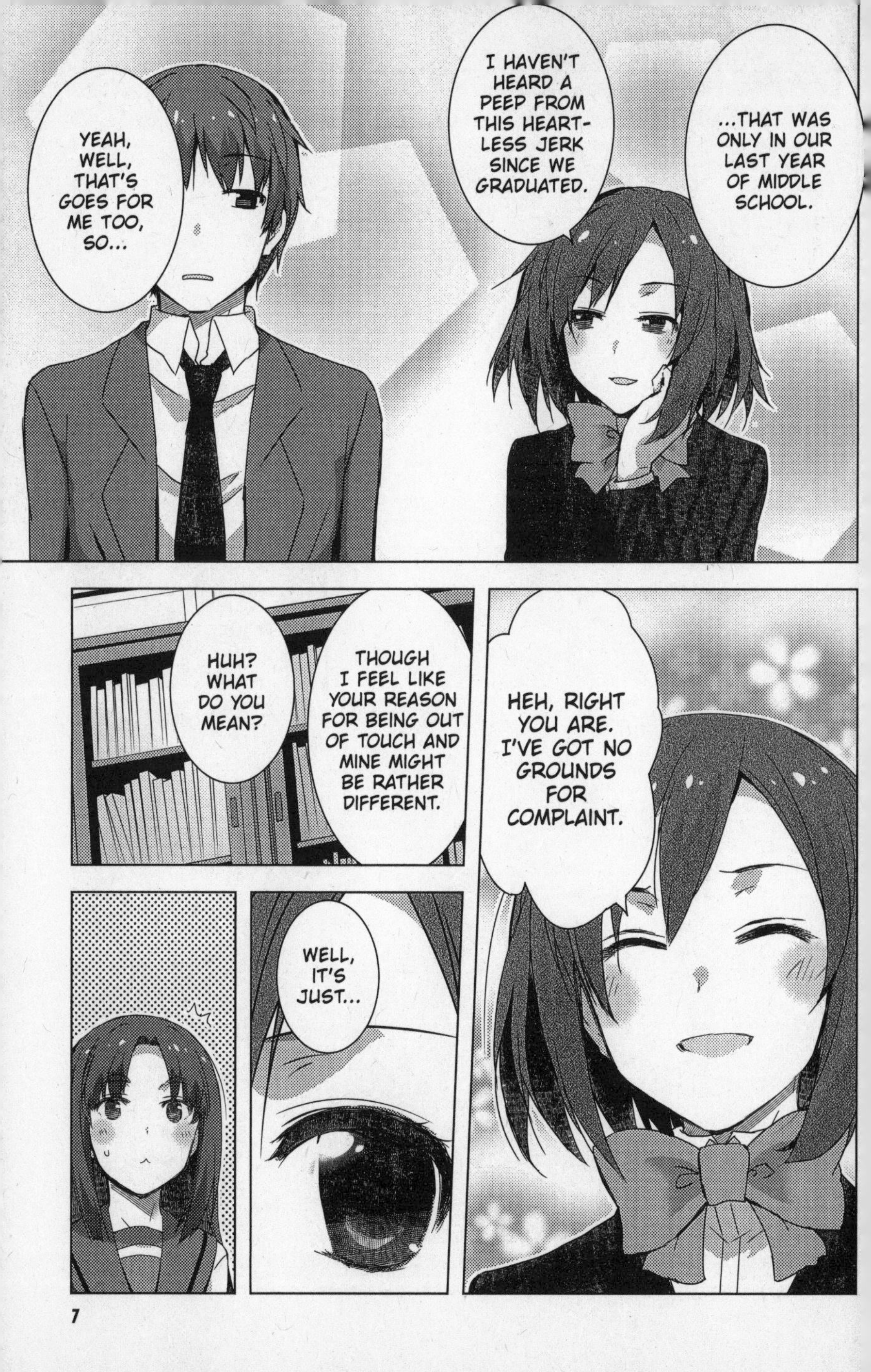
...THAT WAS ONLY IN OUR LAST YEAR OF MIDDLE SCHOOL.
I HAVEN'T HEARD A PEEP FROM THIS HEART-LESS JERK SINCE WE GRADUATED.
YEAH, WELL, THAT'S GOES FOR ME TOO, SO...
HEH, RIGHT YOU ARE. I'VE GOT NO GROUNDS FOR COMPLAINT.
THOUGH I FEEL LIKE YOUR REASON FOR BEING OUT OF TOUCH AND MINE MIGHT BE RATHER DIFFERENT.
HUH? WHAT DO YOU MEAN?
WELL, IT'S JUST...

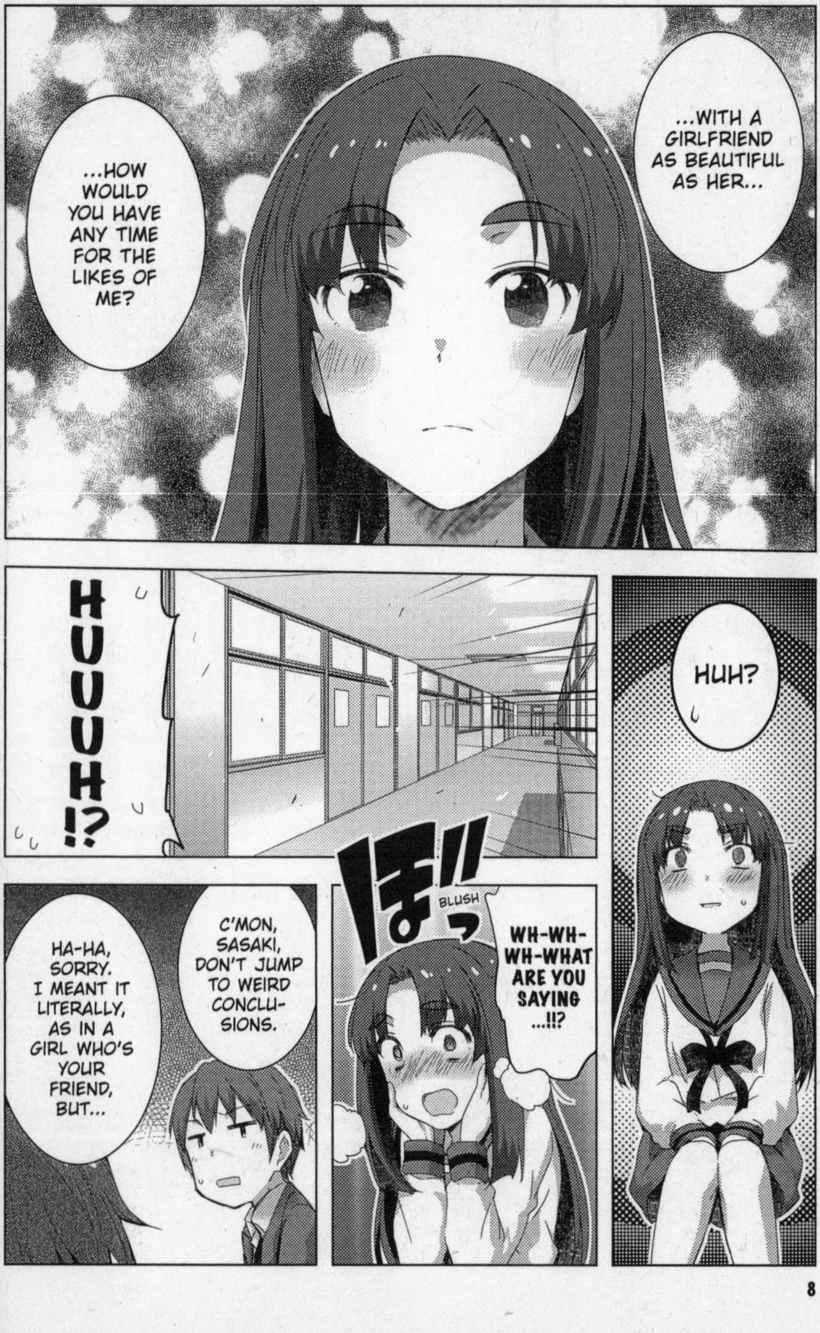
...WITH A GIRLFRIEND AS BEAUTIFUL AS HER...
...HOW WOULD YOU HAVE ANY TIME FOR THE LIKES OF ME?
HUH?
HUUUUH!?
ぼっ
BLUSH
WH-WH-WH-WHAT ARE YOU SAYING ...!!?
C'MON, SASAKI, DON'T JUMP TO WEIRD CONCLU-SIONS.
HA-HA, SORRY. I MEANT IT LITERALLY, AS IN A GIRL WHO'S YOUR FRIEND, BUT...

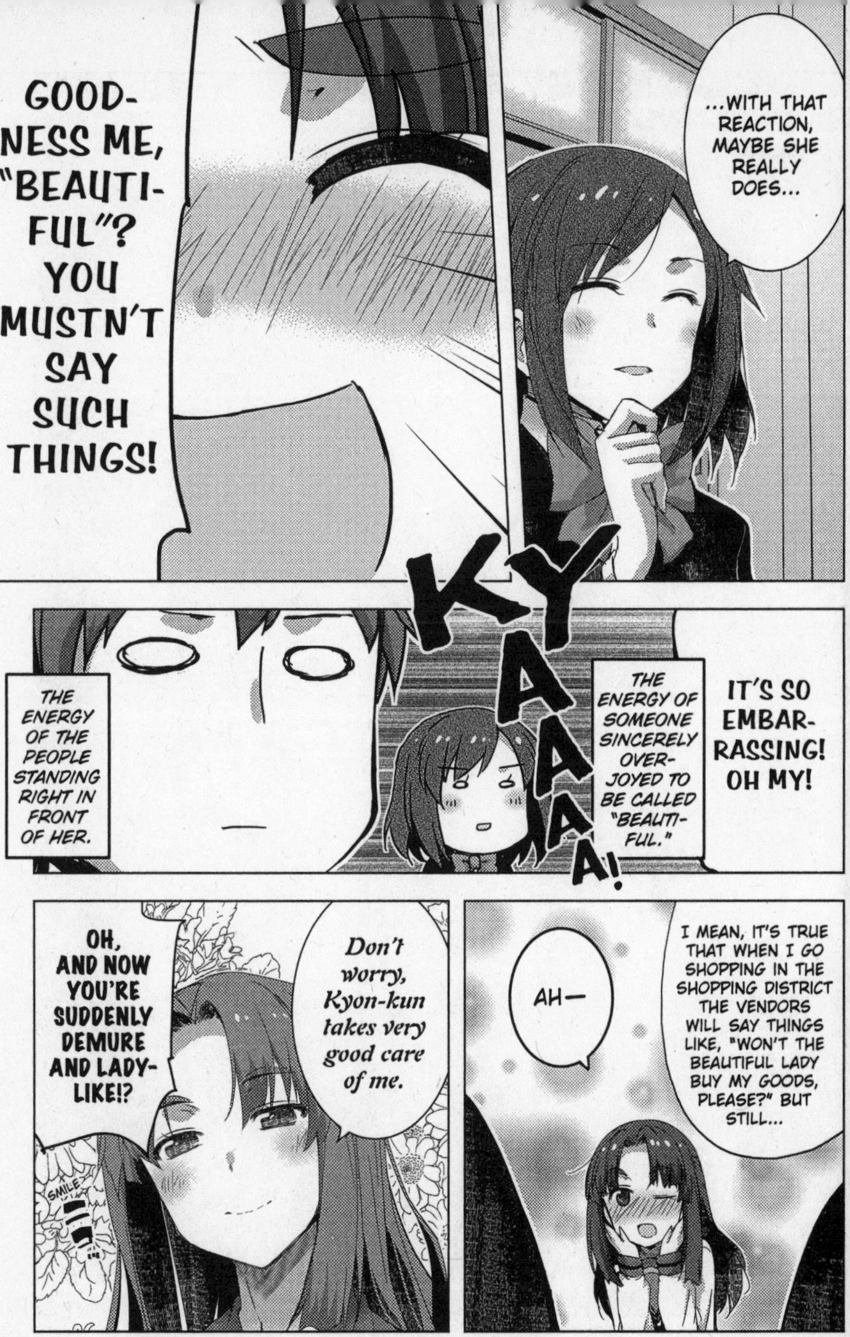
...WITH THAT REACTION, MAYBE SHE REALLY DOES...
GOODNESS ME, "BEAUTIFUL"? YOU MUSTN'T SAY SUCH THINGS!
IT'S SO EMBARRASSING! OH MY!
THE ENERGY OF SOMEONE SINCERELY OVERJOYED TO BE CALLED "BEAUTIFUL."
KYAAAAA!
THE ENERGY OF THE PEOPLE STANDING RIGHT IN FRONT OF HER.
I MEAN, IT'S TRUE THAT WHEN I GO SHOPPING IN THE SHOPPING DISTRICT THE VENDORS WILL SAY THINGS LIKE, "WON'T THE BEAUTIFUL LADY BUY MY GOODS, PLEASE?" BUT STILL...
AH—
Don't worry, Kyon-kun takes very good care of me.
OH, AND NOW YOU'RE SUDDENLY DEMURE AND LADYLIKE!?
SMILE

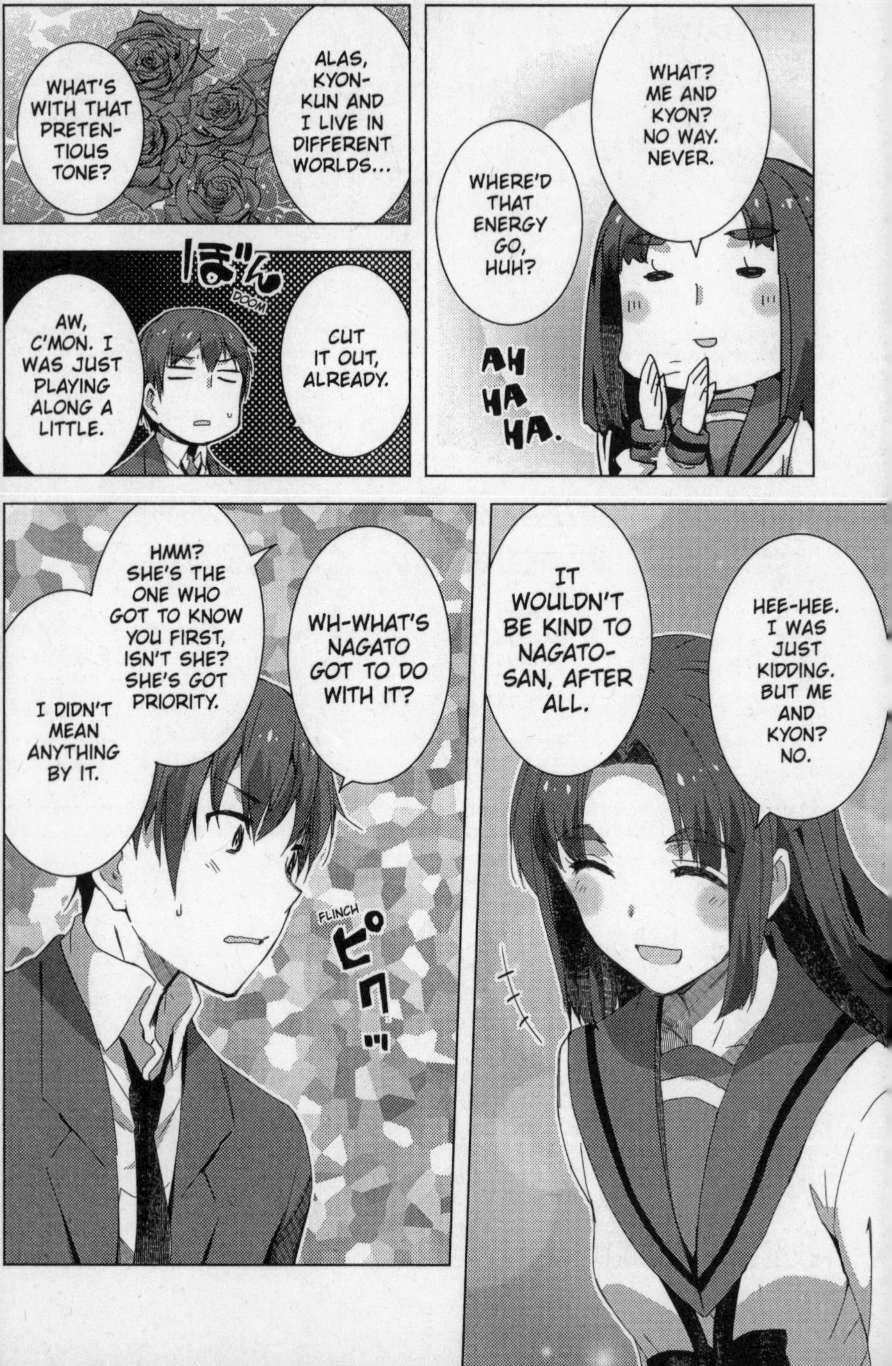
WHAT? ME AND KYON? NO WAY. NEVER.
WHERE'D THAT ENERGY GO, HUH?
AH HA HA.
ALAS, KYON-KUN AND I LIVE IN DIFFERENT WORLDS...
WHAT'S WITH THAT PRETENTIOUS TONE?
ぼん DOOM
CUT IT OUT, ALREADY.
AW, C'MON. I WAS JUST PLAYING ALONG A LITTLE.
HEE-HEE. I WAS JUST KIDDING. BUT ME AND KYON? NO.
IT WOULDN'T BE KIND TO NAGATO-SAN, AFTER ALL.
WH-WHAT'S NAGATO GOT TO DO WITH IT?
FLINCH ピクッ
HMM? SHE'S THE ONE WHO GOT TO KNOW YOU FIRST, ISN'T SHE? SHE'S GOT PRIORITY.
I DIDN'T MEAN ANYTHING BY IT.

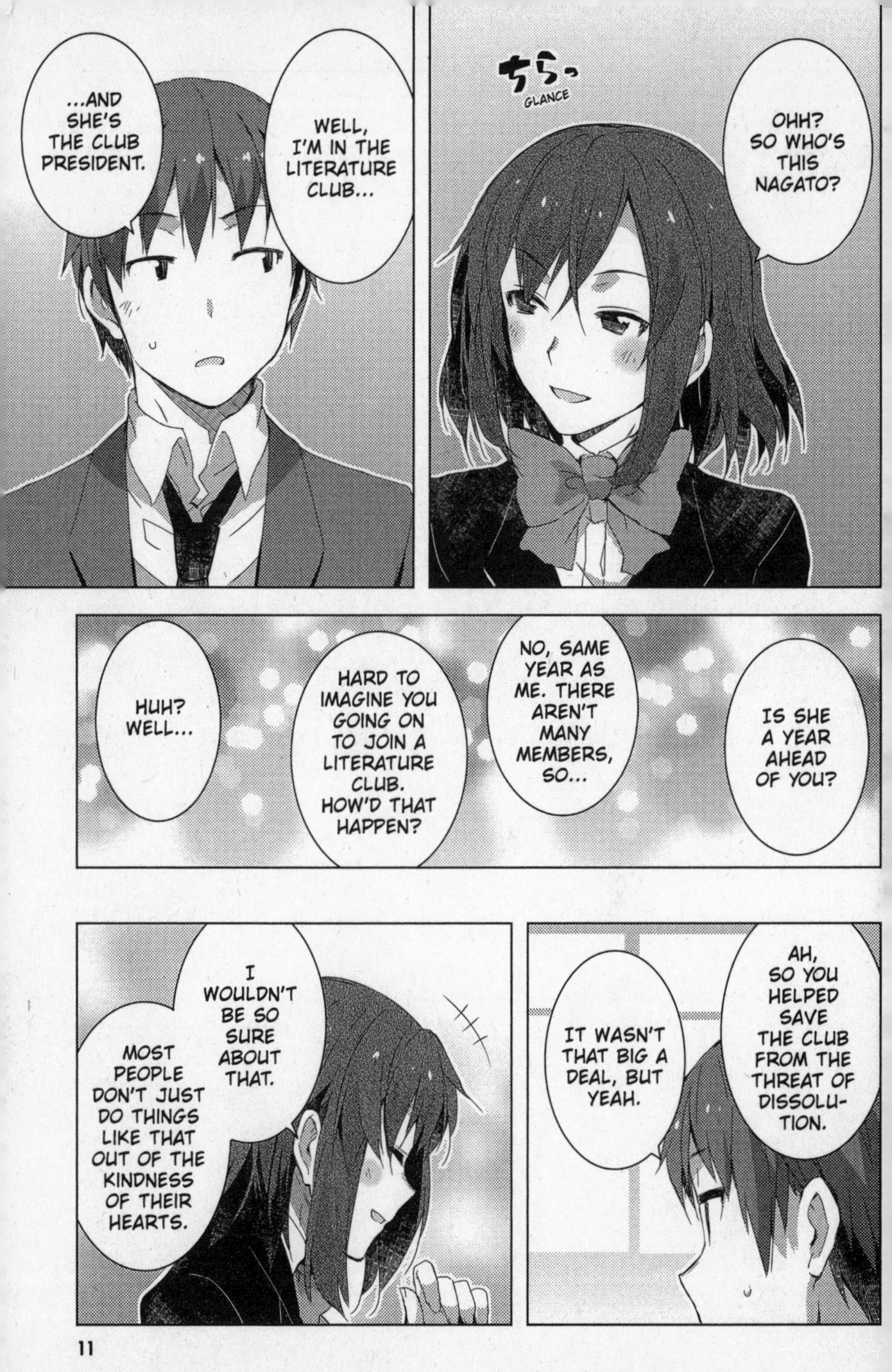
ちらっ
GLANCE
OHH? SO WHO'S THIS NAGATO?
WELL, I'M IN THE LITERATURE CLUB...
...AND SHE'S THE CLUB PRESIDENT.
IS SHE A YEAR AHEAD OF YOU?
NO, SAME YEAR AS ME. THERE AREN'T MANY MEMBERS, SO...
HARD TO IMAGINE YOU GOING ON TO JOIN A LITERATURE CLUB. HOW'D THAT HAPPEN?
HUH? WELL...
AH, SO YOU HELPED SAVE THE CLUB FROM THE THREAT OF DISSOLU-TION.
IT WASN'T THAT BIG A DEAL, BUT YEAH.
I WOULDN'T BE SO SURE ABOUT THAT.
MOST PEOPLE DON'T JUST DO THINGS LIKE THAT OUT OF THE KINDNESS OF THEIR HEARTS.

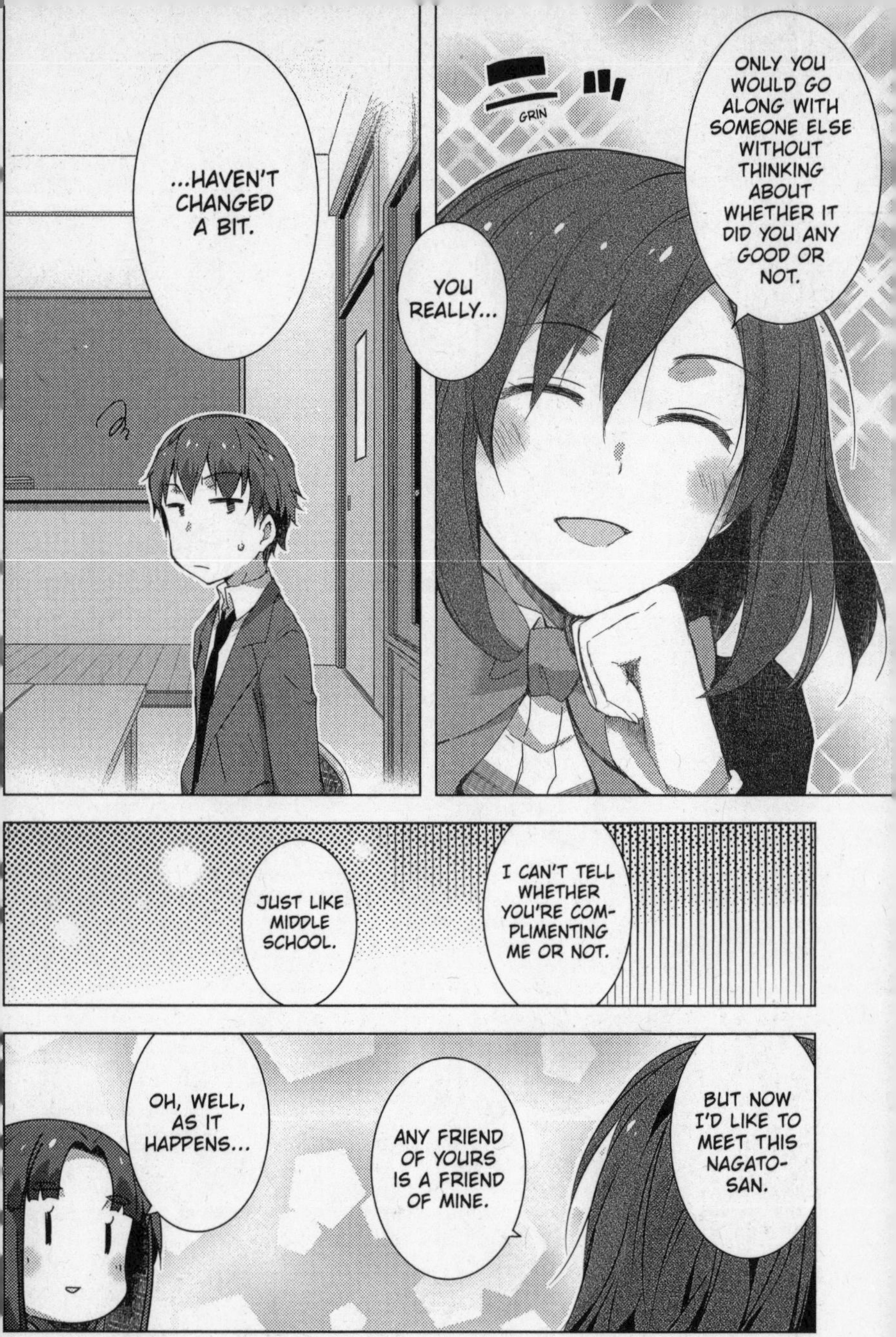
GRIN
ONLY YOU WOULD GO ALONG WITH SOMEONE ELSE WITHOUT THINKING ABOUT WHETHER IT DID YOU ANY GOOD OR NOT.
YOU REALLY...
...HAVEN'T CHANGED A BIT.
I CAN'T TELL WHETHER YOU'RE COM-PLIMENTING ME OR NOT.
JUST LIKE MIDDLE SCHOOL.
BUT NOW I'D LIKE TO MEET THIS NAGATO-SAN.
ANY FRIEND OF YOURS IS A FRIEND OF MINE.
OH, WELL, AS IT HAPPENS...

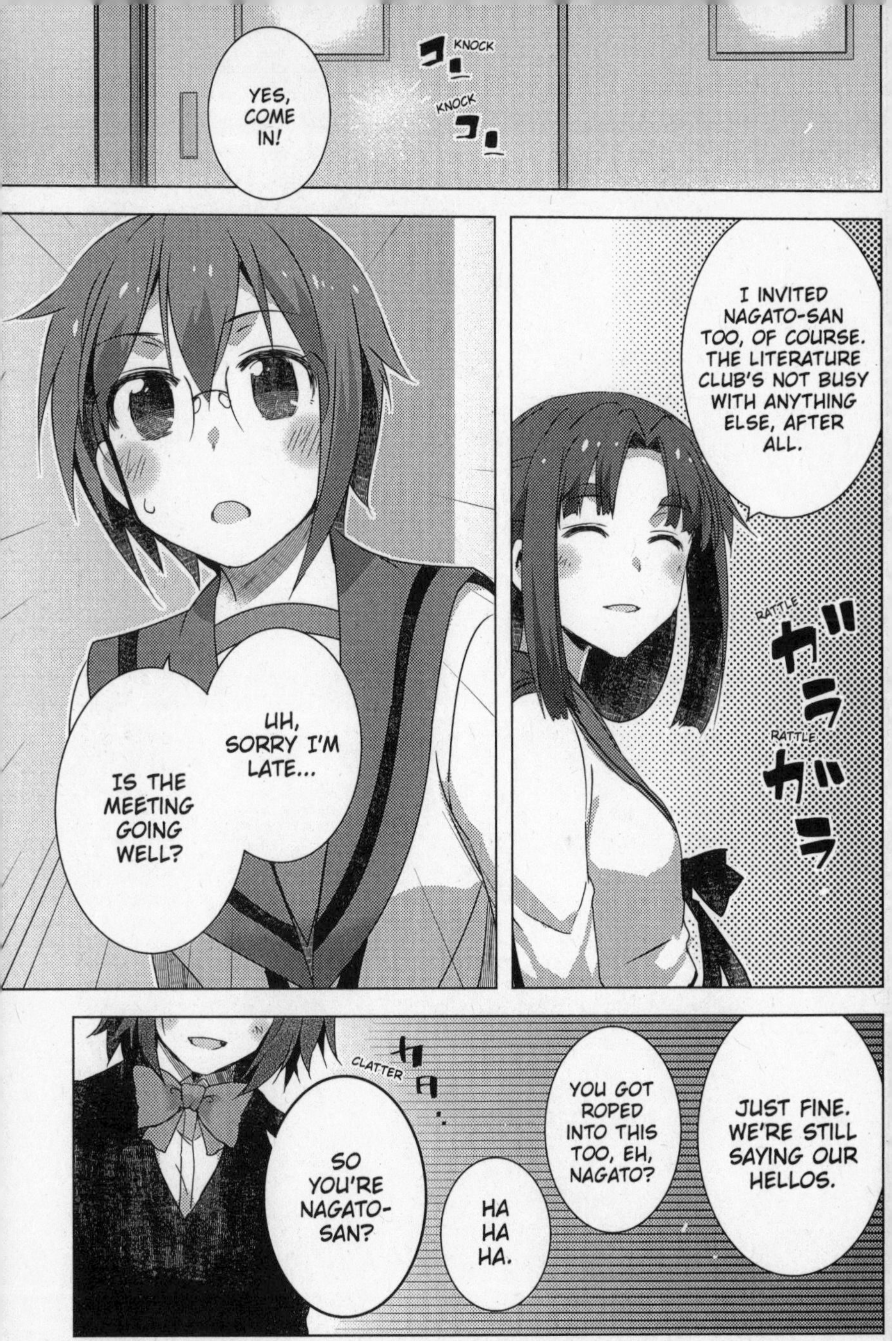
KNOCK
KNOCK
YES, COME IN!
I INVITED NAGATO-SAN TOO, OF COURSE. THE LITERATURE CLUB'S NOT BUSY WITH ANYTHING ELSE, AFTER ALL.
RATTLE
RATTLE
UH, SORRY I'M LATE...
IS THE MEETING GOING WELL?
JUST FINE. WE'RE STILL SAYING OUR HELLOS.
YOU GOT ROPED INTO THIS TOO, EH, NAGATO?
HA HA HA.
CLATTER
SO YOU'RE NAGATO-SAN?

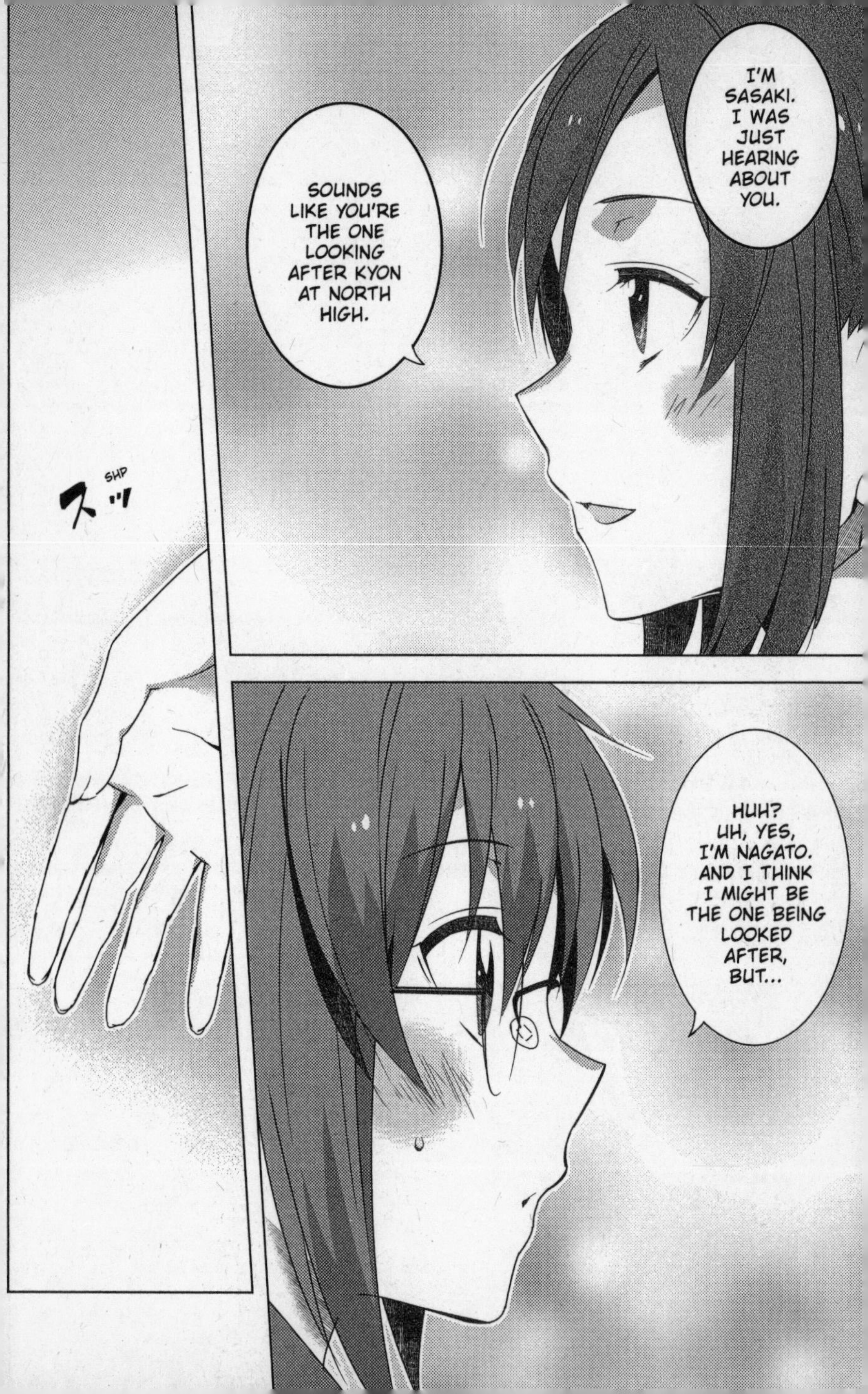
I'M SASAKI. I WAS JUST HEARING ABOUT YOU.
SOUNDS LIKE YOU'RE THE ONE LOOKING AFTER KYON AT NORTH HIGH.
HUH? UH, YES, I'M NAGATO. AND I THINK I MIGHT BE THE ONE BEING LOOKED AFTER, BUT...
スッ
SHP

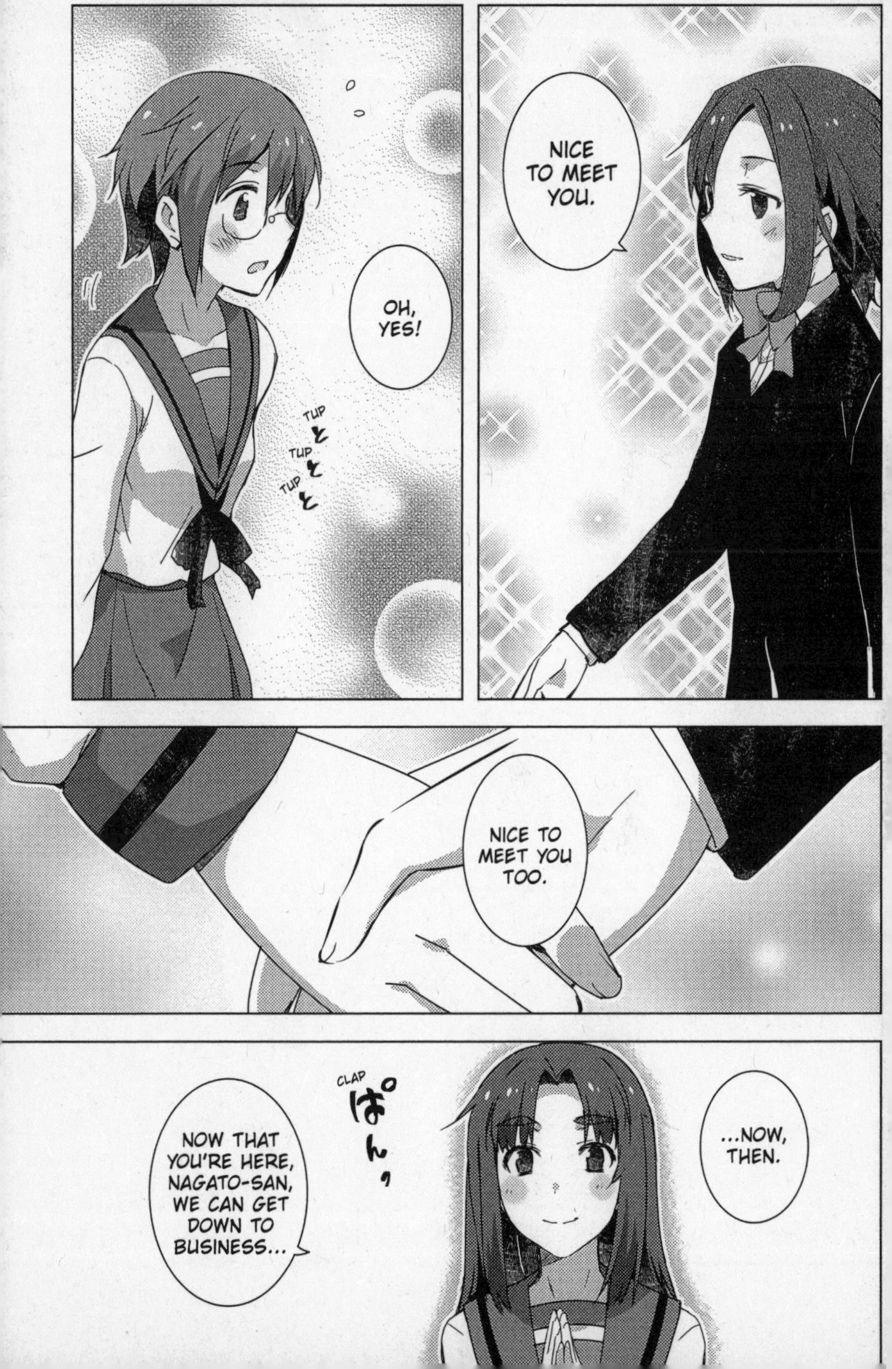
NICE TO MEET YOU.
OH, YES!
TUP
と
TUP
と
TUP
と
NICE TO MEET YOU TOO.
...NOW, THEN.
CLAP
ぱん
NOW THAT YOU'RE HERE, NAGATO-SAN, WE CAN GET DOWN TO BUSINESS...

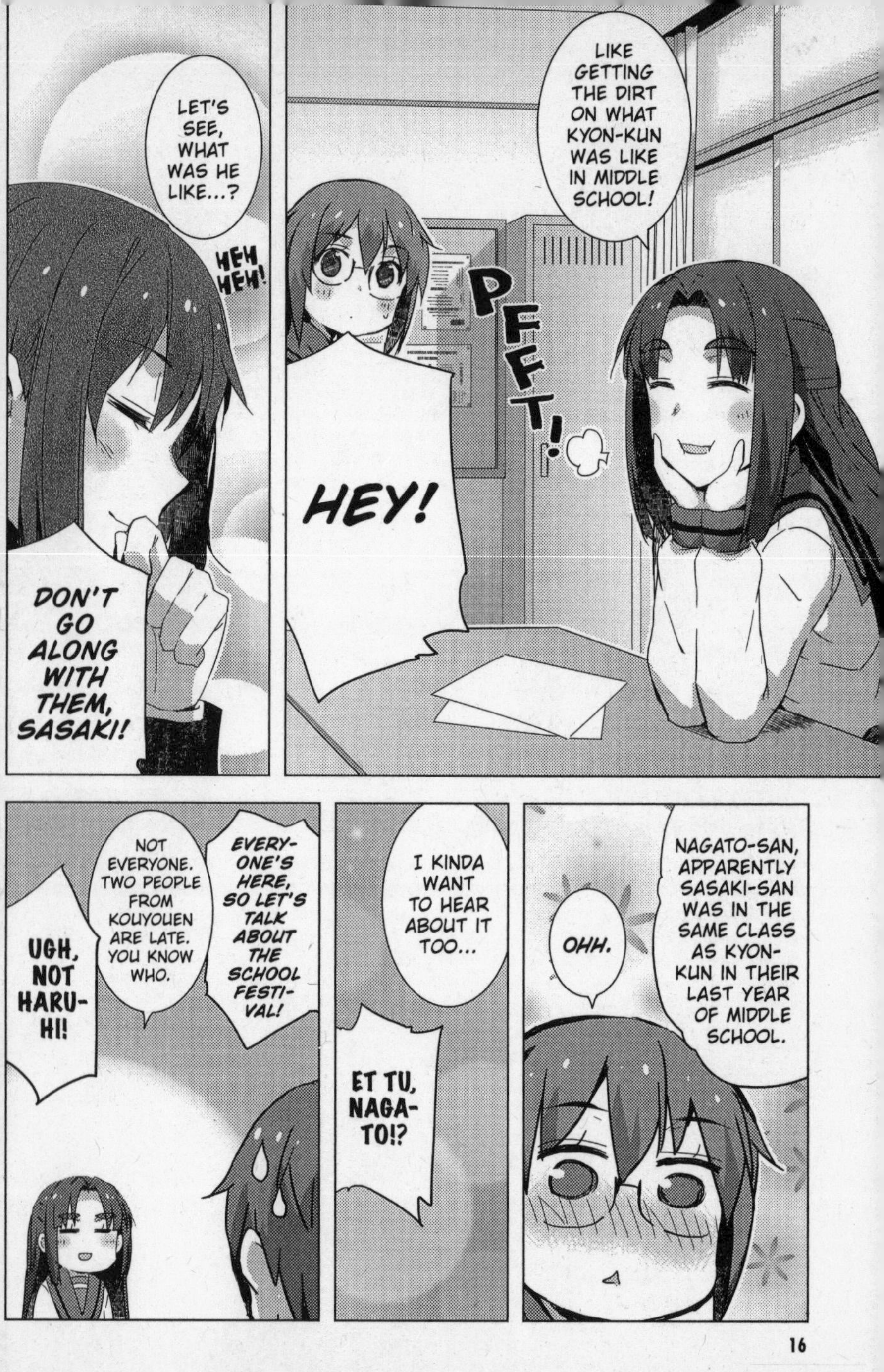
LIKE GETTING THE DIRT ON WHAT KYON-KUN WAS LIKE IN MIDDLE SCHOOL!
PFFT!
HEY!
LET'S SEE, WHAT WAS HE LIKE...?
HEH HEH!
DON'T GO ALONG WITH THEM, SASAKI!
NAGATO-SAN, APPARENTLY SASAKI-SAN WAS IN THE SAME CLASS AS KYON-KUN IN THEIR LAST YEAR OF MIDDLE SCHOOL.
OHH.
I KINDA WANT TO HEAR ABOUT IT TOO...
ET TU, NAGATO!?
EVERYONE'S HERE, SO LET'S TALK ABOUT THE SCHOOL FESTIVAL!
NOT EVERYONE. TWO PEOPLE FROM KOUYOUEN ARE LATE. YOU KNOW WHO.
UGH, NOT HARUHI!

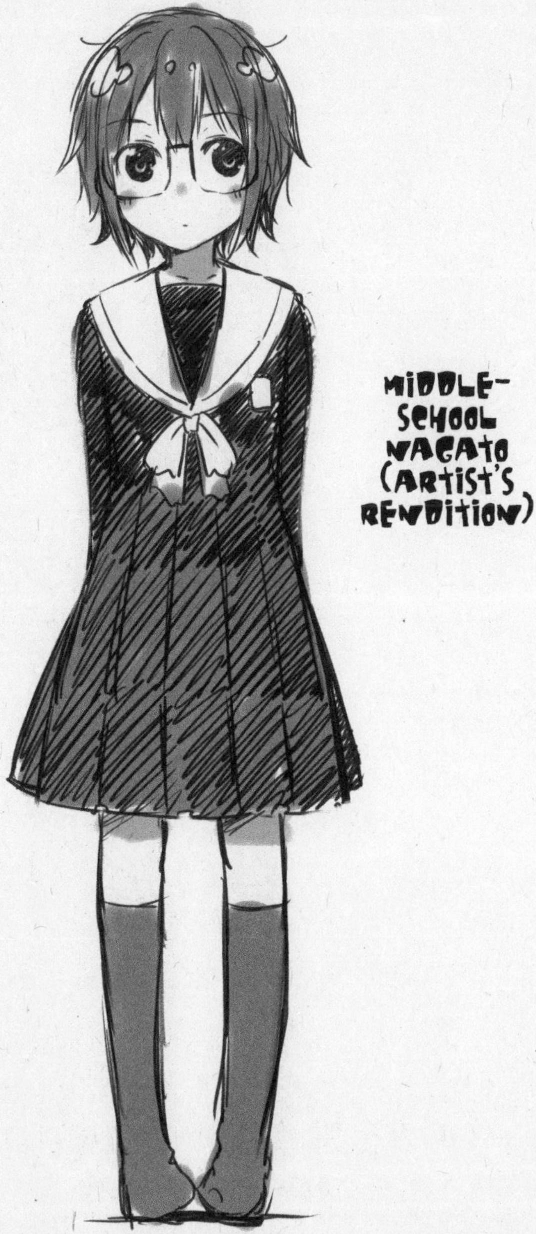
MIDDLE-SCHOOL NAGATO (ARTIST'S RENDITION)

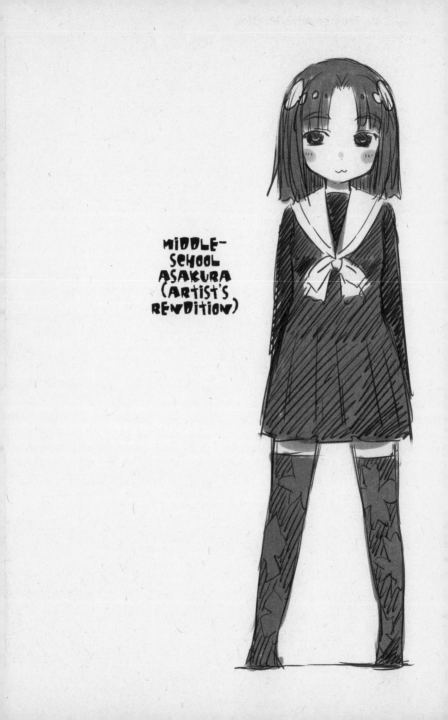

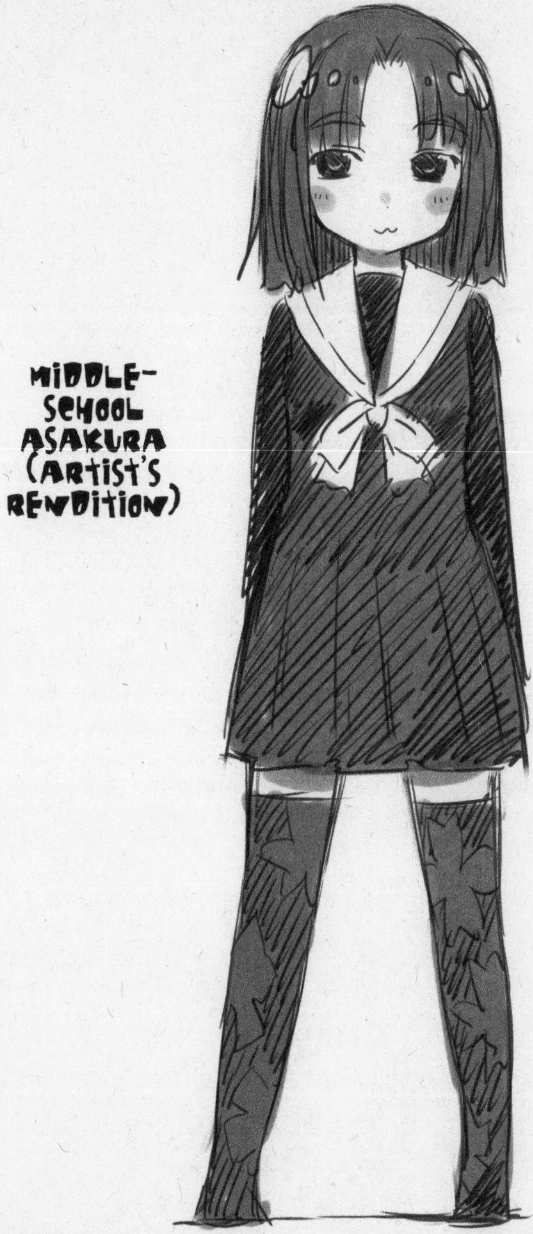
MIDDLE-SCHOOL ASAKURA (ARTIST'S RENDITION)

Epilogue 41>> Programming Meeting

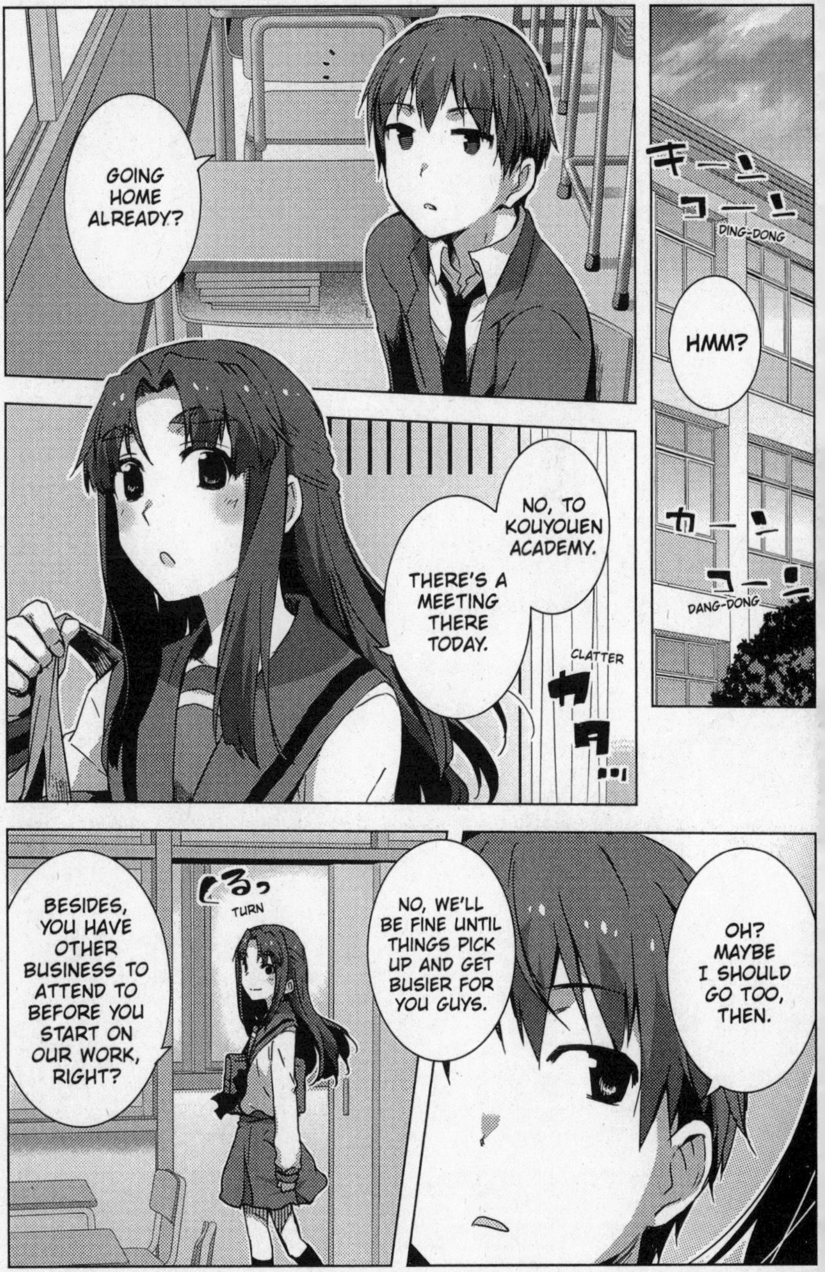
キーン
コーン
DING-DONG
HMM?
カーン
コーン
DANG-DONG
GOING HOME ALREADY?
NO, TO KOUYOUEN ACADEMY.
THERE'S A MEETING THERE TODAY.
CLATTER
カタ…
OH? MAYBE I SHOULD GO TOO, THEN.
NO, WE'LL BE FINE UNTIL THINGS PICK UP AND GET BUSIER FOR YOU GUYS.
くるっ
TURN
BESIDES, YOU HAVE OTHER BUSINESS TO ATTEND TO BEFORE YOU START ON OUR WORK, RIGHT?

Epilogue 41>> Programming Meeting

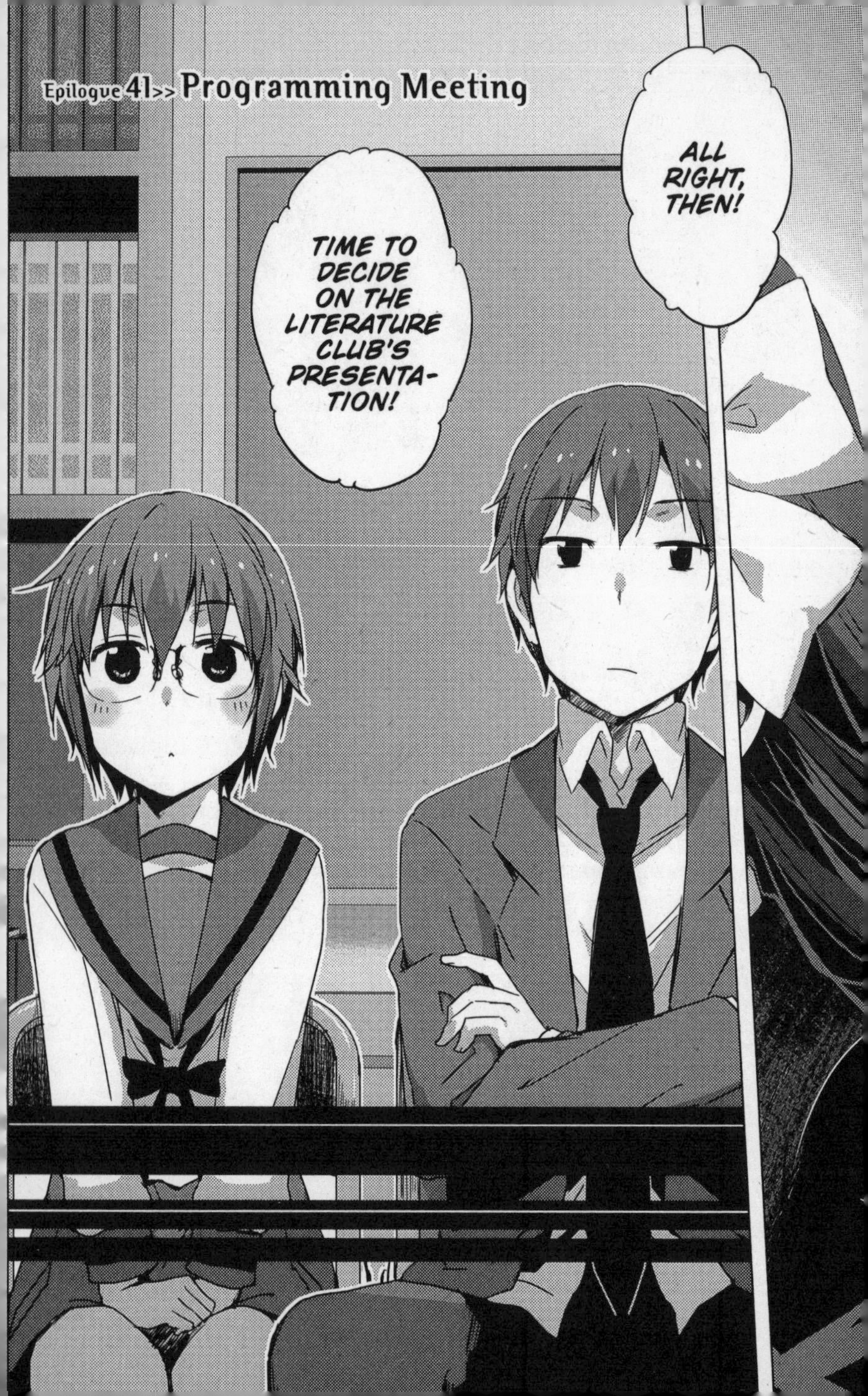
ALL RIGHT, THEN!
TIME TO DECIDE ON THE LITERATURE CLUB'S PRESENTATION!

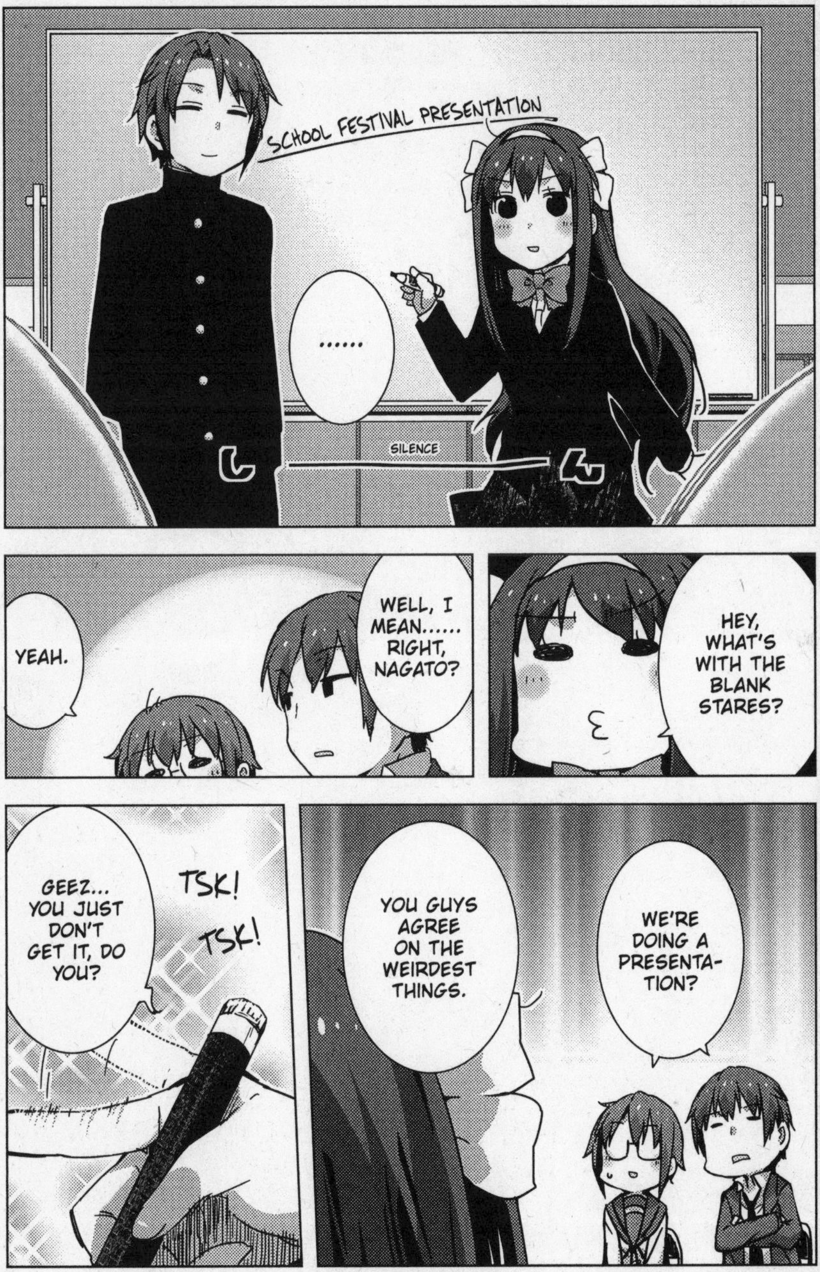
SCHOOL FESTIVAL PRESENTATION
......
SILENCE
HEY, WHAT'S WITH THE BLANK STARES?
WELL, I MEAN...... RIGHT, NAGATO?
YEAH.
WE'RE DOING A PRESENTATION?
YOU GUYS AGREE ON THE WEIRDEST THINGS.
TSK!
TSK!
GEEZ... YOU JUST DON'T GET IT, DO YOU?

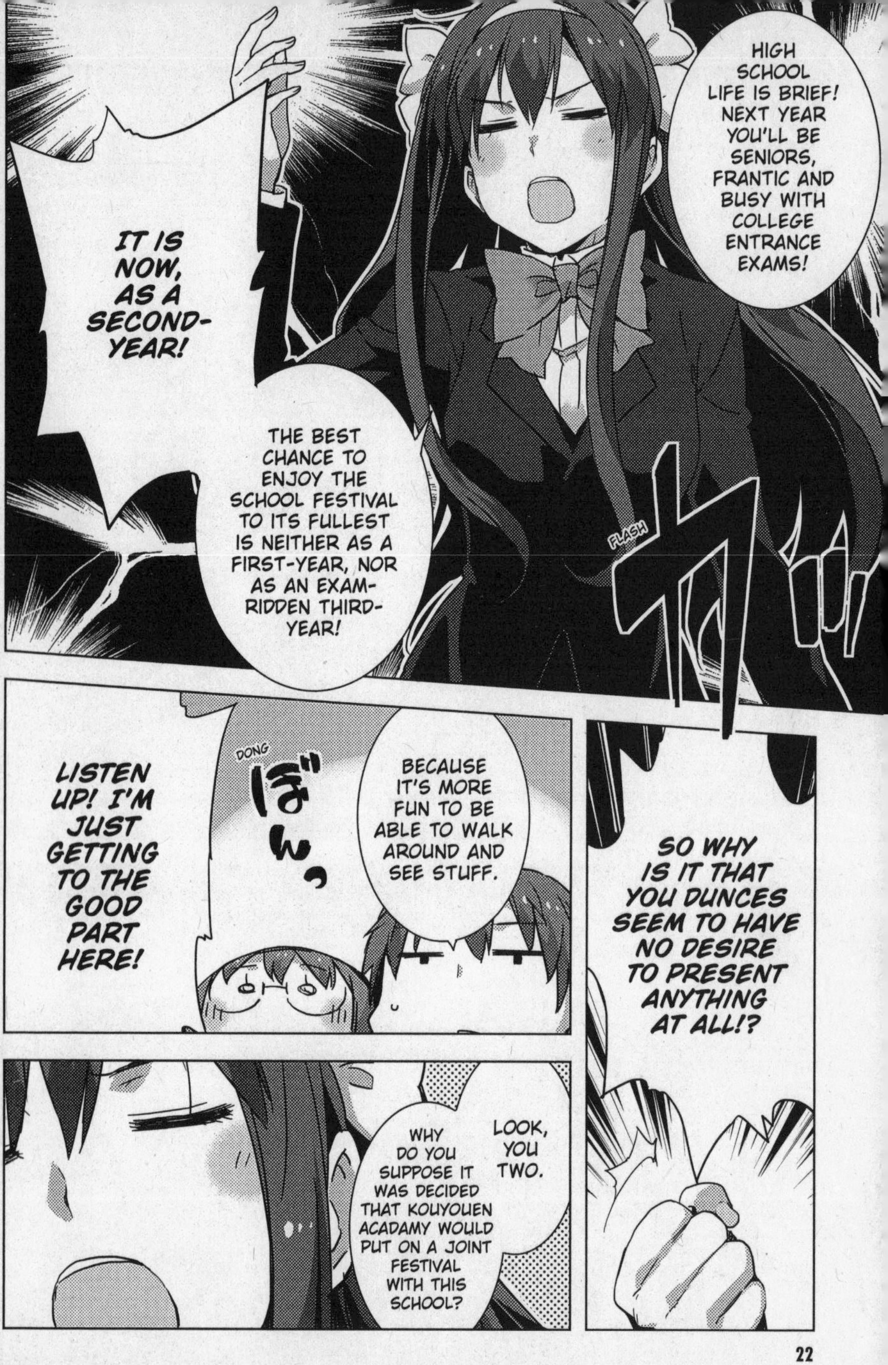
HIGH SCHOOL LIFE IS BRIEF! NEXT YEAR YOU'LL BE SENIORS, FRANTIC AND BUSY WITH COLLEGE ENTRANCE EXAMS!
THE BEST CHANCE TO ENJOY THE SCHOOL FESTIVAL TO ITS FULLEST IS NEITHER AS A FIRST-YEAR, NOR AS AN EXAM-RIDDEN THIRD-YEAR!
IT IS NOW, AS A SECOND-YEAR!
FLASH
SO WHY IS IT THAT YOU DUNCES SEEM TO HAVE NO DESIRE TO PRESENT ANYTHING AT ALL!?
BECAUSE IT'S MORE FUN TO BE ABLE TO WALK AROUND AND SEE STUFF.
DONG
LISTEN UP! I'M JUST GETTING TO THE GOOD PART HERE!
LOOK, YOU TWO.
WHY DO YOU SUPPOSE IT WAS DECIDED THAT KOUYOUEN ACADAMY WOULD PUT ON A JOINT FESTIVAL WITH THIS SCHOOL?

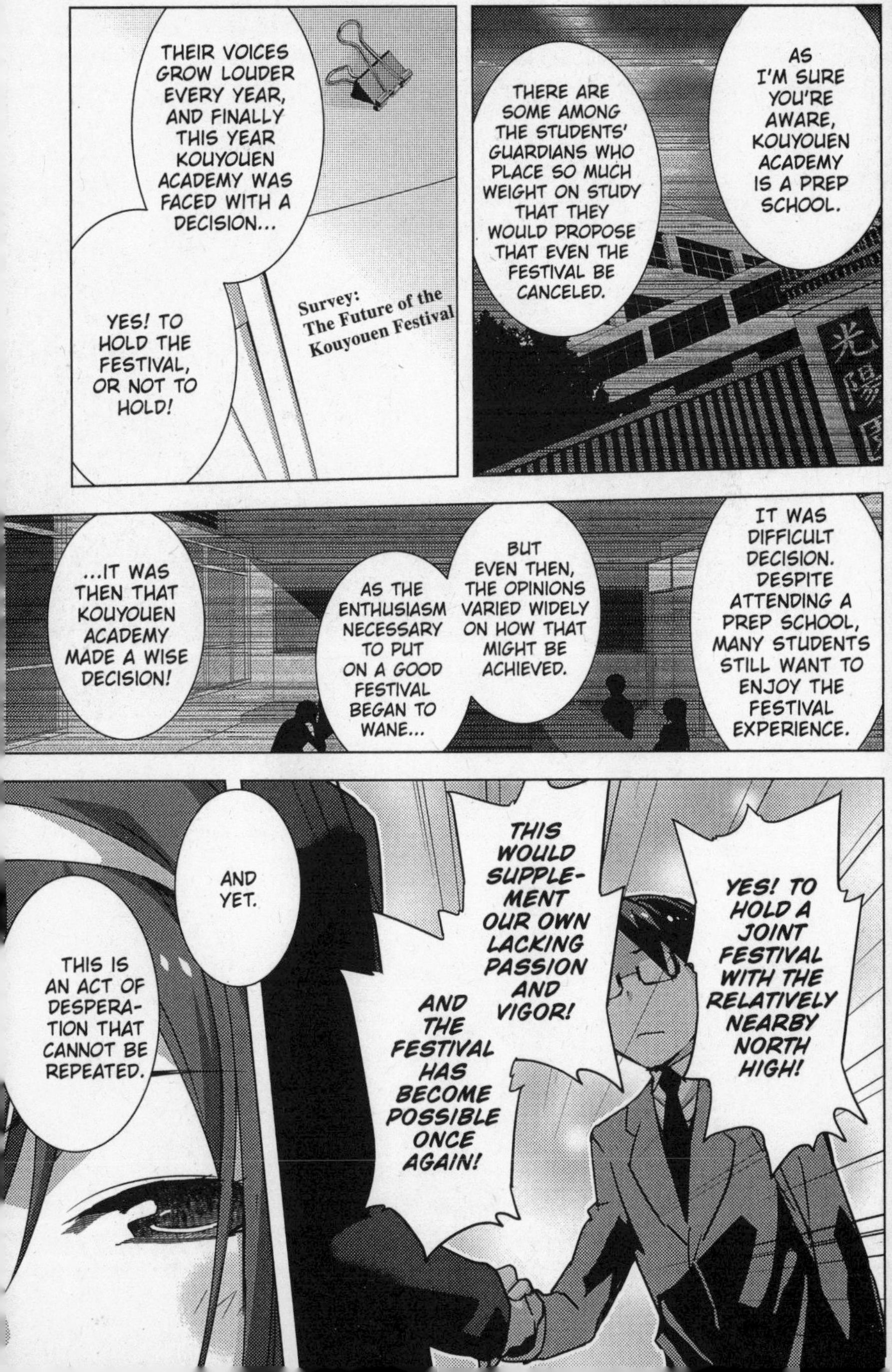
AS I'M SURE YOU'RE AWARE, KOUYOUEN ACADEMY IS A PREP SCHOOL.
THERE ARE SOME AMONG THE STUDENTS' GUARDIANS WHO PLACE SO MUCH WEIGHT ON STUDY THAT THEY WOULD PROPOSE THAT EVEN THE FESTIVAL BE CANCELED.
THEIR VOICES GROW LOUDER EVERY YEAR, AND FINALLY THIS YEAR KOUYOUEN ACADEMY WAS FACED WITH A DECISION...
Survey: The Future of the Kouyouen Festival
YES! TO HOLD THE FESTIVAL, OR NOT TO HOLD!
IT WAS DIFFICULT DECISION. DESPITE ATTENDING A PREP SCHOOL, MANY STUDENTS STILL WANT TO ENJOY THE FESTIVAL EXPERIENCE.
BUT EVEN THEN, THE OPINIONS VARIED WIDELY ON HOW THAT MIGHT BE ACHIEVED.
AS THE ENTHUSIASM NECESSARY TO PUT ON A GOOD FESTIVAL BEGAN TO WANE...
...IT WAS THEN THAT KOUYOUEN ACADEMY MADE A WISE DECISION!
YES! TO HOLD A JOINT FESTIVAL WITH THE RELATIVELY NEARBY NORTH HIGH!
THIS WOULD SUPPLEMENT OUR OWN LACKING PASSION AND VIGOR!
AND THE FESTIVAL HAS BECOME POSSIBLE ONCE AGAIN!
AND YET.
THIS IS AN ACT OF DESPERATION THAT CANNOT BE REPEATED.

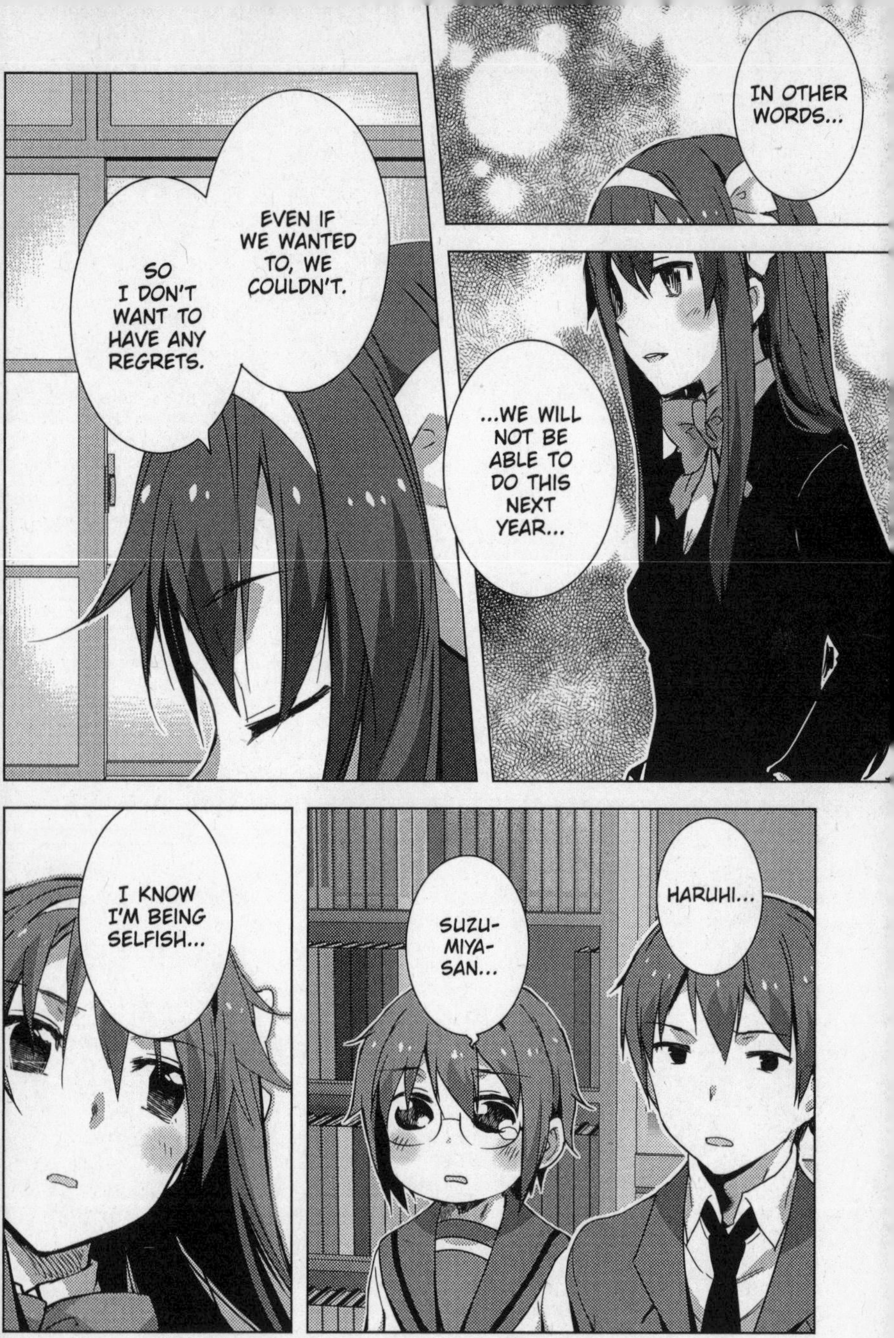
IN OTHER WORDS...
...WE WILL NOT BE ABLE TO DO THIS NEXT YEAR...
EVEN IF WE WANTED TO, WE COULDN'T.
SO I DON'T WANT TO HAVE ANY REGRETS.
HARUHI...
SUZU-MIYA-SAN...
I KNOW I'M BEING SELFISH...

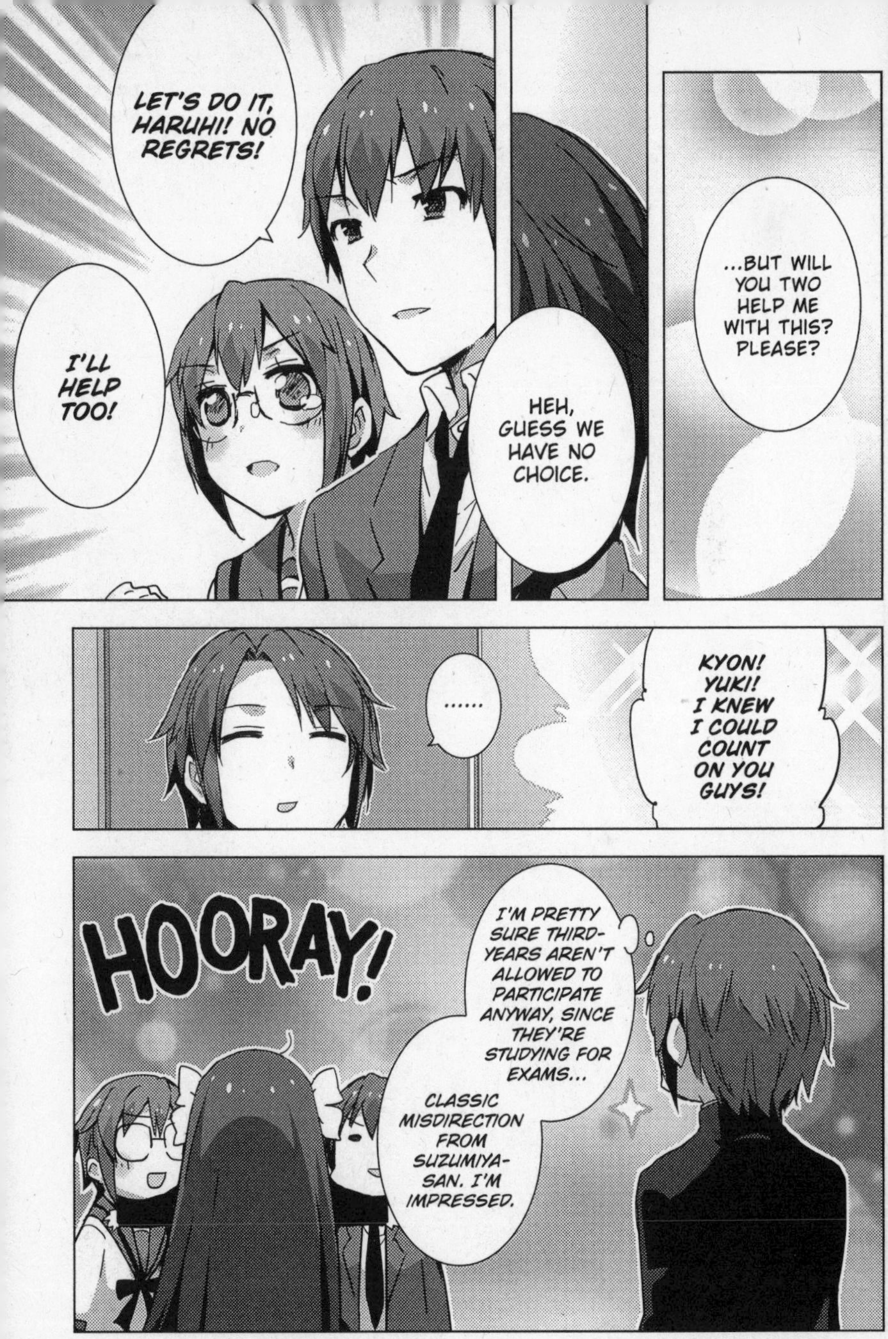
...BUT WILL YOU TWO HELP ME WITH THIS? PLEASE?
HEH, GUESS WE HAVE NO CHOICE.
LET'S DO IT, HARUHI! NO REGRETS!
I'LL HELP TOO!
KYON! YUKI! I KNEW I COULD COUNT ON YOU GUYS!
......
I'M PRETTY SURE THIRD-YEARS AREN'T ALLOWED TO PARTICIPATE ANYWAY, SINCE THEY'RE STUDYING FOR EXAMS...
CLASSIC MISDIRECTION FROM SUZUMIYA-SAN. I'M IMPRESSED.
HOORAY!

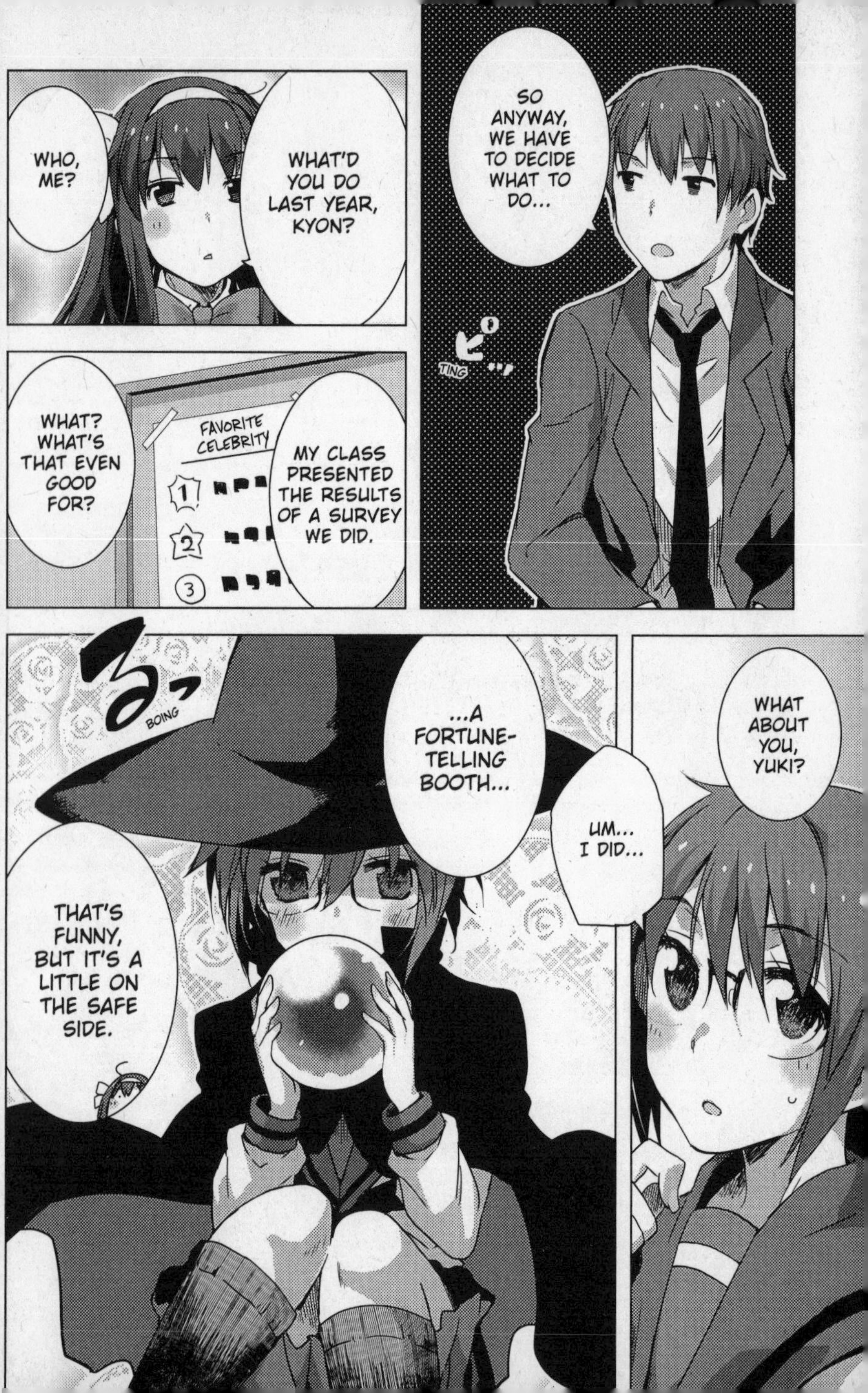
SO ANYWAY, WE HAVE TO DECIDE WHAT TO DO...
TING
WHAT'D YOU DO LAST YEAR, KYON?
WHO, ME?
MY CLASS PRESENTED THE RESULTS OF A SURVEY WE DID.
FAVORITE CELEBRITY
WHAT? WHAT'S THAT EVEN GOOD FOR?
WHAT ABOUT YOU, YUKI?
UM... I DID...
...A FORTUNE-TELLING BOOTH...
BOING
THAT'S FUNNY, BUT IT'S A LITTLE ON THE SAFE SIDE.

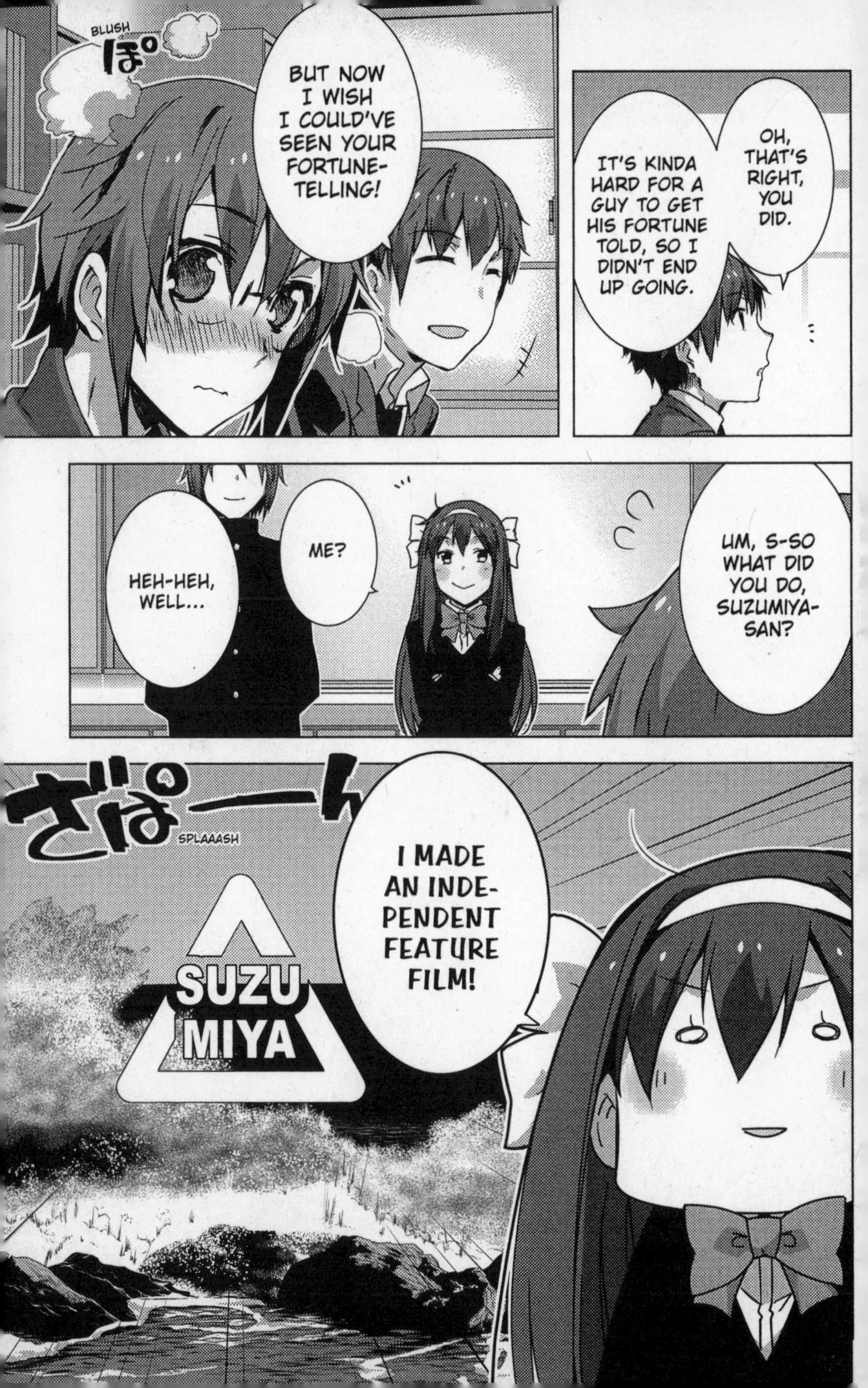
OH, THAT'S RIGHT, YOU DID.
IT'S KINDA HARD FOR A GUY TO GET HIS FORTUNE TOLD, SO I DIDN'T END UP GOING.
BUT NOW I WISH I COULD'VE SEEN YOUR FORTUNE-TELLING!
ぽ
BLUSH
UM, S-SO WHAT DID YOU DO, SUZUMIYA-SAN?
ME?
HEH-HEH, WELL...
I MADE AN INDE-PENDENT FEATURE FILM!
ざぱーーん
SPLAAASH
SUZU MIYA

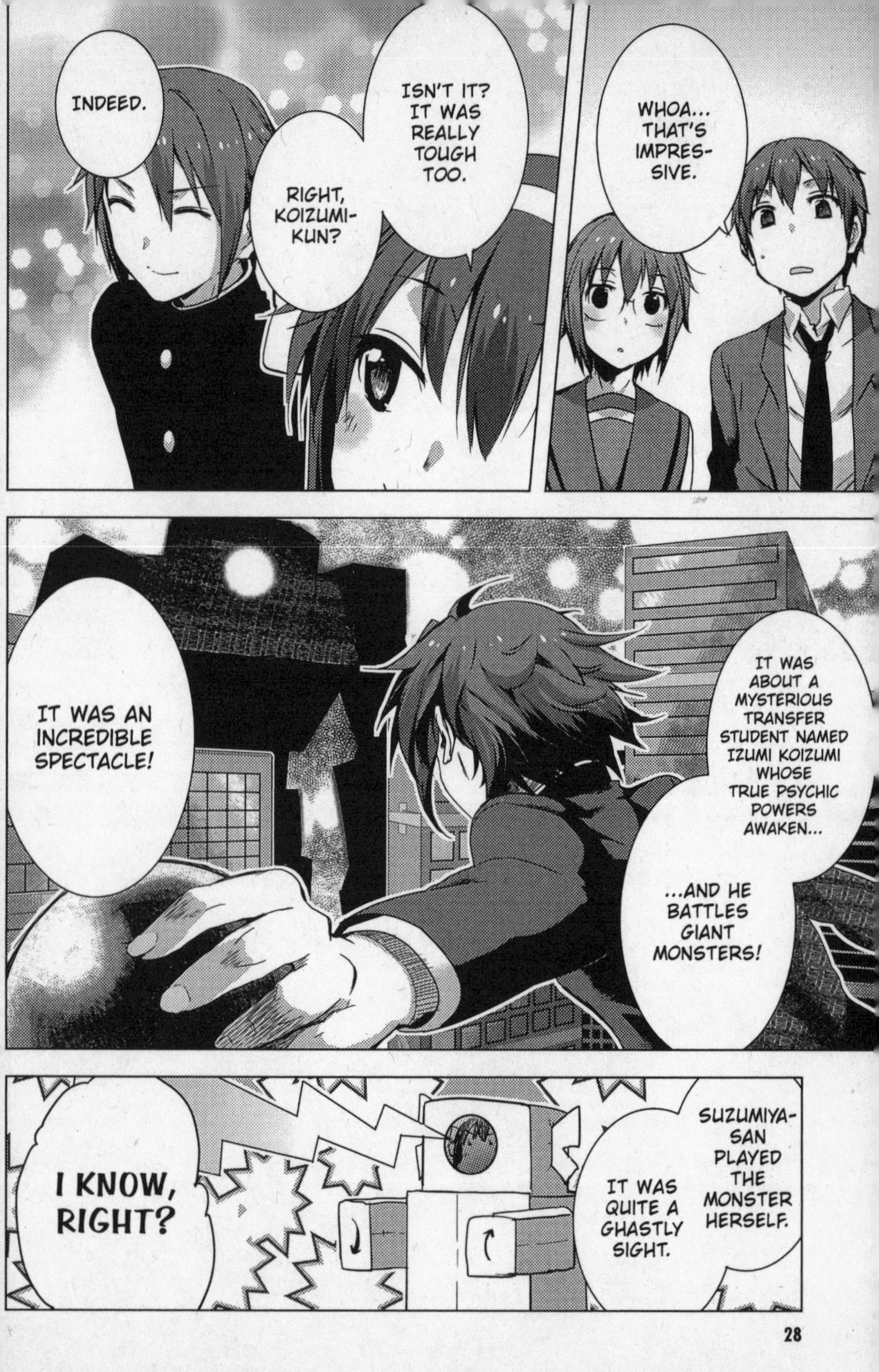
WHOA... THAT'S IMPRES-SIVE.
ISN'T IT? IT WAS REALLY TOUGH TOO.
RIGHT, KOIZUMI-KUN?
INDEED.
IT WAS ABOUT A MYSTERIOUS TRANSFER STUDENT NAMED IZUMI KOIZUMI WHOSE TRUE PSYCHIC POWERS AWAKEN...
...AND HE BATTLES GIANT MONSTERS!
IT WAS AN INCREDIBLE SPECTACLE!
SUZUMIYA-SAN PLAYED THE MONSTER HERSELF.
IT WAS QUITE A GHASTLY SIGHT.
I KNOW, RIGHT?

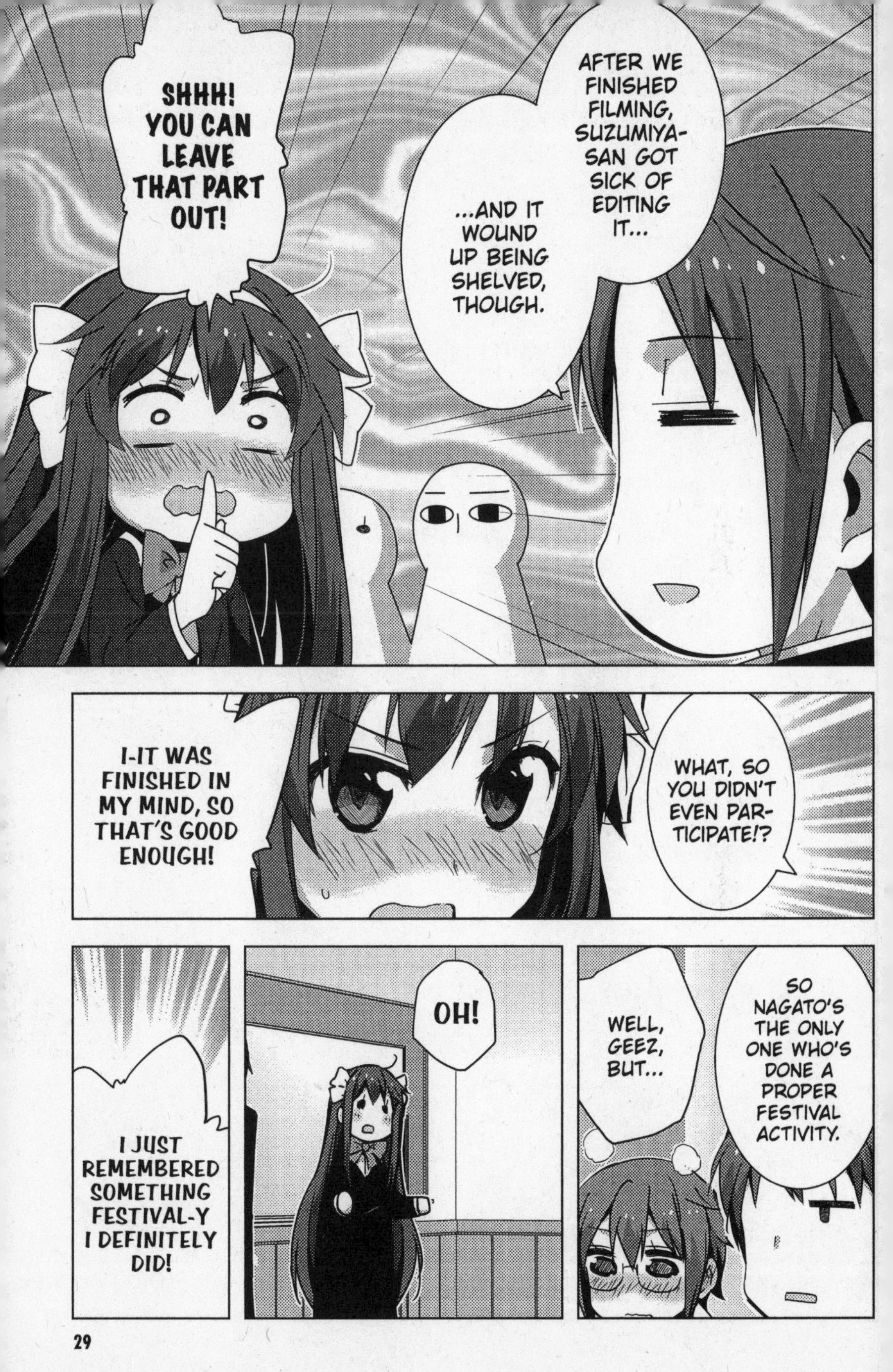
AFTER WE FINISHED FILMING, SUZUMIYA-SAN GOT SICK OF EDITING IT...
...AND IT WOUND UP BEING SHELVED, THOUGH.
SHHH! YOU CAN LEAVE THAT PART OUT!
WHAT, SO YOU DIDN'T EVEN PAR-TICIPATE!?
I-IT WAS FINISHED IN MY MIND, SO THAT'S GOOD ENOUGH!
SO NAGATO'S THE ONLY ONE WHO'S DONE A PROPER FESTIVAL ACTIVITY.
WELL, GEEZ, BUT...
OH!
I JUST REMEMBERED SOMETHING FESTIVAL-Y I DEFINITELY DID!

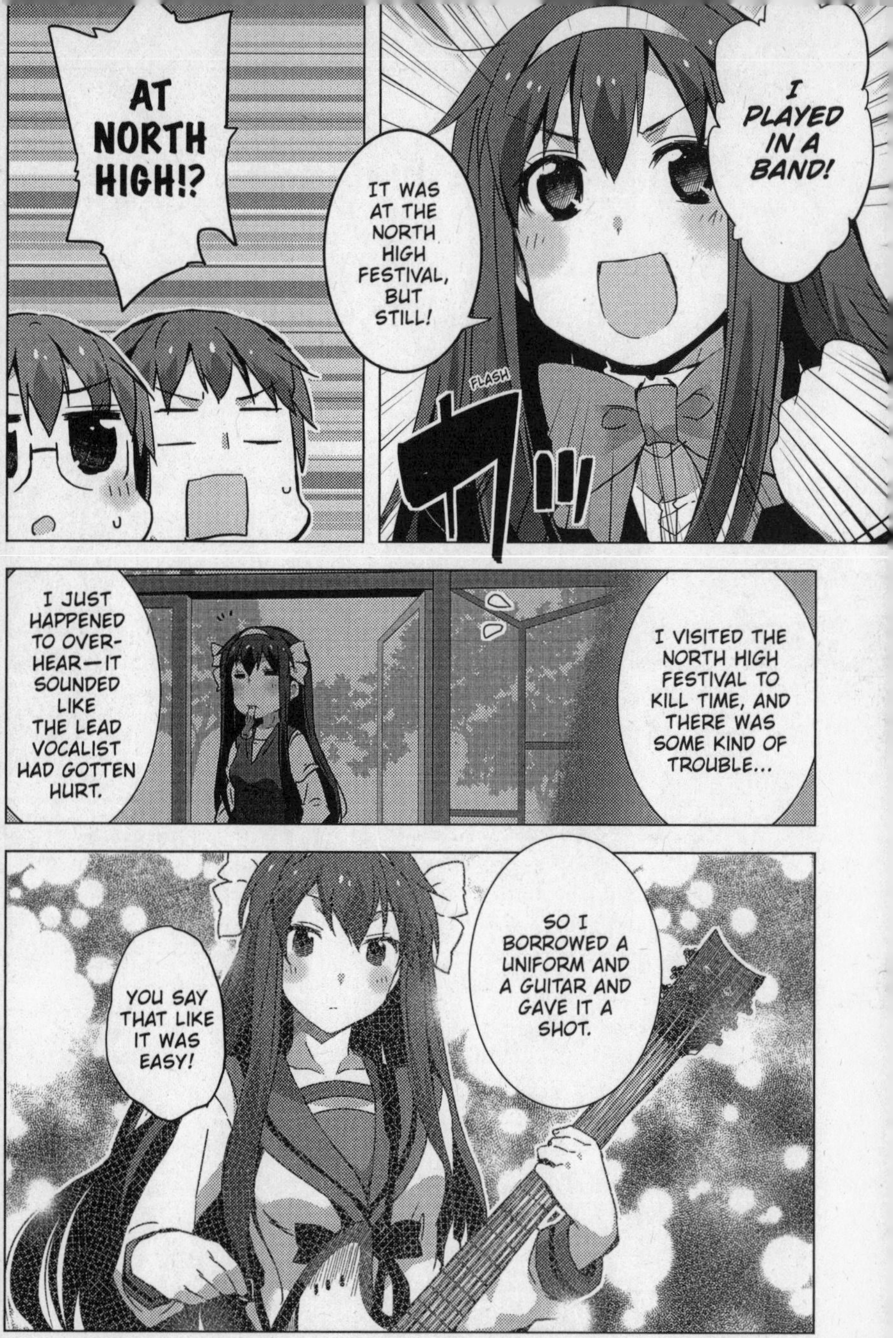
I PLAYED IN A BAND!
IT WAS AT THE NORTH HIGH FESTIVAL, BUT STILL!
FLASH
AT NORTH HIGH!?
I VISITED THE NORTH HIGH FESTIVAL TO KILL TIME, AND THERE WAS SOME KIND OF TROUBLE...
I JUST HAPPENED TO OVER-HEAR—IT SOUNDED LIKE THE LEAD VOCALIST HAD GOTTEN HURT.
SO I BORROWED A UNIFORM AND A GUITAR AND GAVE IT A SHOT.
YOU SAY THAT LIKE IT WAS EASY!

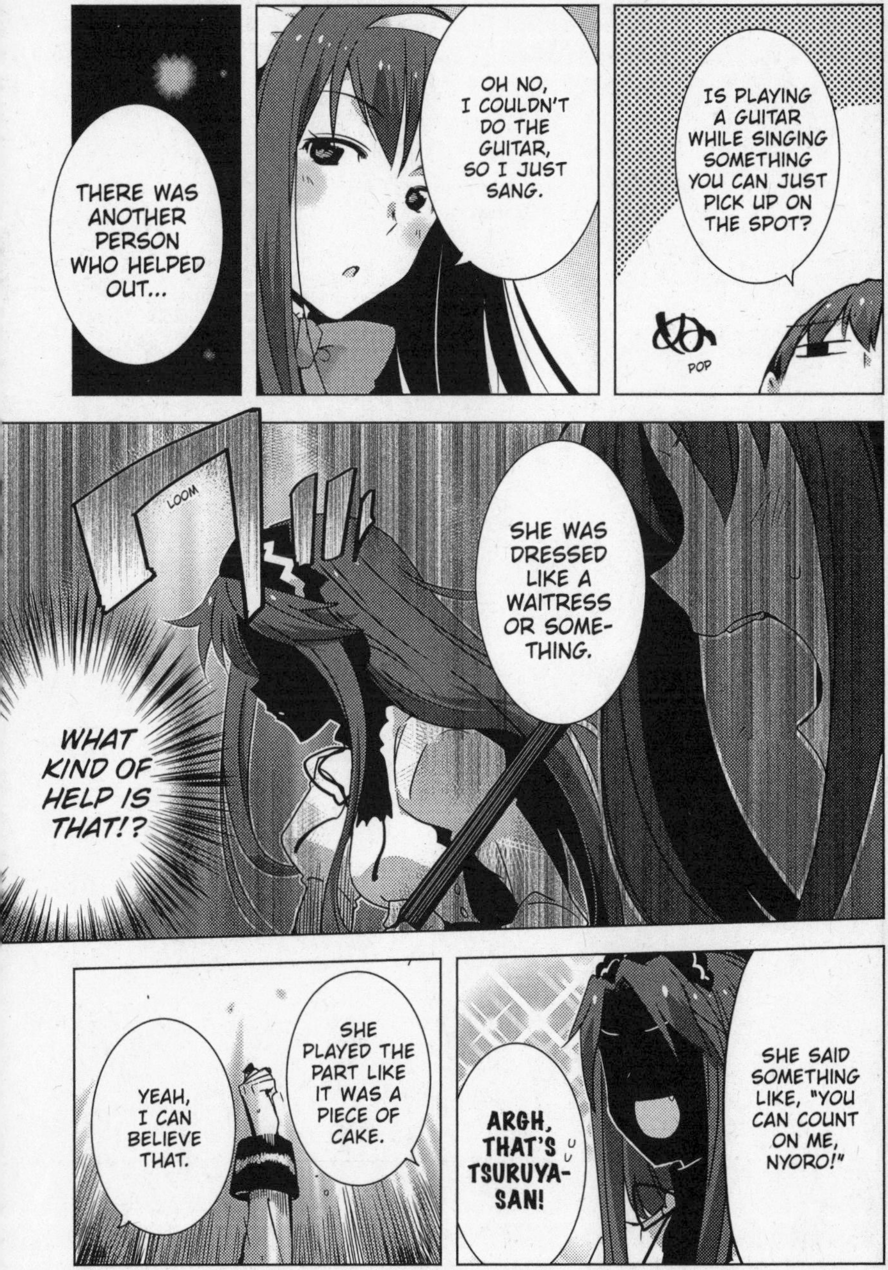
IS PLAYING A GUITAR WHILE SINGING SOMETHING YOU CAN JUST PICK UP ON THE SPOT?
ぬ
POP
OH NO, I COULDN'T DO THE GUITAR, SO I JUST SANG.
THERE WAS ANOTHER PERSON WHO HELPED OUT...
SHE WAS DRESSED LIKE A WAITRESS OR SOME-THING.
LOOM
WHAT KIND OF HELP IS THAT!?
SHE SAID SOMETHING LIKE, "YOU CAN COUNT ON ME, NYORO!"
ARGH, THAT'S TSURUYA-SAN!
SHE PLAYED THE PART LIKE IT WAS A PIECE OF CAKE.
YEAH, I CAN BELIEVE THAT.

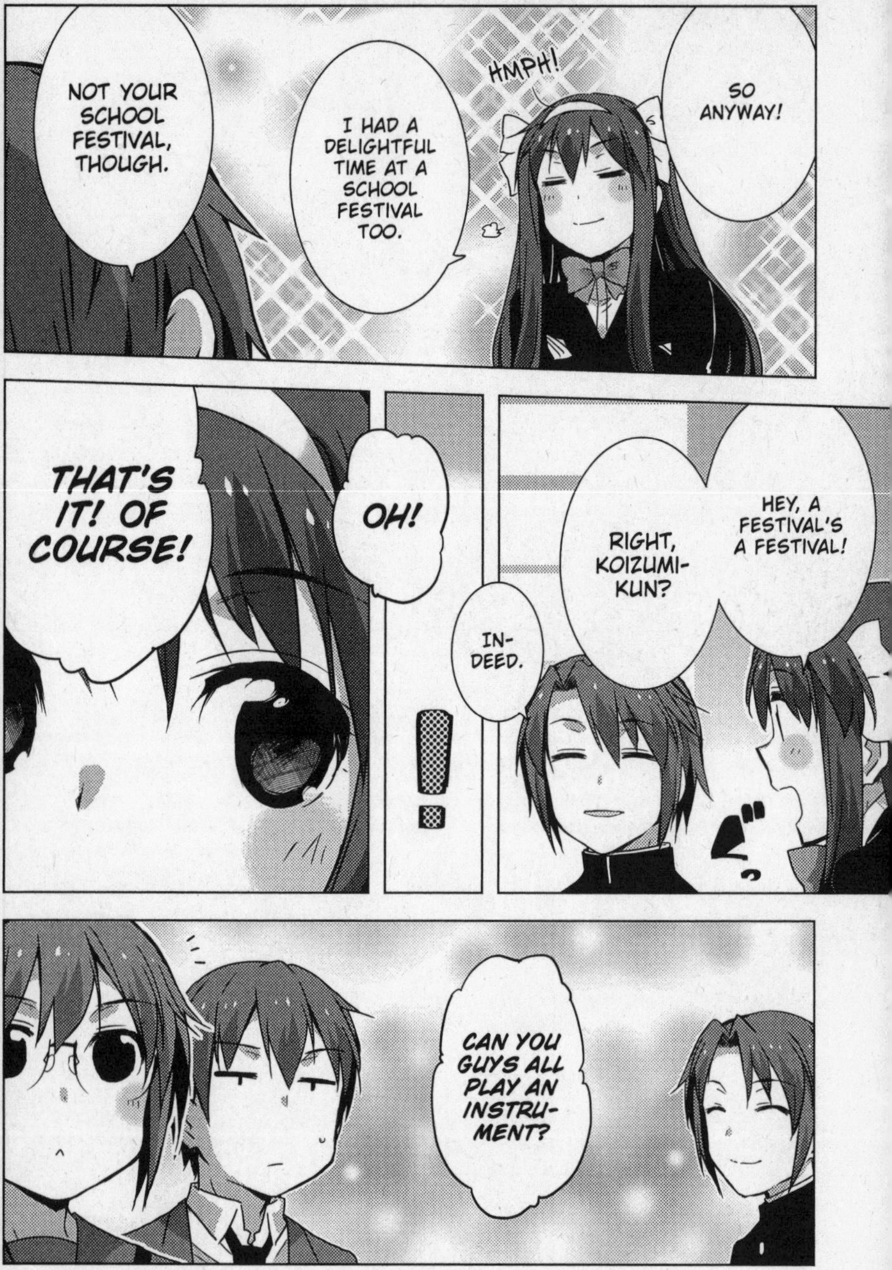
SO ANYWAY!
HMPH!
I HAD A DELIGHTFUL TIME AT A SCHOOL FESTIVAL TOO.
NOT YOUR SCHOOL FESTIVAL, THOUGH.
HEY, A FESTIVAL'S A FESTIVAL!
RIGHT, KOIZUMI-KUN?
IN-DEED.
!
OH!
THAT'S IT! OF COURSE!
CAN YOU GUYS ALL PLAY AN INSTRUMENT?

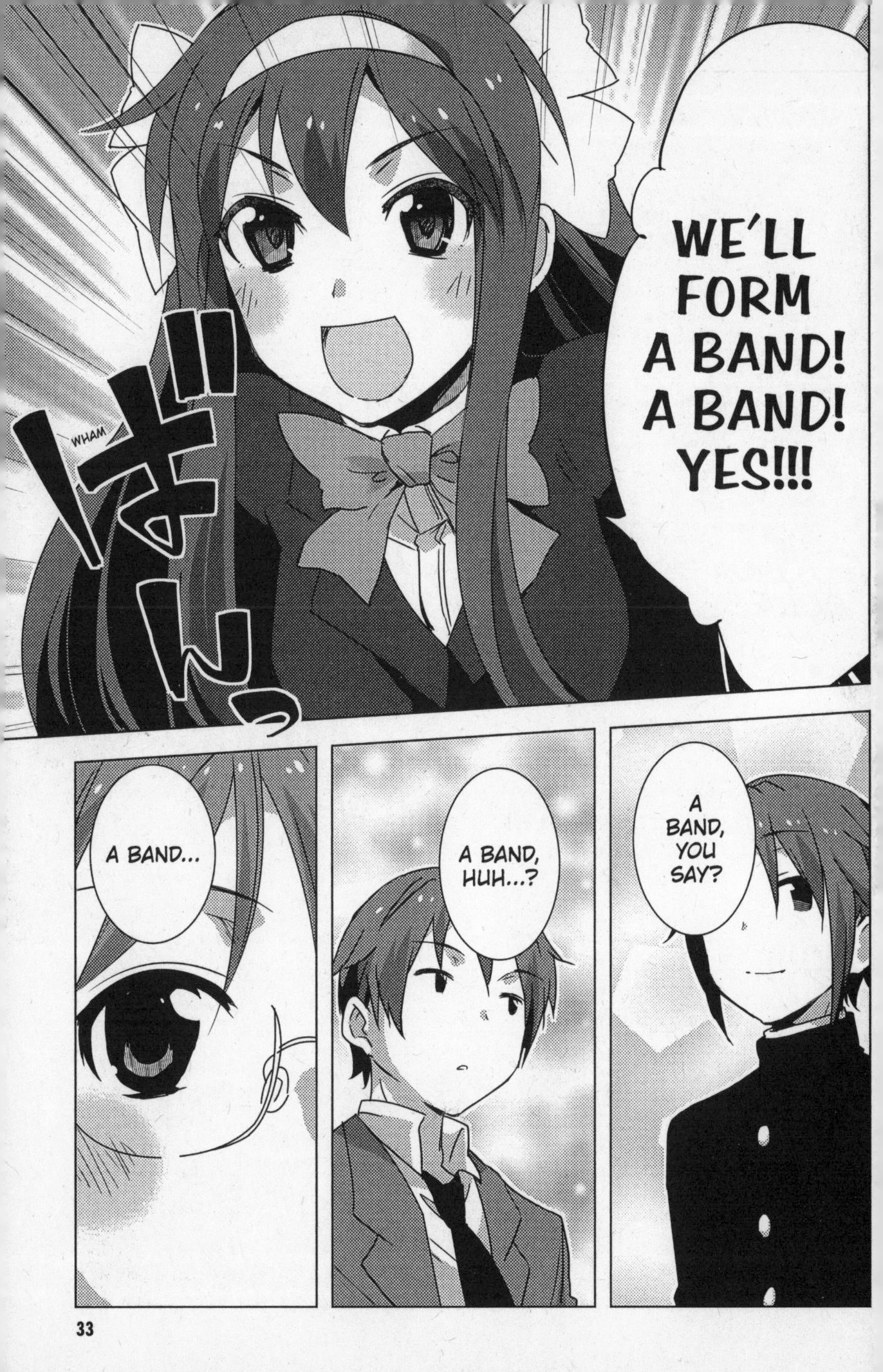
WE'LL FORM A BAND! A BAND! YES!!!
ばんっ
WHAM
A BAND, YOU SAY?
A BAND, HUH...?
A BAND...

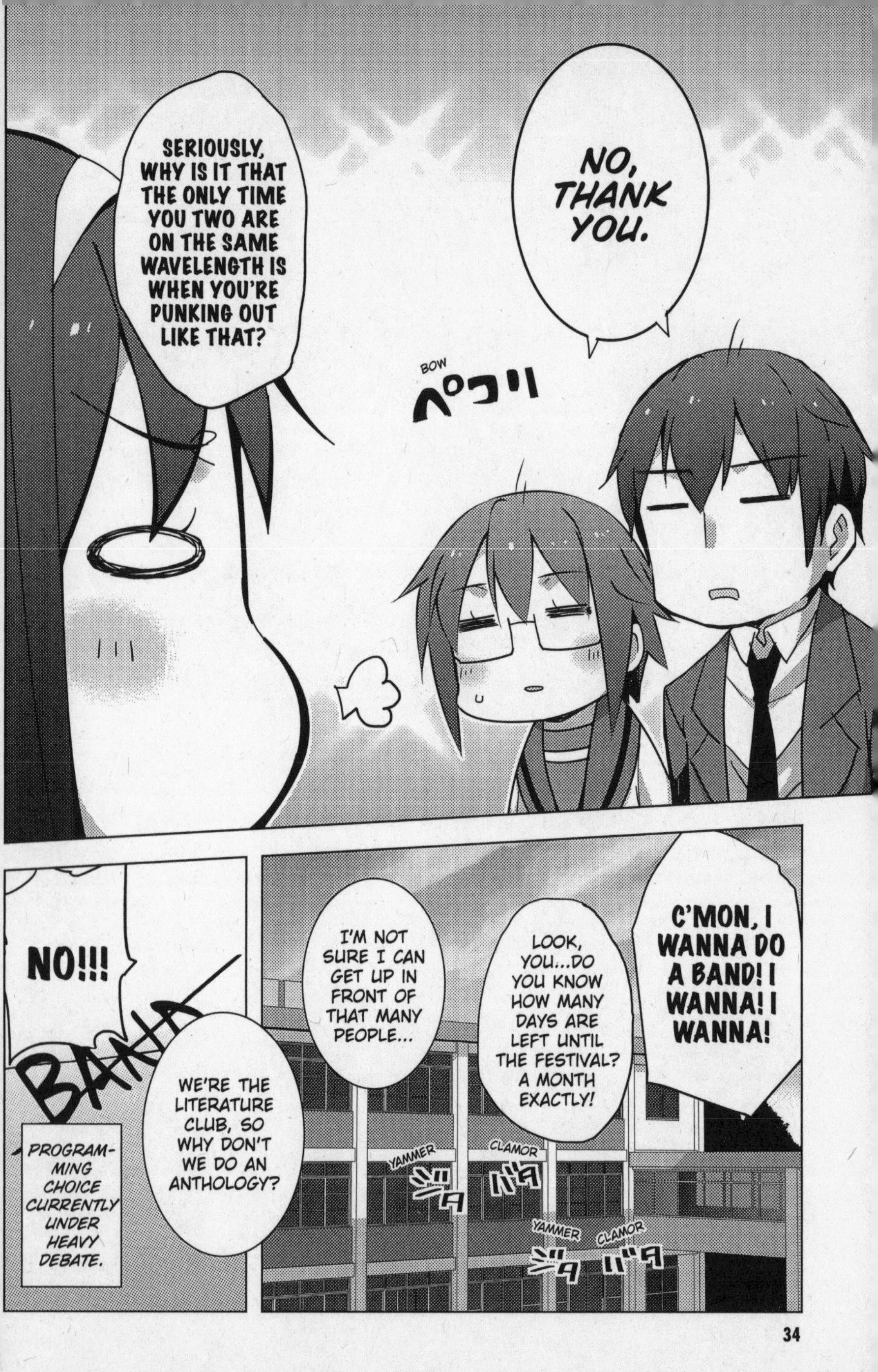

NO, THANK YOU.
BOW
ペコリ
SERIOUSLY, WHY IS IT THAT THE ONLY TIME YOU TWO ARE ON THE SAME WAVELENGTH IS WHEN YOU'RE PUNKING OUT LIKE THAT?
C'MON, I WANNA DO A BAND! I WANNA! I WANNA!
LOOK, YOU...DO YOU KNOW HOW MANY DAYS ARE LEFT UNTIL THE FESTIVAL? A MONTH EXACTLY!
I'M NOT SURE I CAN GET UP IN FRONT OF THAT MANY PEOPLE...
WE'RE THE LITERATURE CLUB, SO WHY DON'T WE DO AN ANTHOLOGY?
YAMMER
ジタ
CLAMOR
バタ
YAMMER
ジタ
CLAMOR
バタ
NO!!!
PROGRAM-MING CHOICE CURRENTLY UNDER HEAVY DEBATE.

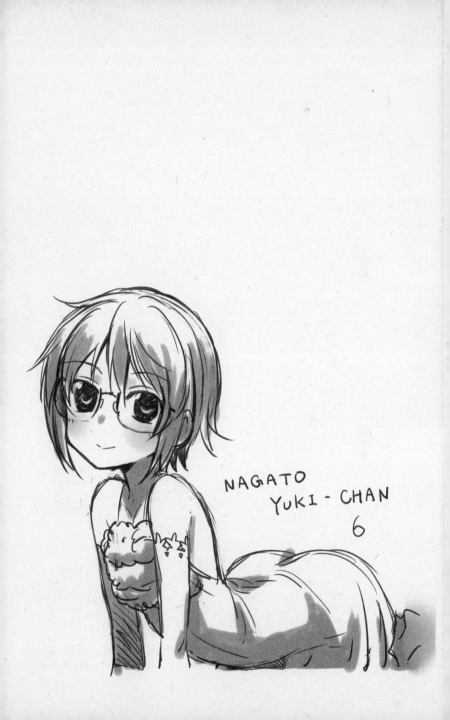

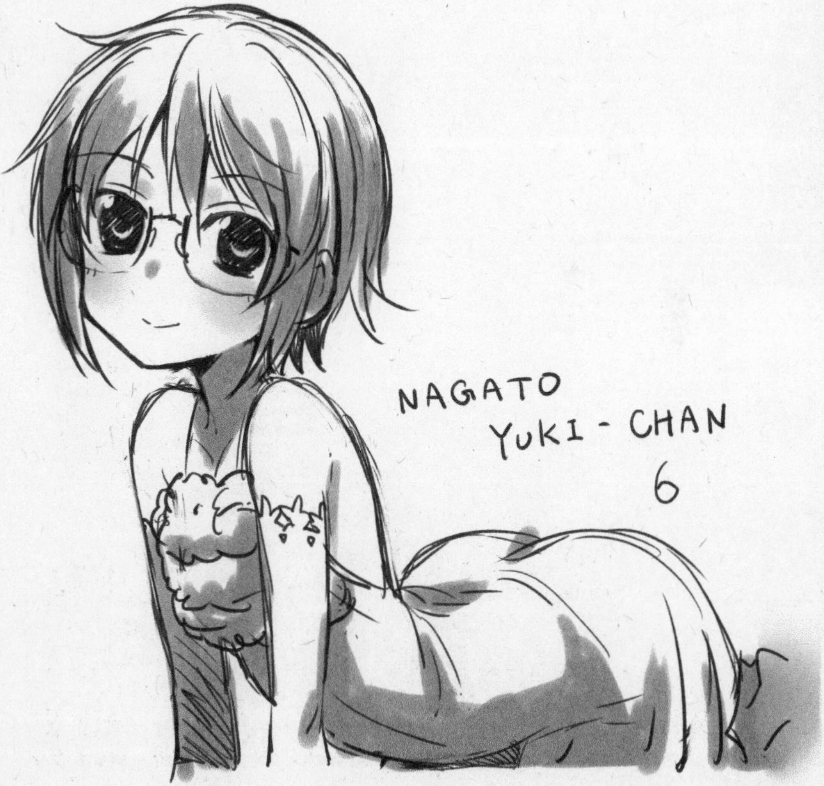
NAGATO
YUKI - CHAN
6

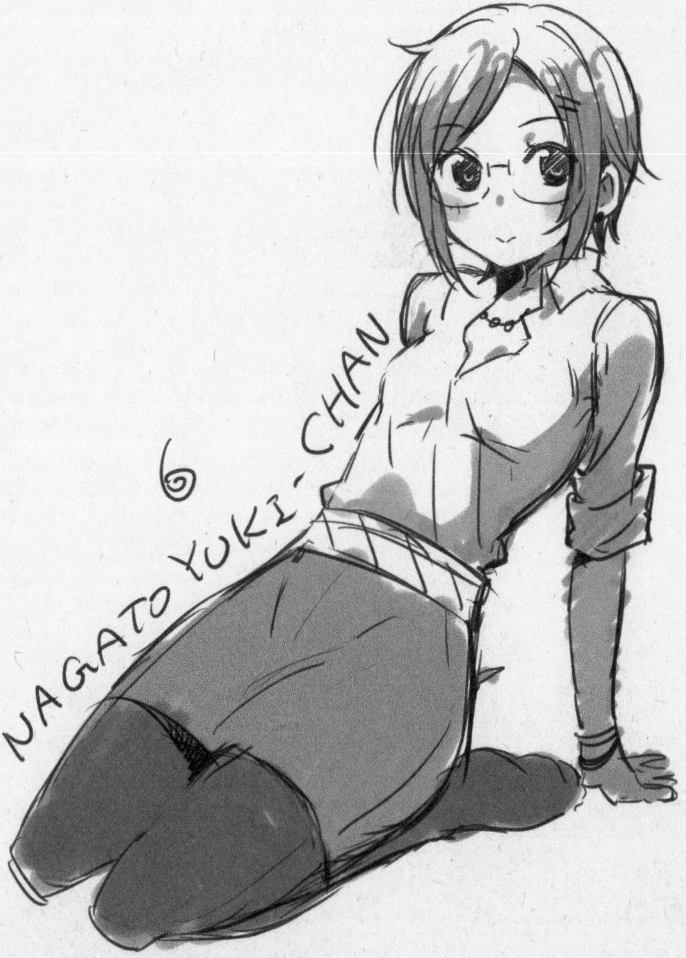
NAGATO YUKI-CHAN
6

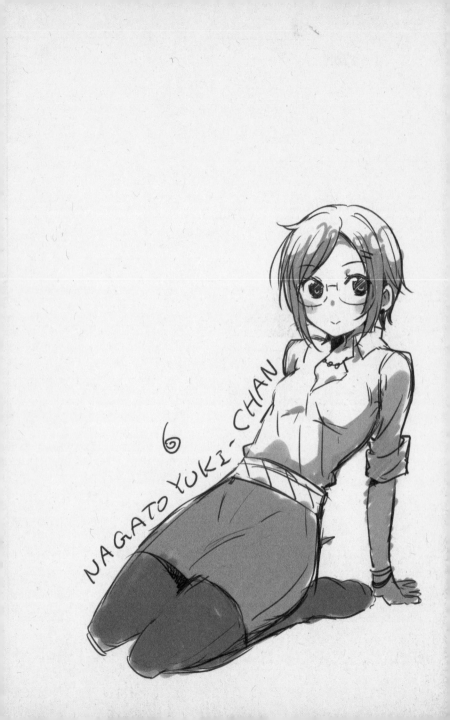

Epilogue 42>> Going Home

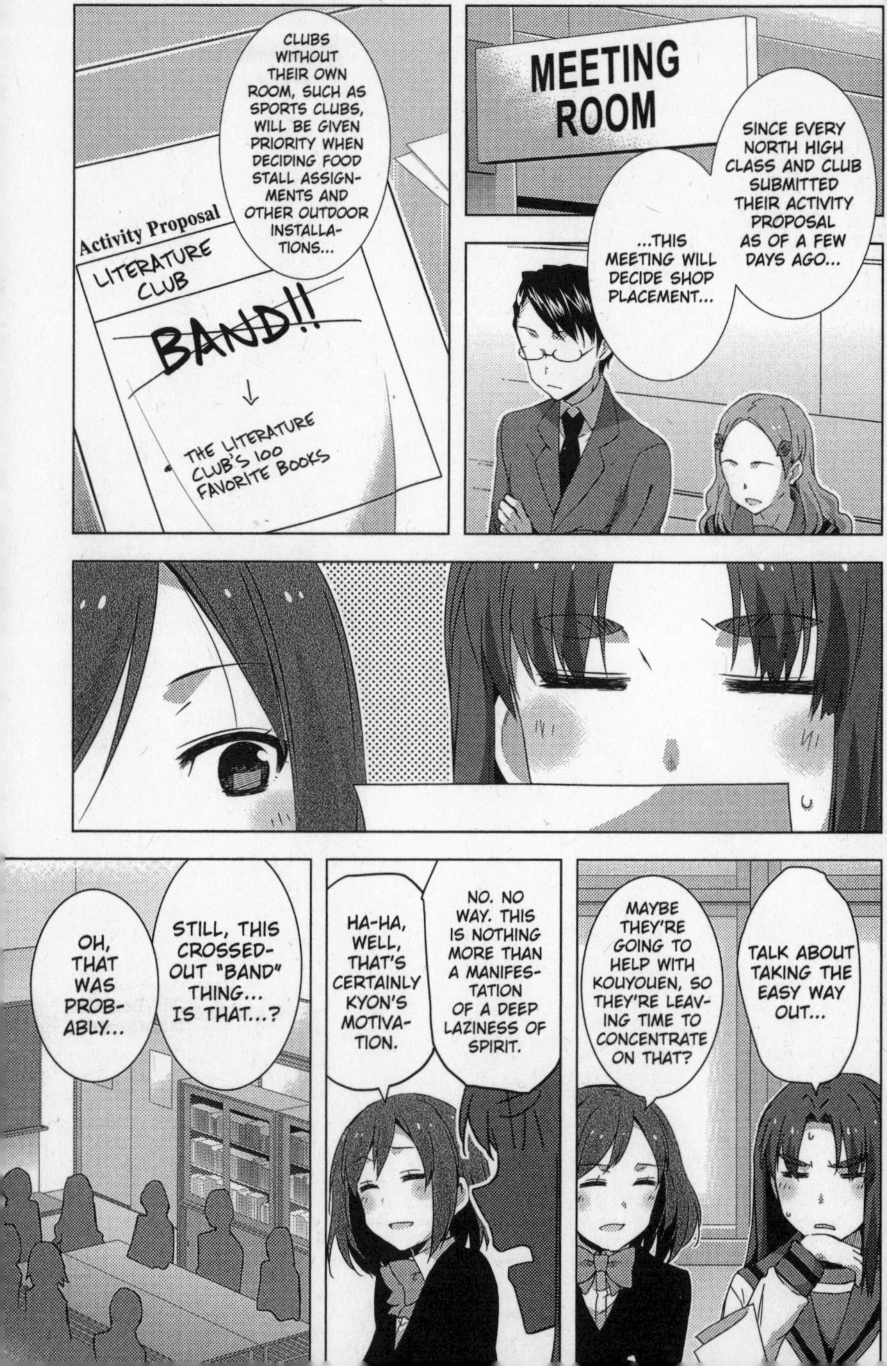
MEETING ROOM
SINCE EVERY NORTH HIGH CLASS AND CLUB SUBMITTED THEIR ACTIVITY PROPOSAL AS OF A FEW DAYS AGO...
...THIS MEETING WILL DECIDE SHOP PLACEMENT...
CLUBS WITHOUT THEIR OWN ROOM, SUCH AS SPORTS CLUBS, WILL BE GIVEN PRIORITY WHEN DECIDING FOOD STALL ASSIGNMENTS AND OTHER OUTDOOR INSTALLATIONS...
Activity Proposal
LITERATURE CLUB
BAND!!
THE LITERATURE CLUB'S 100 FAVORITE BOOKS
TALK ABOUT TAKING THE EASY WAY OUT...
MAYBE THEY'RE GOING TO HELP WITH KOUYOUEN, SO THEY'RE LEAVING TIME TO CONCENTRATE ON THAT?
NO. NO WAY. THIS IS NOTHING MORE THAN A MANIFESTATION OF A DEEP LAZINESS OF SPIRIT.
HA-HA, WELL, THAT'S CERTAINLY KYON'S MOTIVATION.
STILL, THIS CROSSED-OUT "BAND" THING... IS THAT...?
OH, THAT WAS PROBABLY...

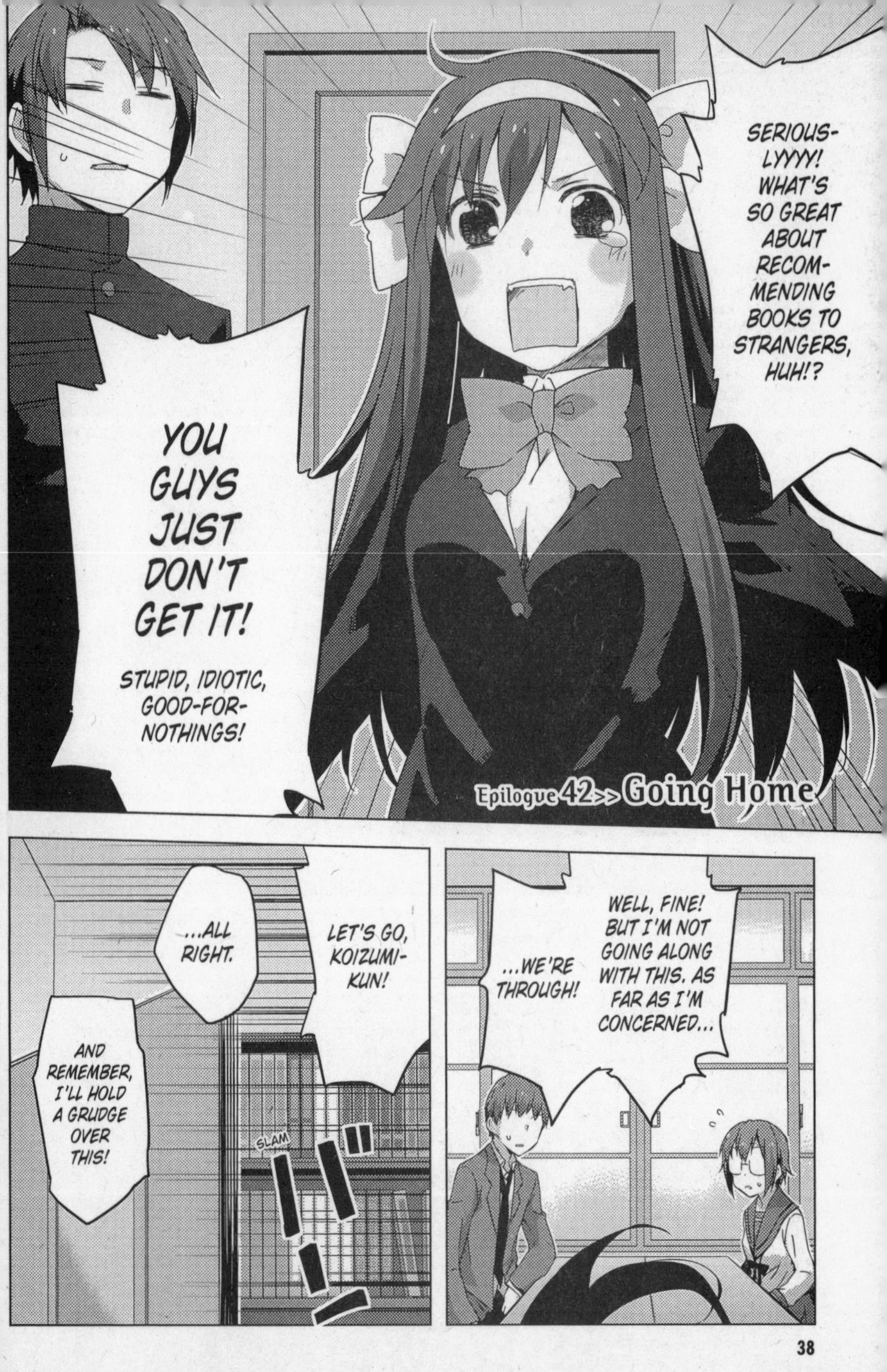
SERIOUS-LYYYY! WHAT'S SO GREAT ABOUT RECOM-MENDING BOOKS TO STRANGERS, HUH!?
YOU GUYS JUST DON'T GET IT!
STUPID, IDIOTIC, GOOD-FOR-NOTHINGS!
Epilogue 42>> Going Home
WELL, FINE! BUT I'M NOT GOING ALONG WITH THIS. AS FAR AS I'M CONCERNED...
...WE'RE THROUGH!
LET'S GO, KOIZUMI-KUN!
...ALL RIGHT.
AND REMEMBER, I'LL HOLD A GRUDGE OVER THIS!
SLAM

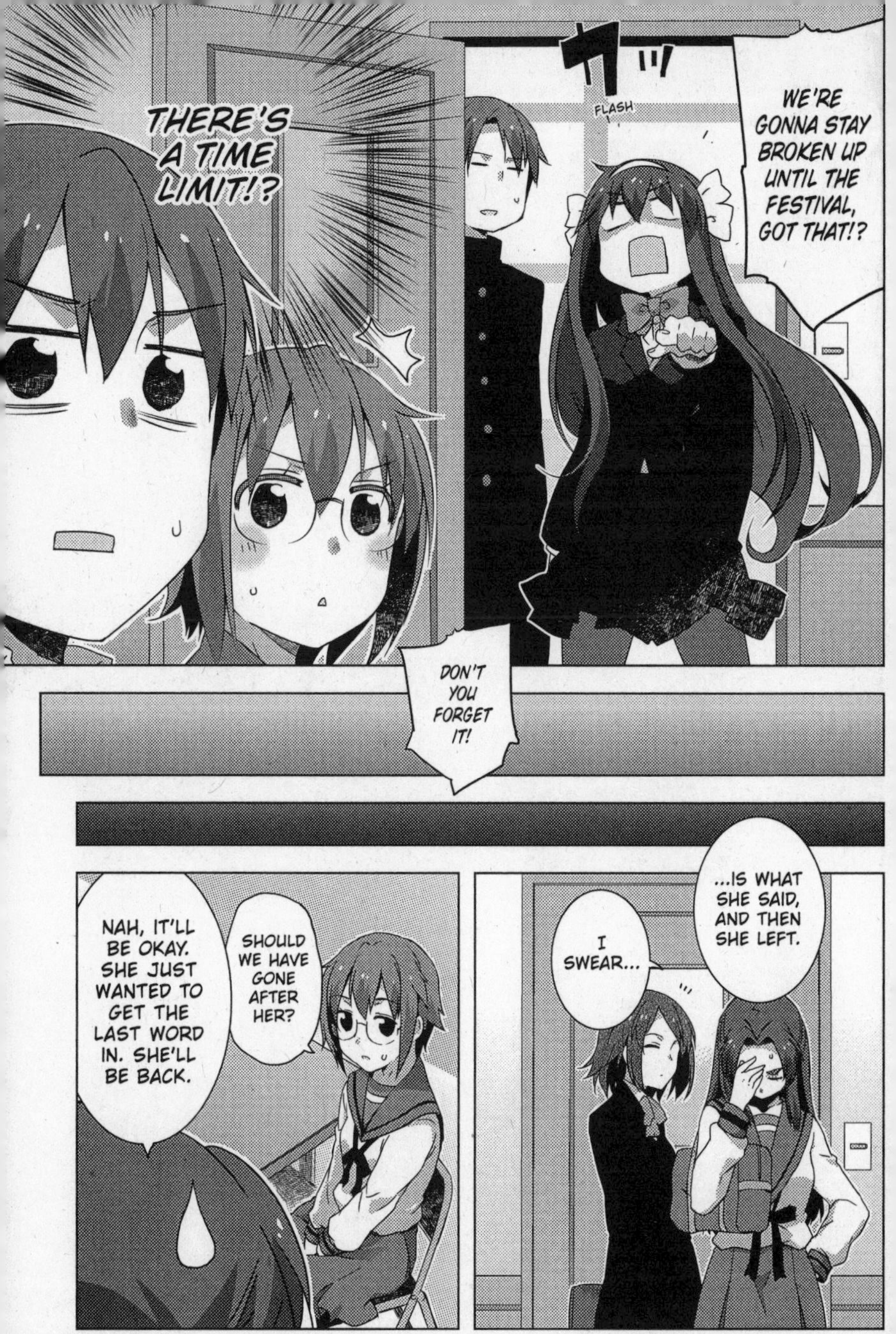
WE'RE GONNA STAY BROKEN UP UNTIL THE FESTIVAL, GOT THAT!?
FLASH
DON'T YOU FORGET IT!
THERE'S A TIME LIMIT!?
...IS WHAT SHE SAID, AND THEN SHE LEFT.
I SWEAR...
SHOULD WE HAVE GONE AFTER HER?
NAH, IT'LL BE OKAY. SHE JUST WANTED TO GET THE LAST WORD IN. SHE'LL BE BACK.

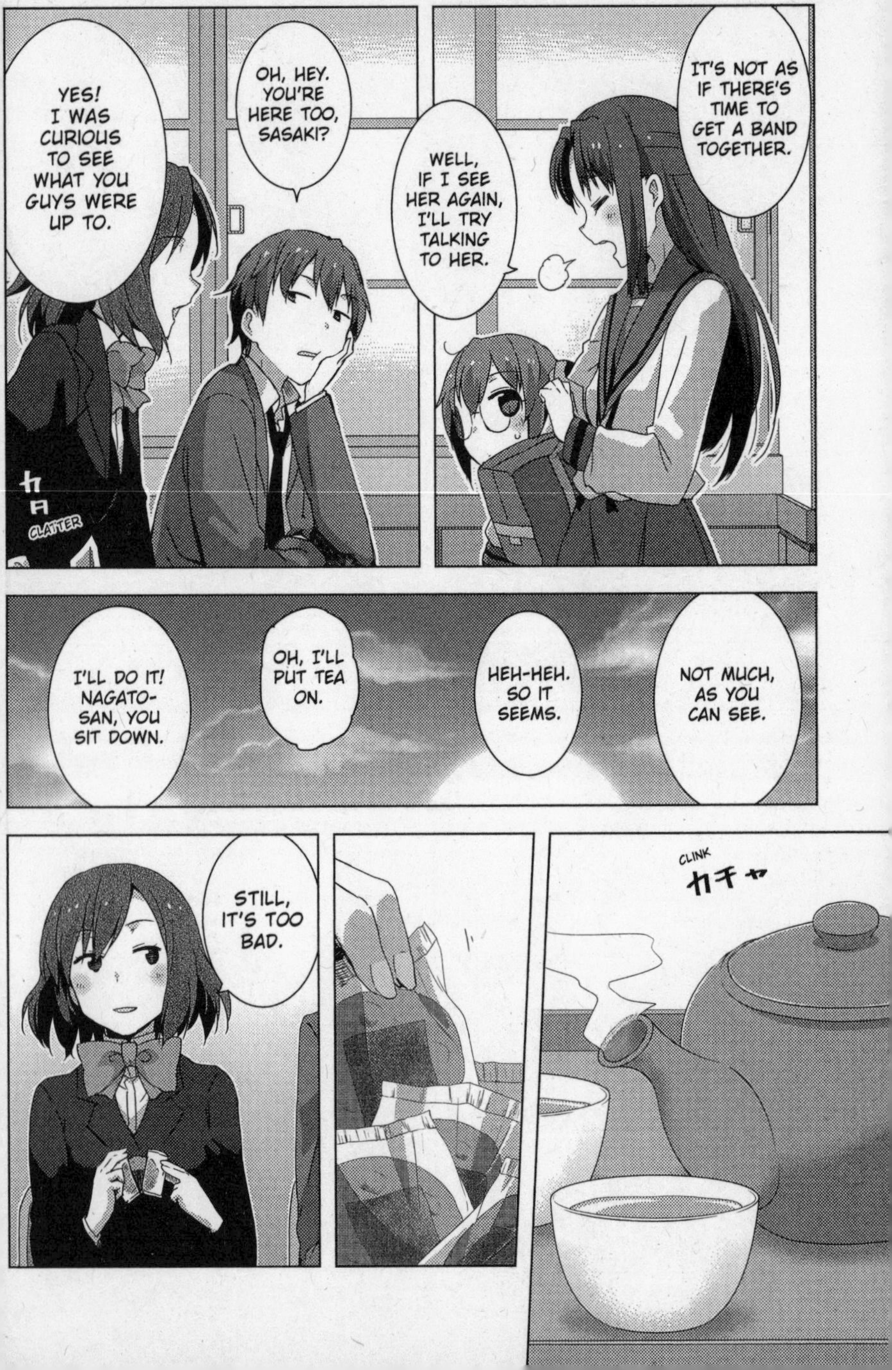
IT'S NOT AS IF THERE'S TIME TO GET A BAND TOGETHER.
WELL, IF I SEE HER AGAIN, I'LL TRY TALKING TO HER.
OH, HEY. YOU'RE HERE TOO, SASAKI?
YES! I WAS CURIOUS TO SEE WHAT YOU GUYS WERE UP TO.
カタ
CLATTER
NOT MUCH, AS YOU CAN SEE.
HEH-HEH. SO IT SEEMS.
OH, I'LL PUT TEA ON.
I'LL DO IT! NAGATO-SAN, YOU SIT DOWN.
CLINK
カチャ
STILL, IT'S TOO BAD.

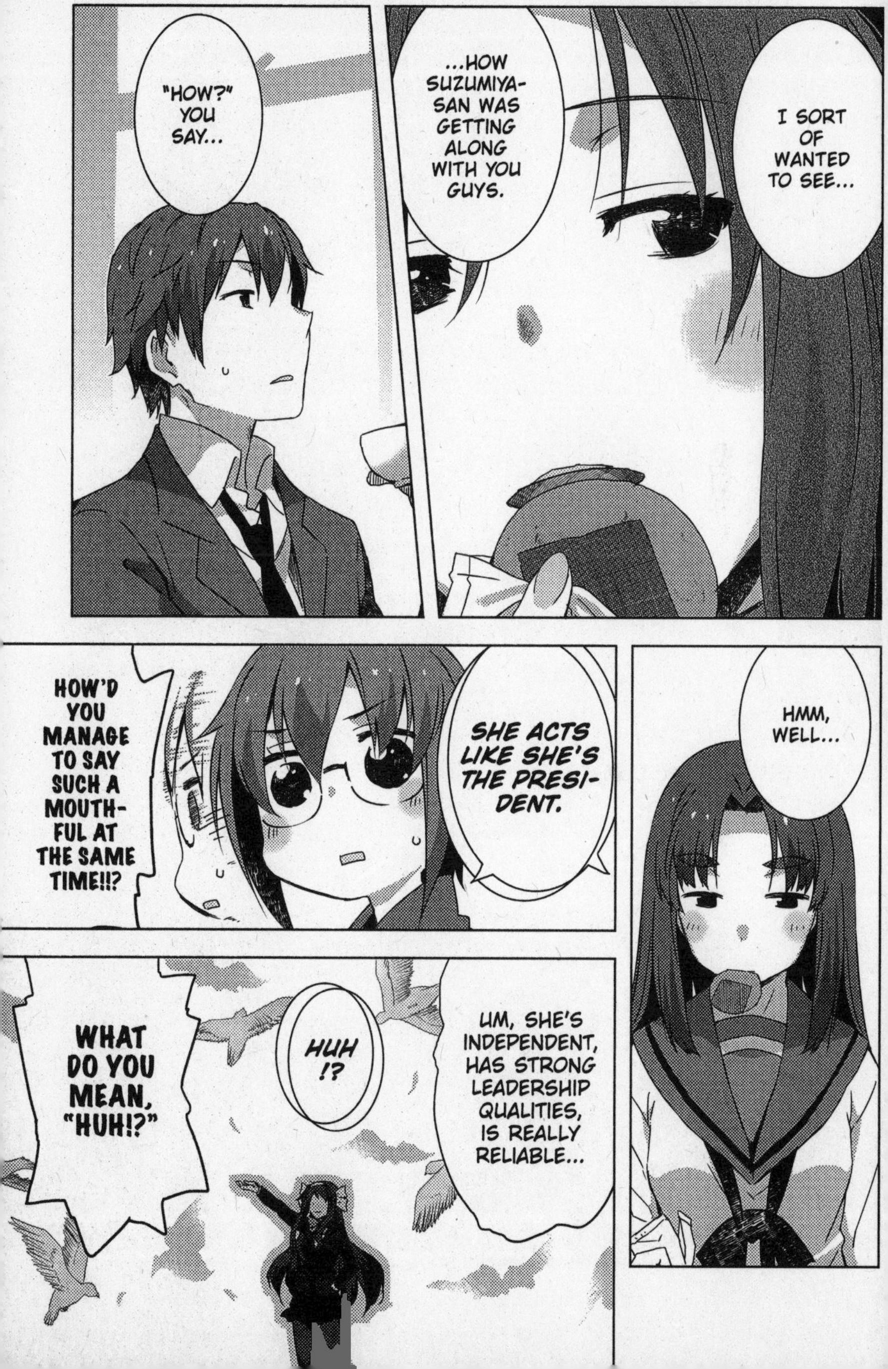
I SORT OF WANTED TO SEE...
...HOW SUZUMIYA-SAN WAS GETTING ALONG WITH YOU GUYS.
"HOW?" YOU SAY...
HMM, WELL...
SHE ACTS LIKE SHE'S THE PRESI-DENT.
HOW'D YOU MANAGE TO SAY SUCH A MOUTH-FUL AT THE SAME TIME!!?
UM, SHE'S INDEPENDENT, HAS STRONG LEADERSHIP QUALITIES, IS REALLY RELIABLE...
HUH !?
WHAT DO YOU MEAN, "HUH!?"

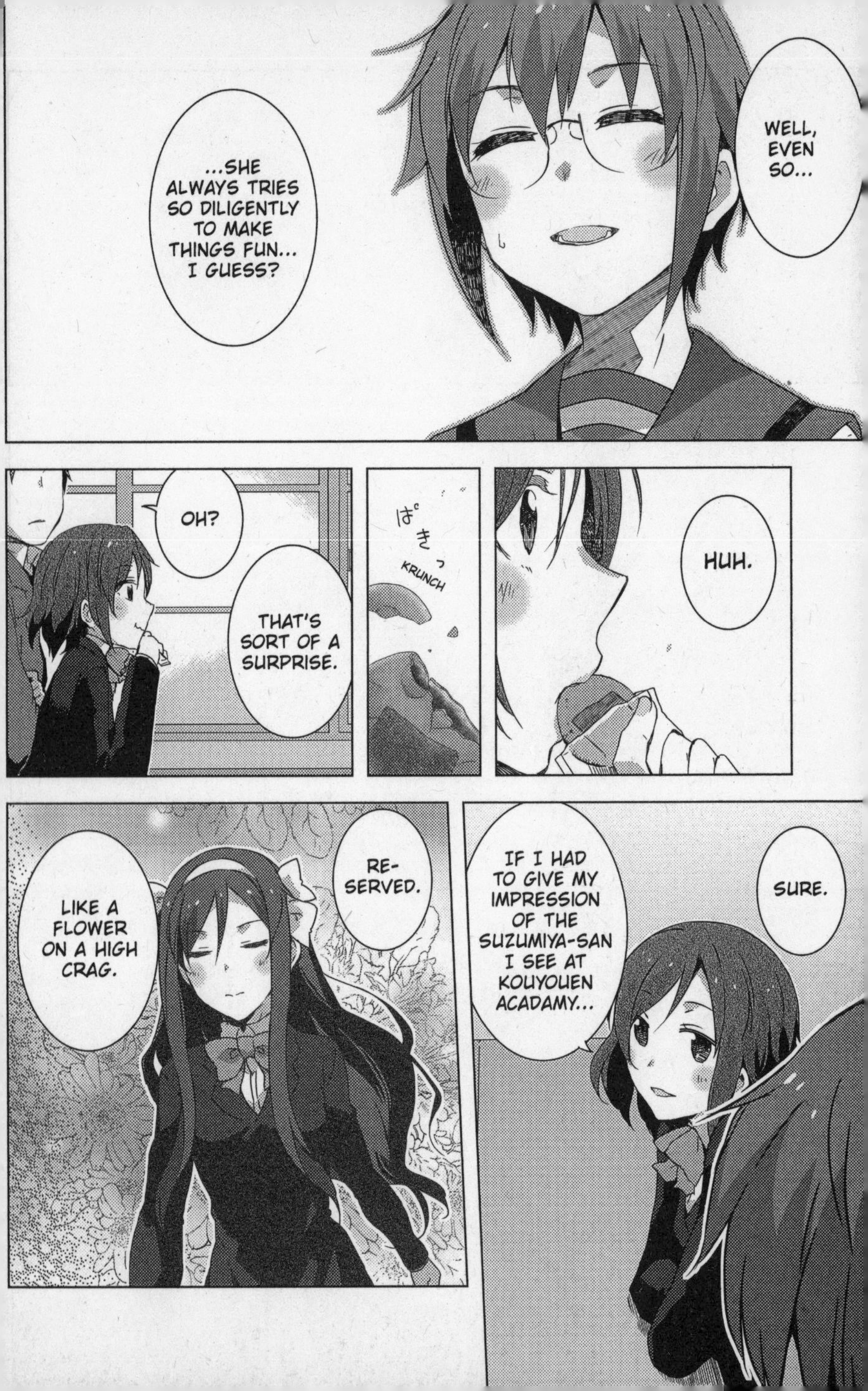
WELL, EVEN SO...
...SHE ALWAYS TRIES SO DILIGENTLY TO MAKE THINGS FUN... I GUESS?
HUH.
ぱきっ
KRUNCH
OH?
THAT'S SORT OF A SURPRISE.
SURE.
IF I HAD TO GIVE MY IMPRESSION OF THE SUZUMIYA-SAN I SEE AT KOUYOUEN ACADAMY...
RE-SERVED.
LIKE A FLOWER ON A HIGH CRAG.

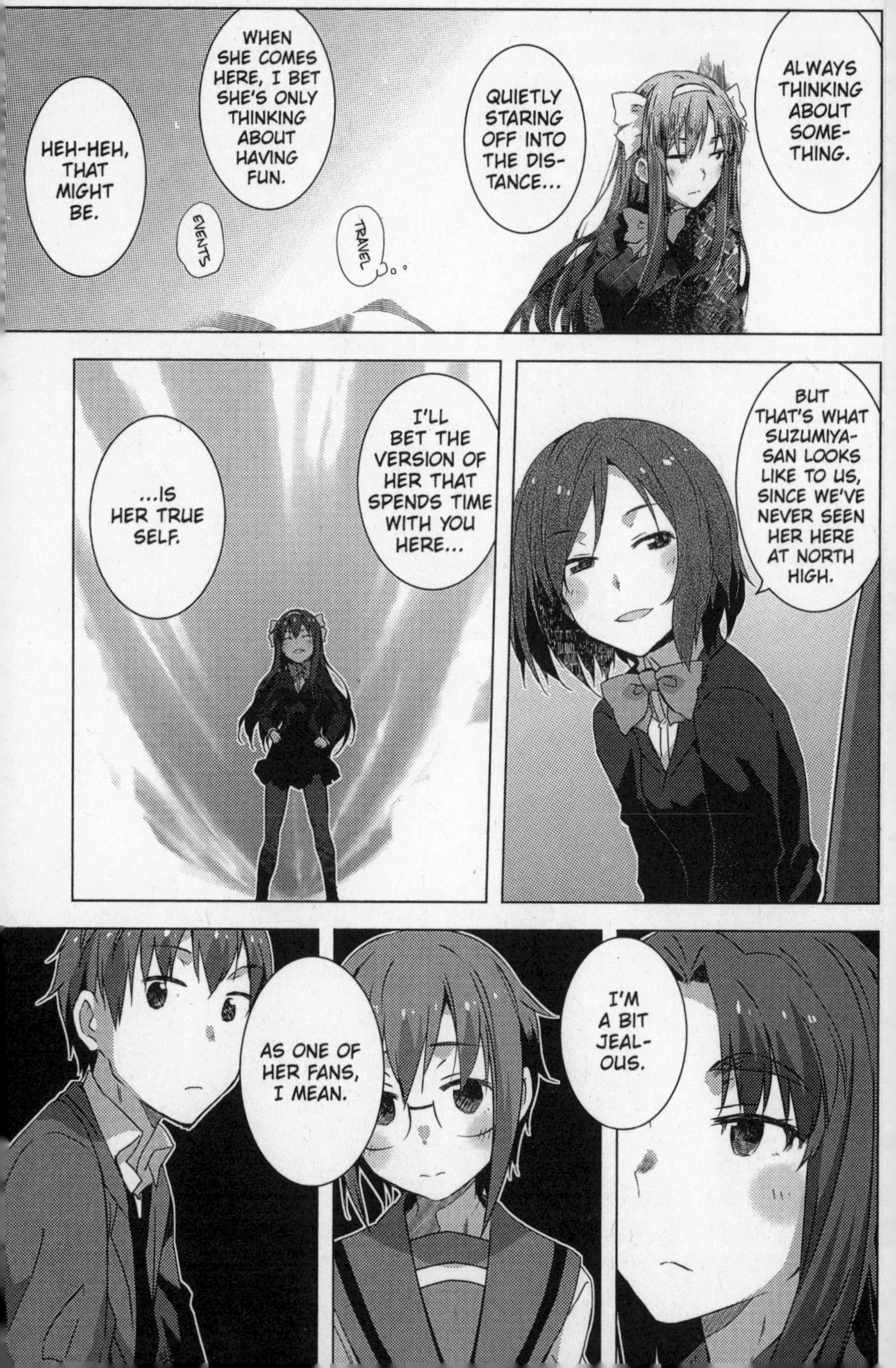
ALWAYS THINKING ABOUT SOME-THING.
QUIETLY STARING OFF INTO THE DIS-TANCE...
WHEN SHE COMES HERE, I BET SHE'S ONLY THINKING ABOUT HAVING FUN.
TRAVEL
EVENTS
HEH-HEH, THAT MIGHT BE.
BUT THAT'S WHAT SUZUMIYA-SAN LOOKS LIKE TO US, SINCE WE'VE NEVER SEEN HER HERE AT NORTH HIGH.
I'LL BET THE VERSION OF HER THAT SPENDS TIME WITH YOU HERE...
...IS HER TRUE SELF.
I'M A BIT JEAL-OUS.
AS ONE OF HER FANS, I MEAN.

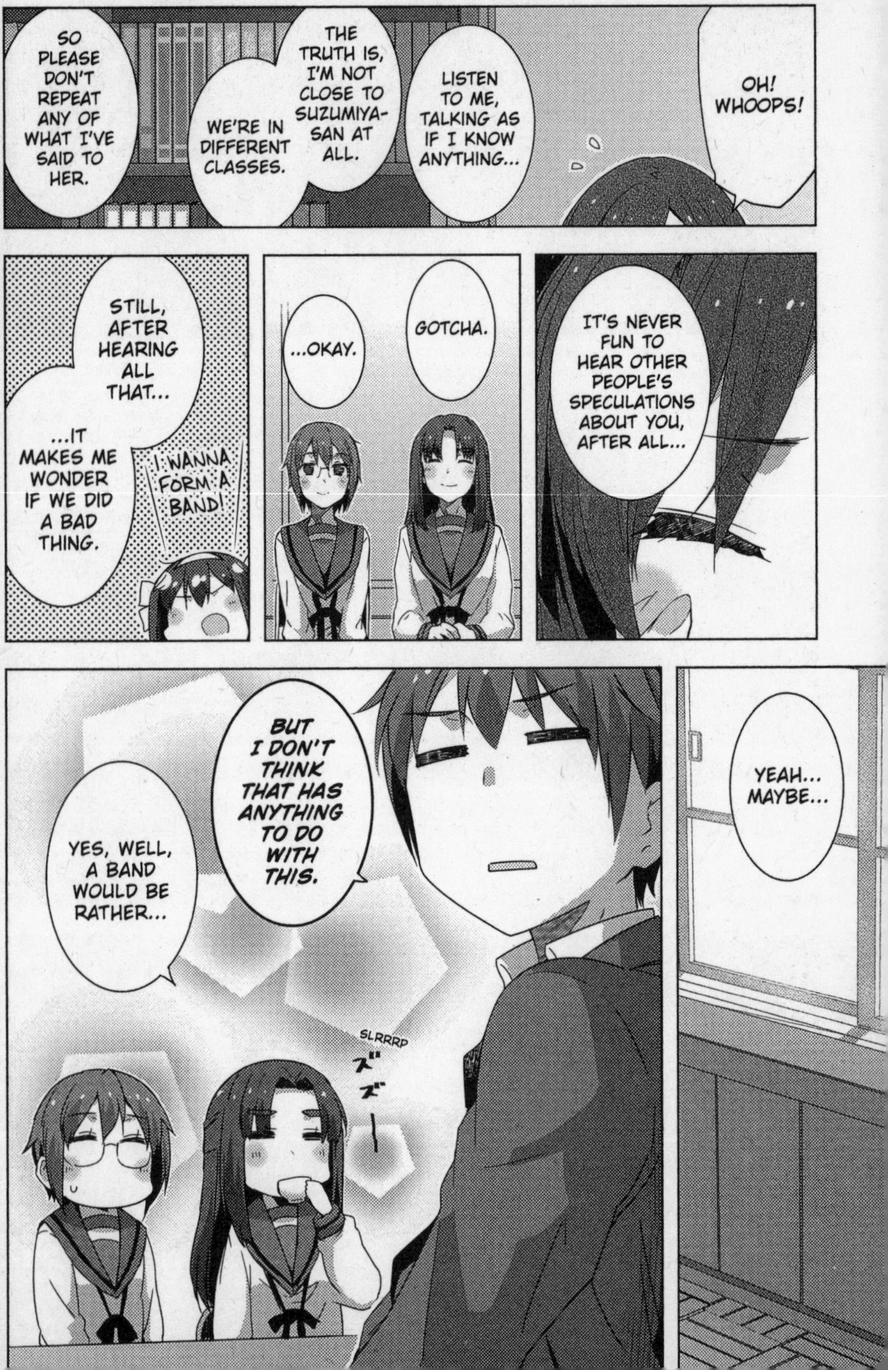
OH! WHOOPS!
LISTEN TO ME, TALKING AS IF I KNOW ANYTHING...
THE TRUTH IS, I'M NOT CLOSE TO SUZUMIYA-SAN AT ALL.
WE'RE IN DIFFERENT CLASSES.
SO PLEASE DON'T REPEAT ANY OF WHAT I'VE SAID TO HER.
IT'S NEVER FUN TO HEAR OTHER PEOPLE'S SPECULATIONS ABOUT YOU, AFTER ALL...
GOTCHA.
...OKAY.
STILL, AFTER HEARING ALL THAT...
I WANNA FORM A BAND!
...IT MAKES ME WONDER IF WE DID A BAD THING.
YEAH... MAYBE...
BUT I DON'T THINK THAT HAS ANYTHING TO DO WITH THIS.
YES, WELL, A BAND WOULD BE RATHER...
SLRRRP
ズズー

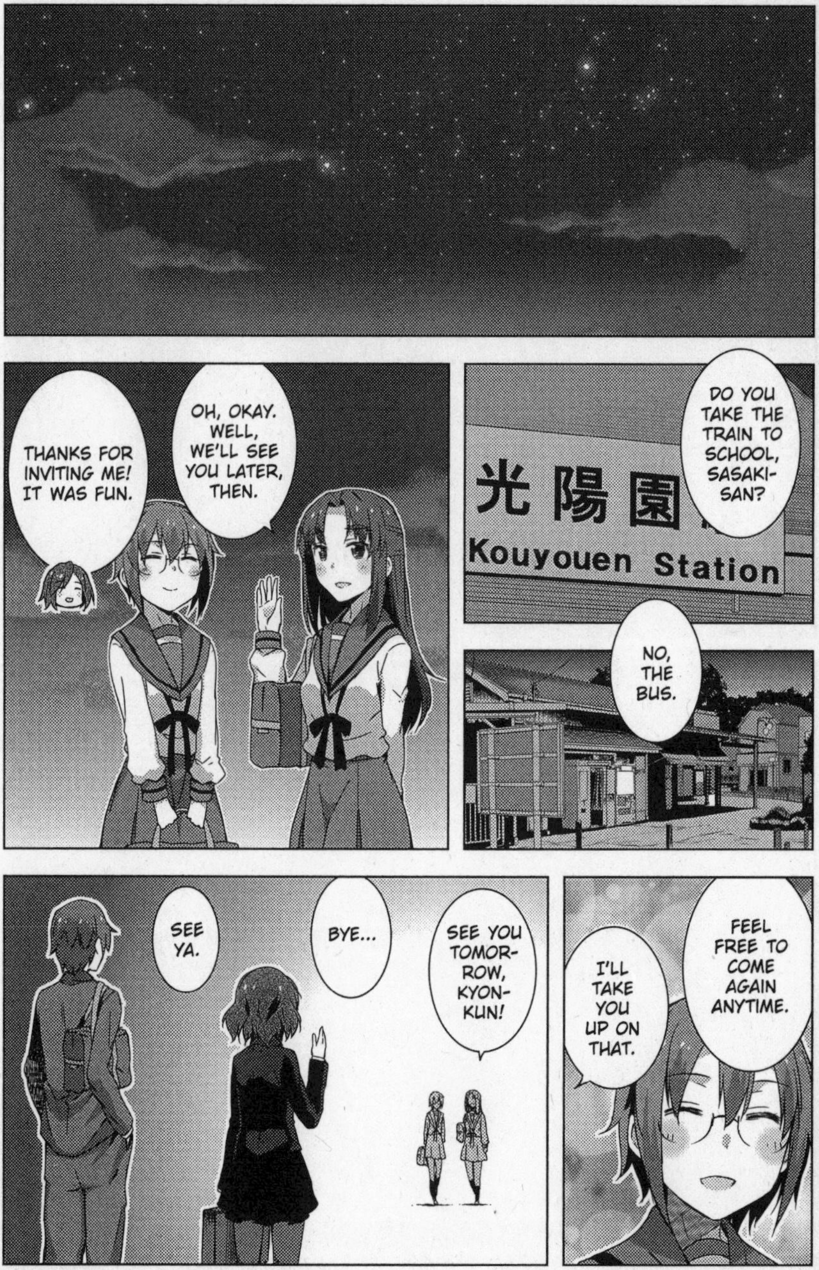
光陽園
Kouyouen Station
DO YOU TAKE THE TRAIN TO SCHOOL, SASAKI-SAN?
NO, THE BUS.
OH, OKAY. WELL, WE'LL SEE YOU LATER, THEN.
THANKS FOR INVITING ME! IT WAS FUN.
FEEL FREE TO COME AGAIN ANYTIME.
I'LL TAKE YOU UP ON THAT.
SEE YOU TOMOR-ROW, KYON-KUN!
BYE...
SEE YA.

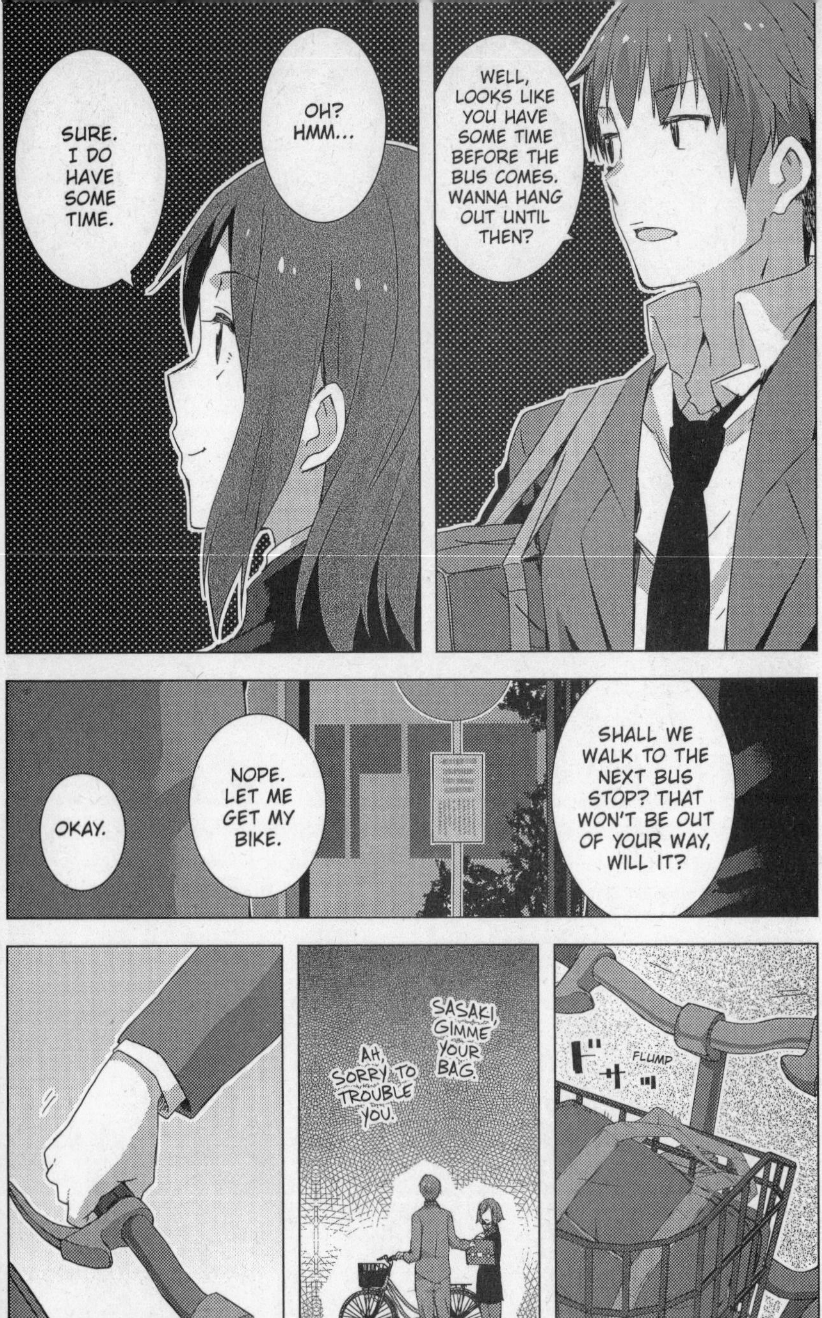
WELL, LOOKS LIKE YOU HAVE SOME TIME BEFORE THE BUS COMES. WANNA HANG OUT UNTIL THEN?
OH? HMM...
SURE. I DO HAVE SOME TIME.
SHALL WE WALK TO THE NEXT BUS STOP? THAT WON'T BE OUT OF YOUR WAY, WILL IT?
NOPE. LET ME GET MY BIKE.
OKAY.
ドサッ
FLUMP
SASAKI, GIMME YOUR BAG.
AH, SORRY TO TROUBLE YOU.

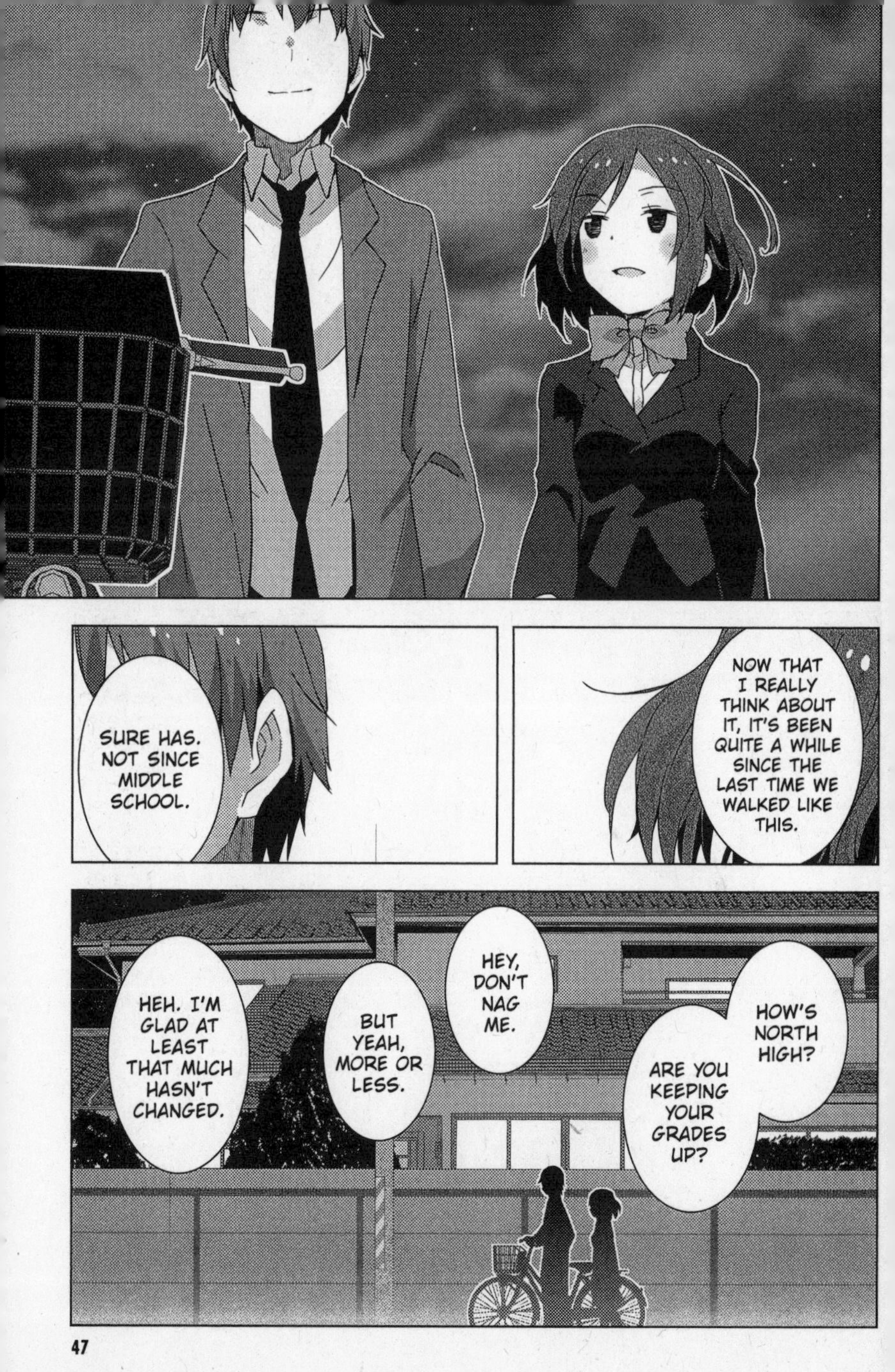
NOW THAT I REALLY THINK ABOUT IT, IT'S BEEN QUITE A WHILE SINCE THE LAST TIME WE WALKED LIKE THIS.
SURE HAS. NOT SINCE MIDDLE SCHOOL.
HOW'S NORTH HIGH?
ARE YOU KEEPING YOUR GRADES UP?
HEY, DON'T NAG ME.
BUT YEAH, MORE OR LESS.
HEH. I'M GLAD AT LEAST THAT MUCH HASN'T CHANGED.

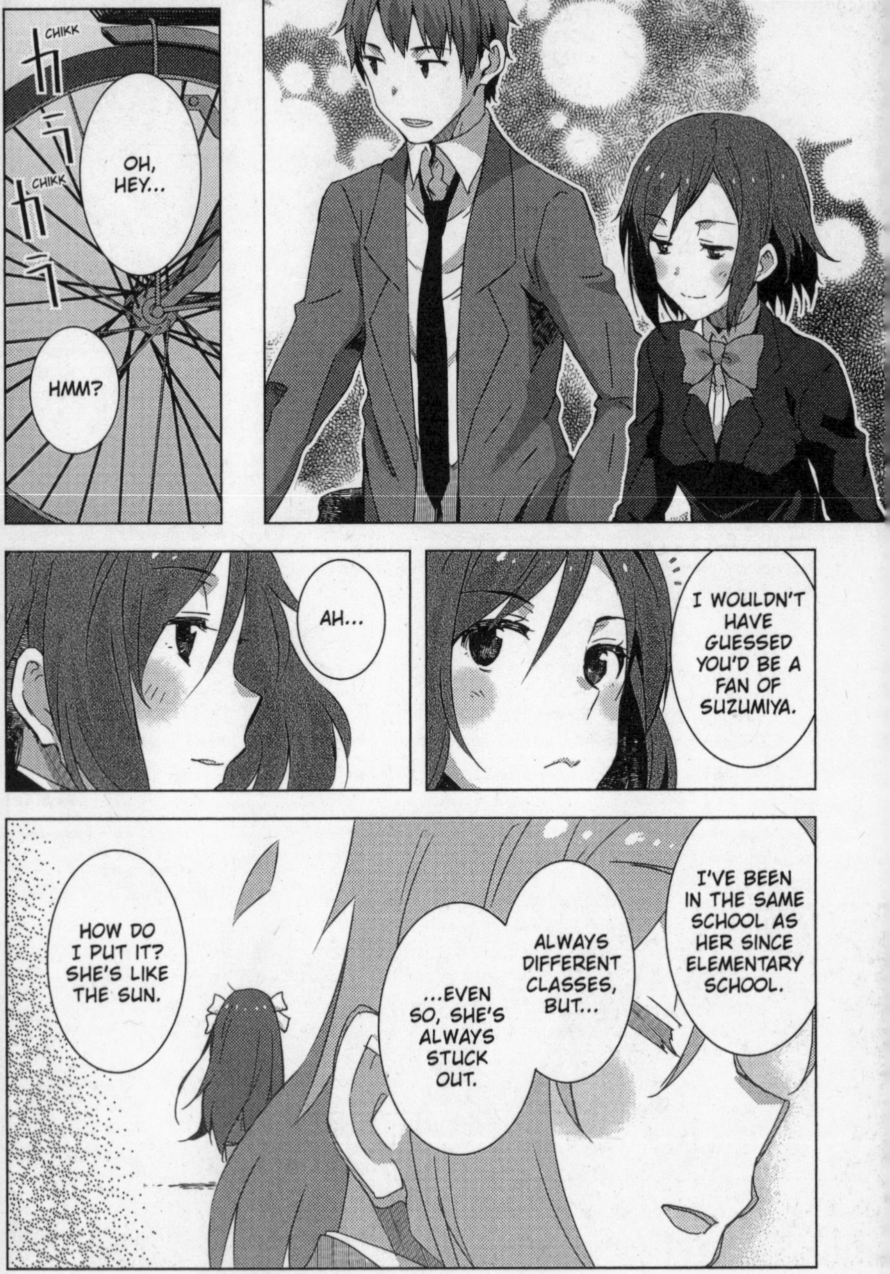
CHIKK
OH, HEY...
CHIKK
HMM?
I WOULDN'T HAVE GUESSED YOU'D BE A FAN OF SUZUMIYA.
AH...
I'VE BEEN IN THE SAME SCHOOL AS HER SINCE ELEMENTARY SCHOOL.
ALWAYS DIFFERENT CLASSES, BUT...
...EVEN SO, SHE'S ALWAYS STUCK OUT.
HOW DO I PUT IT? SHE'S LIKE THE SUN.

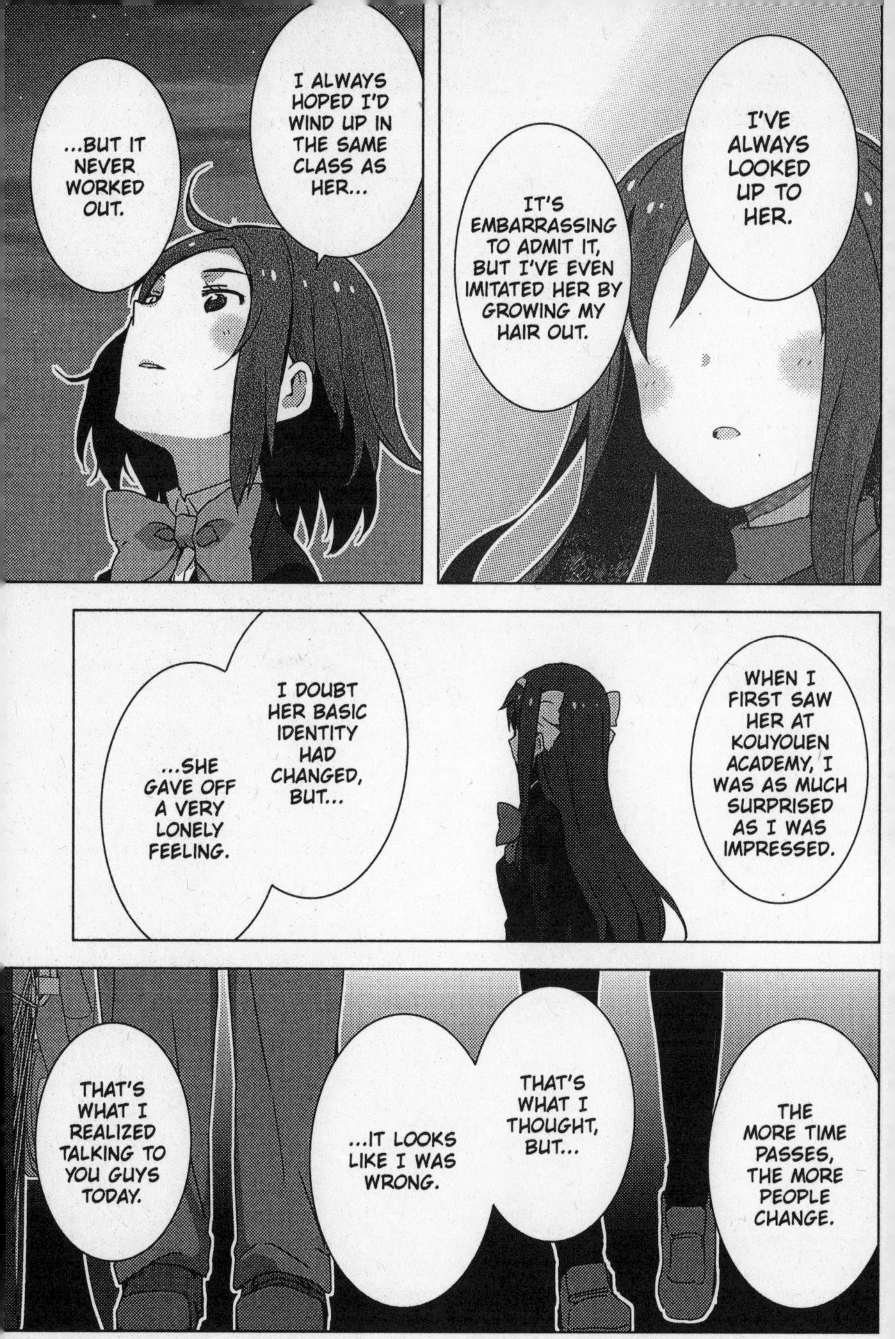
I'VE ALWAYS LOOKED UP TO HER.
IT'S EMBARRASSING TO ADMIT IT, BUT I'VE EVEN IMITATED HER BY GROWING MY HAIR OUT.
I ALWAYS HOPED I'D WIND UP IN THE SAME CLASS AS HER...
...BUT IT NEVER WORKED OUT.
WHEN I FIRST SAW HER AT KOUYOUEN ACADEMY, I WAS AS MUCH SURPRISED AS I WAS IMPRESSED.
I DOUBT HER BASIC IDENTITY HAD CHANGED, BUT...
...SHE GAVE OFF A VERY LONELY FEELING.
THE MORE TIME PASSES, THE MORE PEOPLE CHANGE.
THAT'S WHAT I THOUGHT, BUT...
...IT LOOKS LIKE I WAS WRONG.
THAT'S WHAT I REALIZED TALKING TO YOU GUYS TODAY.

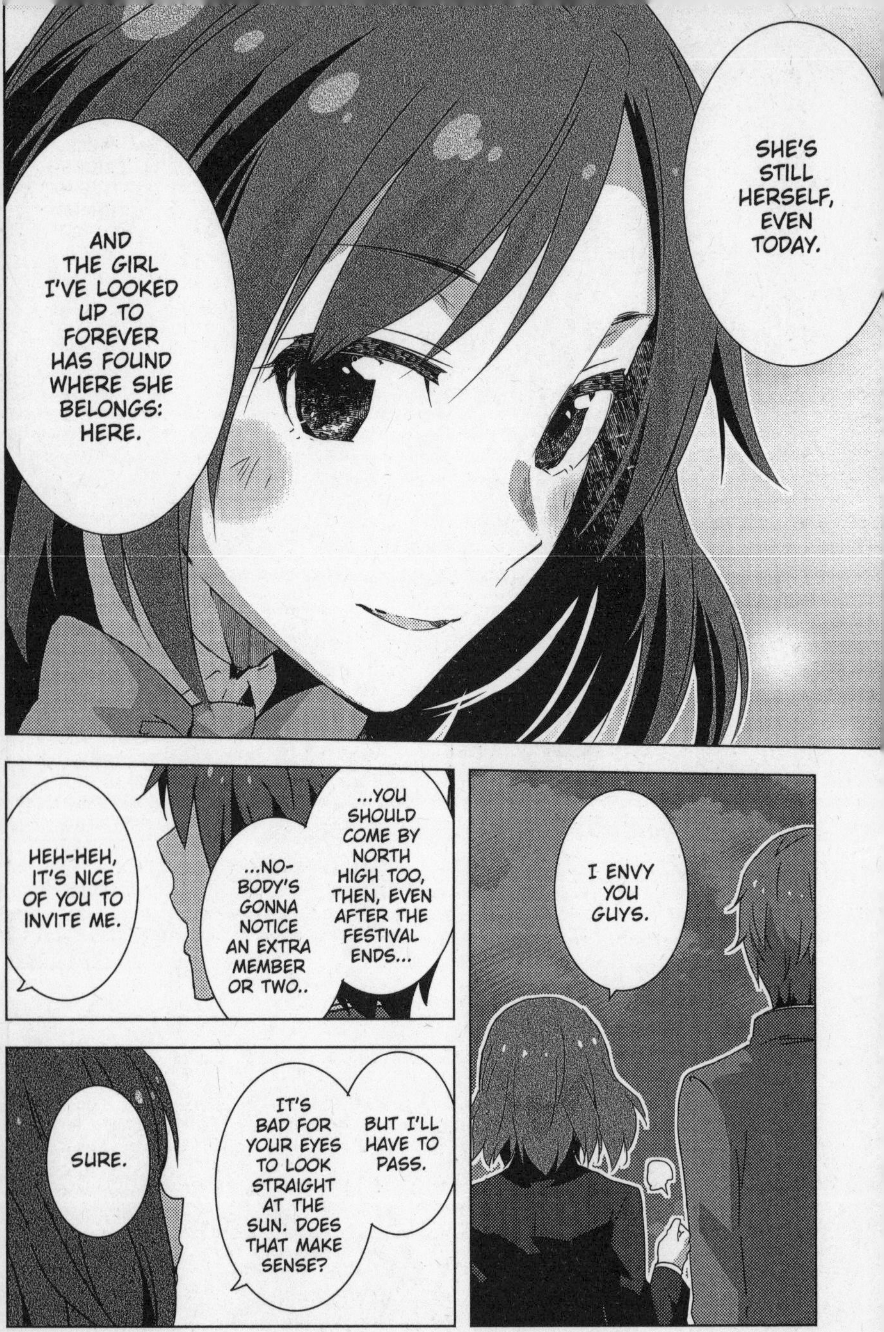
SHE'S STILL HERSELF, EVEN TODAY.
AND THE GIRL I'VE LOOKED UP TO FOREVER HAS FOUND WHERE SHE BELONGS: HERE.
I ENVY YOU GUYS.
...YOU SHOULD COME BY NORTH HIGH TOO, THEN, EVEN AFTER THE FESTIVAL ENDS...
...NO-BODY'S GONNA NOTICE AN EXTRA MEMBER OR TWO..
HEH-HEH, IT'S NICE OF YOU TO INVITE ME.
BUT I'LL HAVE TO PASS.
IT'S BAD FOR YOUR EYES TO LOOK STRAIGHT AT THE SUN. DOES THAT MAKE SENSE?
SURE.

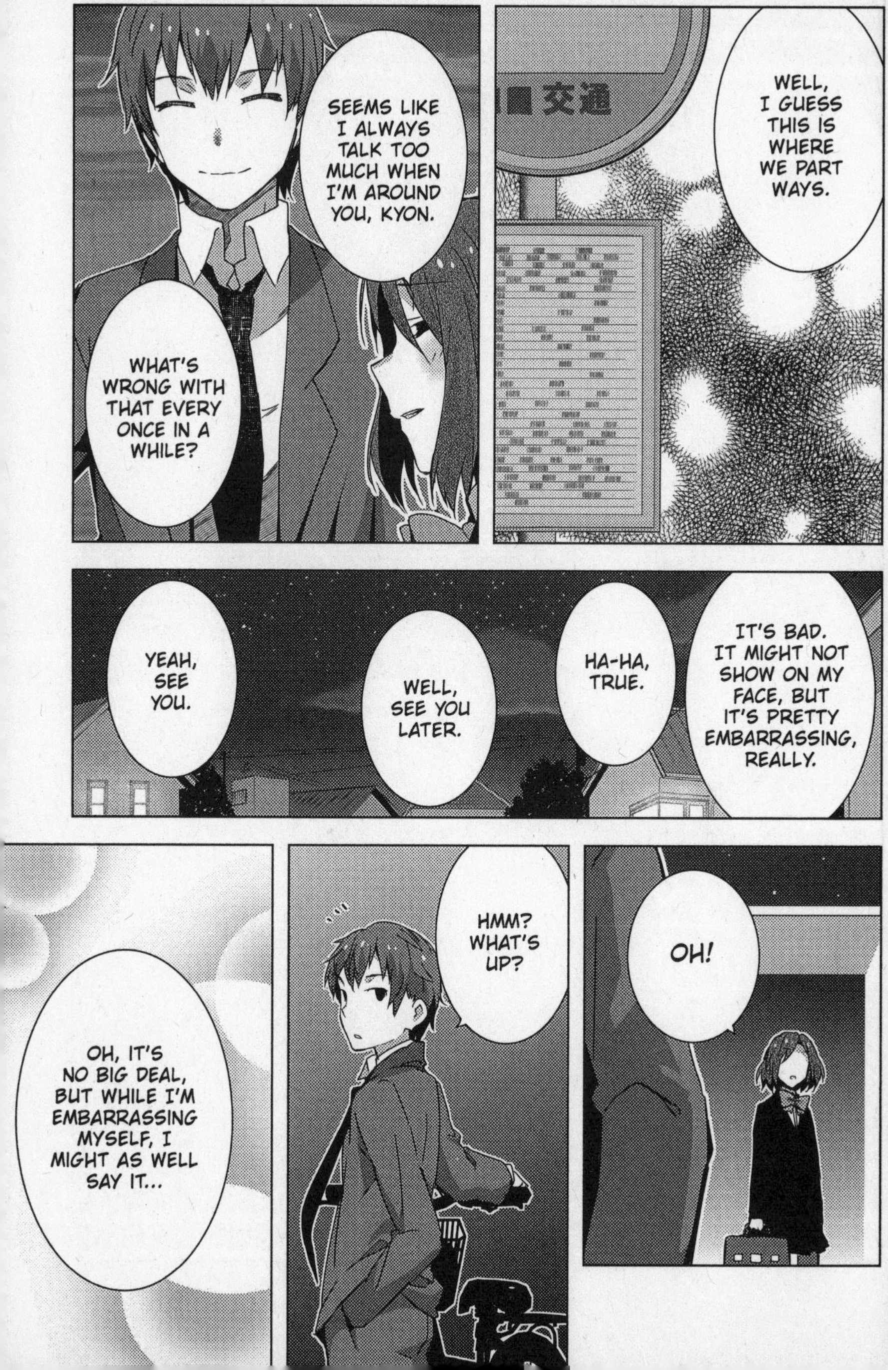
交通
WELL, I GUESS THIS IS WHERE WE PART WAYS.
SEEMS LIKE I ALWAYS TALK TOO MUCH WHEN I'M AROUND YOU, KYON.
WHAT'S WRONG WITH THAT EVERY ONCE IN A WHILE?
IT'S BAD. IT MIGHT NOT SHOW ON MY FACE, BUT IT'S PRETTY EMBARRASSING, REALLY.
HA-HA, TRUE.
WELL, SEE YOU LATER.
YEAH, SEE YOU.
OH!
HMM? WHAT'S UP?
OH, IT'S NO BIG DEAL, BUT WHILE I'M EMBARRASSING MYSELF, I MIGHT AS WELL SAY IT...

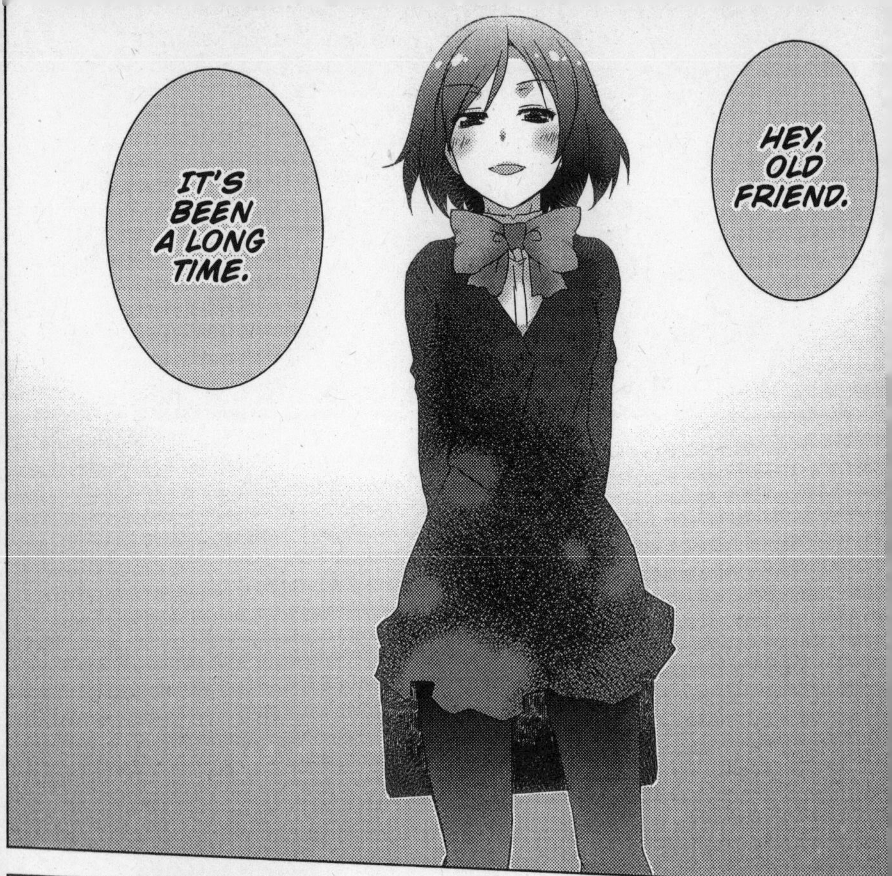
HEY, OLD FRIEND.
IT'S BEEN A LONG TIME.

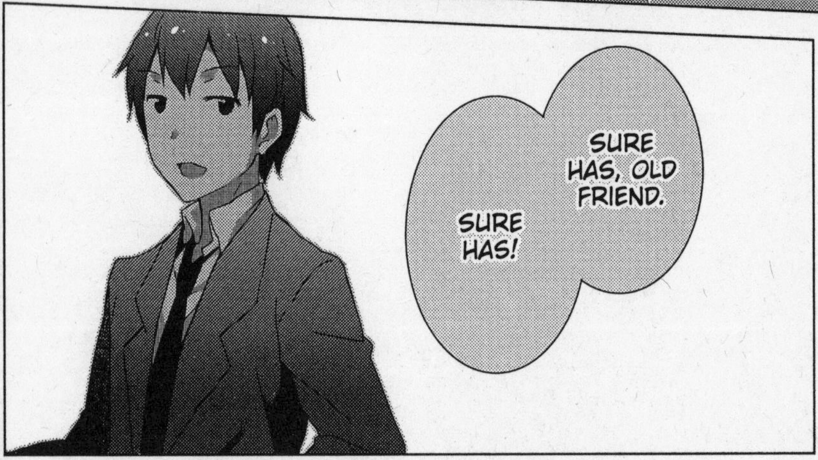
SURE HAS, OLD FRIEND.
SURE HAS!

Epilogue 43>> Festival Preparation (Kyon) 1

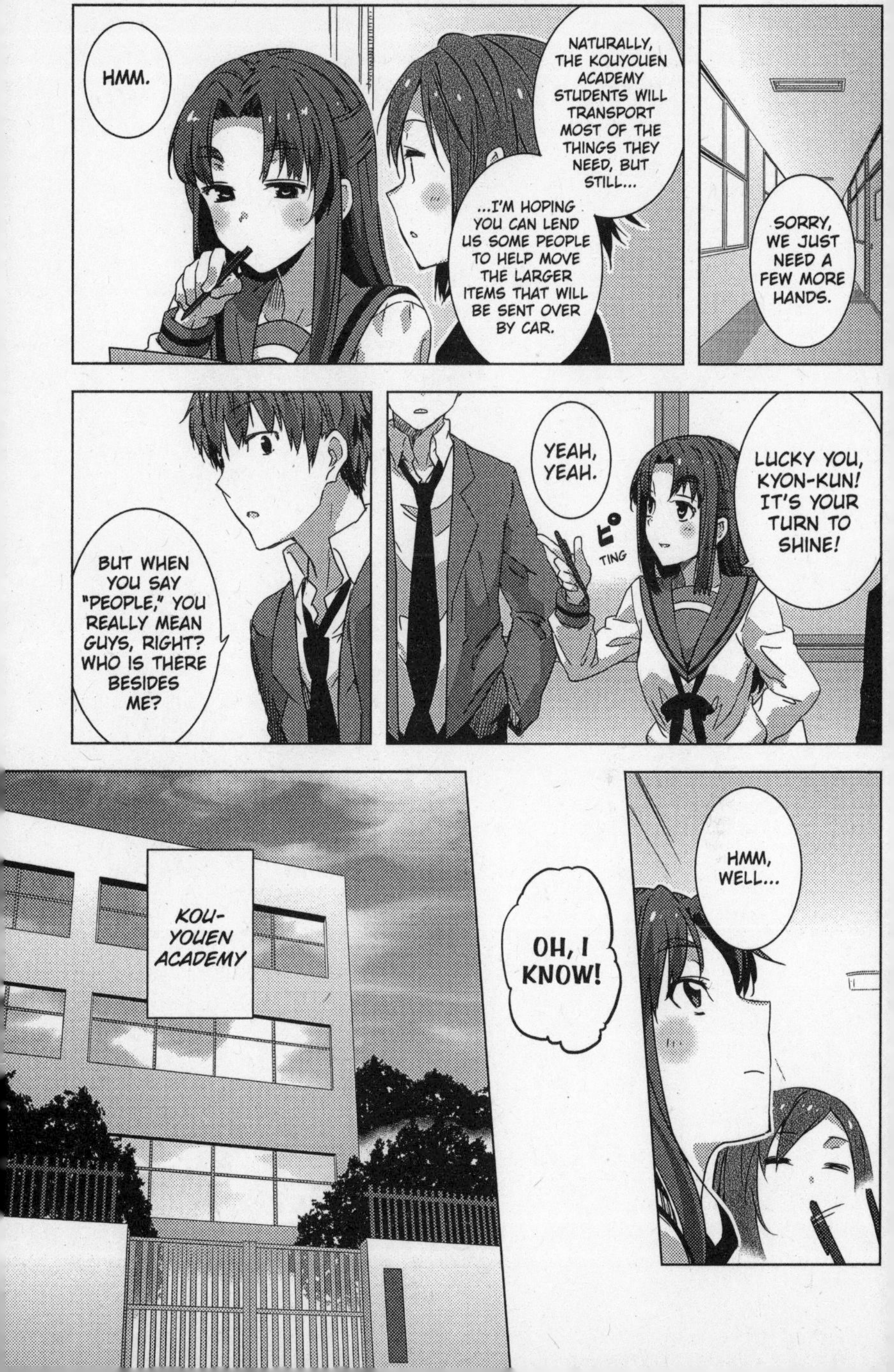
SORRY, WE JUST NEED A FEW MORE HANDS.
NATURALLY, THE KOUYOUEN ACADEMY STUDENTS WILL TRANSPORT MOST OF THE THINGS THEY NEED, BUT STILL...
...I'M HOPING YOU CAN LEND US SOME PEOPLE TO HELP MOVE THE LARGER ITEMS THAT WILL BE SENT OVER BY CAR.
HMM.
LUCKY YOU, KYON-KUN! IT'S YOUR TURN TO SHINE!
ピ
TING
YEAH, YEAH.
BUT WHEN YOU SAY "PEOPLE," YOU REALLY MEAN GUYS, RIGHT? WHO IS THERE BESIDES ME?
HMM, WELL...
OH, I KNOW!
KOU-YOUEN ACADEMY

Epilogue 43>> Festival Preparation (Kyon) 1

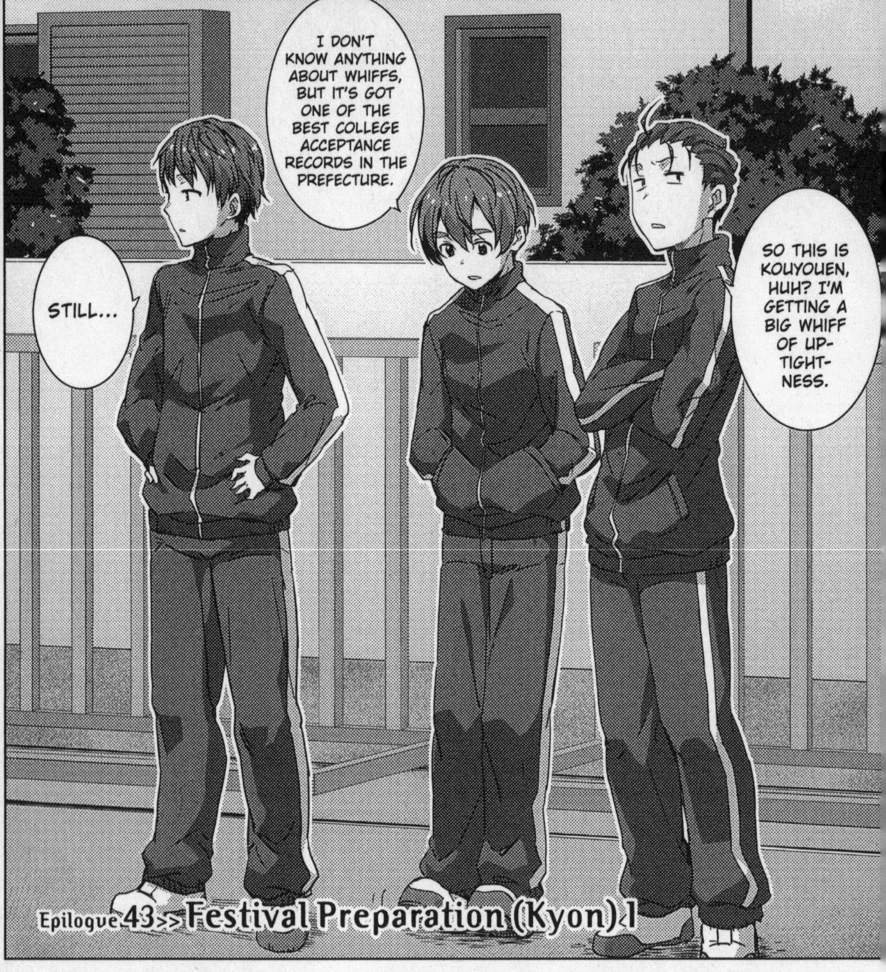
SO THIS IS KOUYOUEN, HUH? I'M GETTING A BIG WHIFF OF UP-TIGHT-NESS.
I DON'T KNOW ANYTHING ABOUT WHIFFS, BUT IT'S GOT ONE OF THE BEST COLLEGE ACCEPTANCE RECORDS IN THE PREFECTURE.
STILL...

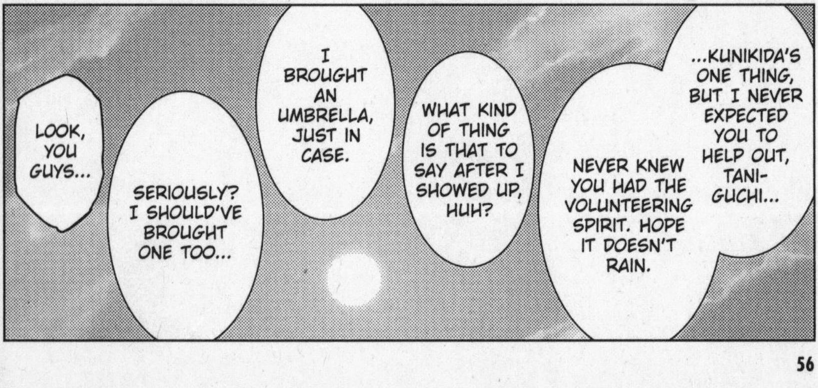
...KUNIKIDA'S ONE THING, BUT I NEVER EXPECTED YOU TO HELP OUT, TANI-GUCHI...
NEVER KNEW YOU HAD THE VOLUNTEERING SPIRIT. HOPE IT DOESN'T RAIN.
WHAT KIND OF THING IS THAT TO SAY AFTER I SHOWED UP, HUH?
I BROUGHT AN UMBRELLA, JUST IN CASE.
SERIOUSLY? I SHOULD'VE BROUGHT ONE TOO...
LOOK, YOU GUYS...

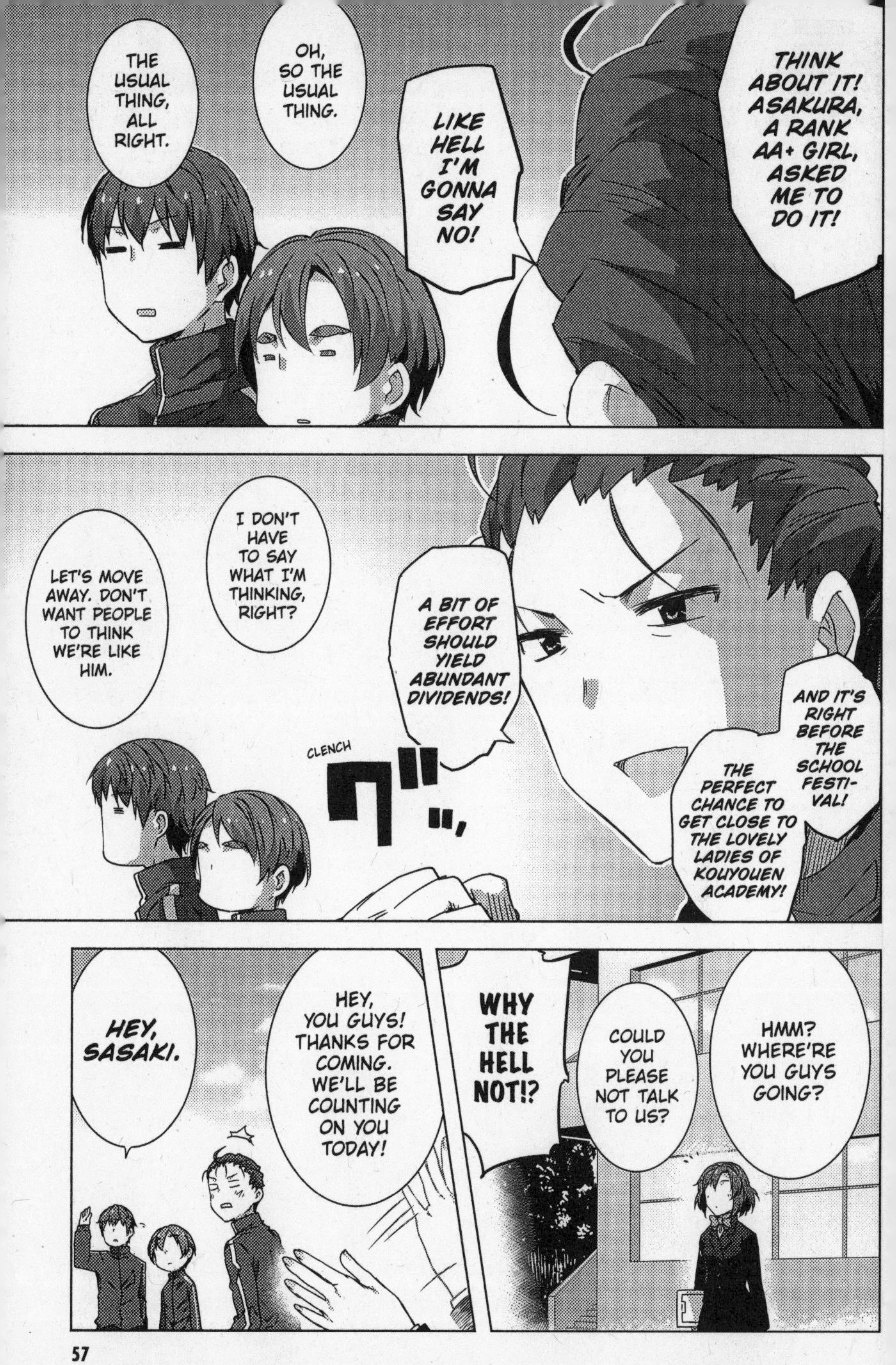
THINK ABOUT IT! ASAKURA, A RANK AA+ GIRL, ASKED ME TO DO IT!
LIKE HELL I'M GONNA SAY NO!
OH, SO THE USUAL THING.
THE USUAL THING, ALL RIGHT.
AND IT'S RIGHT BEFORE THE SCHOOL FESTI-VAL!
THE PERFECT CHANCE TO GET CLOSE TO THE LOVELY LADIES OF KOUYOUEN ACADEMY!
A BIT OF EFFORT SHOULD YIELD ABUNDANT DIVIDENDS!
CLENCH
I DON'T HAVE TO SAY WHAT I'M THINKING, RIGHT?
LET'S MOVE AWAY. DON'T WANT PEOPLE TO THINK WE'RE LIKE HIM.
HMM? WHERE'RE YOU GUYS GOING?
COULD YOU PLEASE NOT TALK TO US?
WHY THE HELL NOT!?
HEY, YOU GUYS! THANKS FOR COMING. WE'LL BE COUNTING ON YOU TODAY!
HEY, SASAKI.

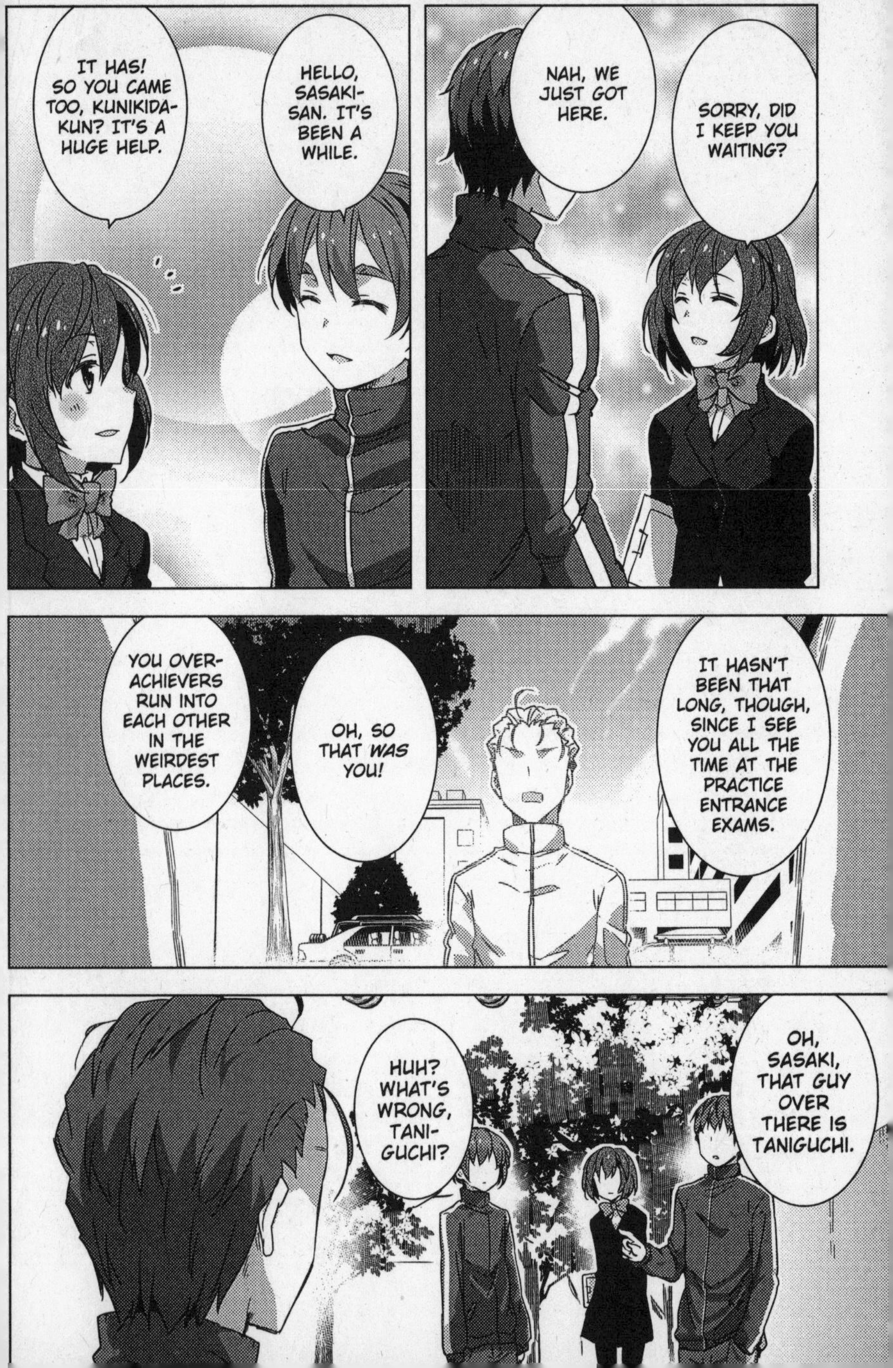
SORRY, DID I KEEP YOU WAITING?
NAH, WE JUST GOT HERE.
HELLO, SASAKI-SAN. IT'S BEEN A WHILE.
IT HAS! SO YOU CAME TOO, KUNIKIDA-KUN? IT'S A HUGE HELP.
IT HASN'T BEEN THAT LONG, THOUGH, SINCE I SEE YOU ALL THE TIME AT THE PRACTICE ENTRANCE EXAMS.
OH, SO THAT *WAS* YOU!
YOU OVER-ACHIEVERS RUN INTO EACH OTHER IN THE WEIRDEST PLACES.
OH, SASAKI, THAT GUY OVER THERE IS TANIGUCHI.
HUH? WHAT'S WRONG, TANI-GUCHI?

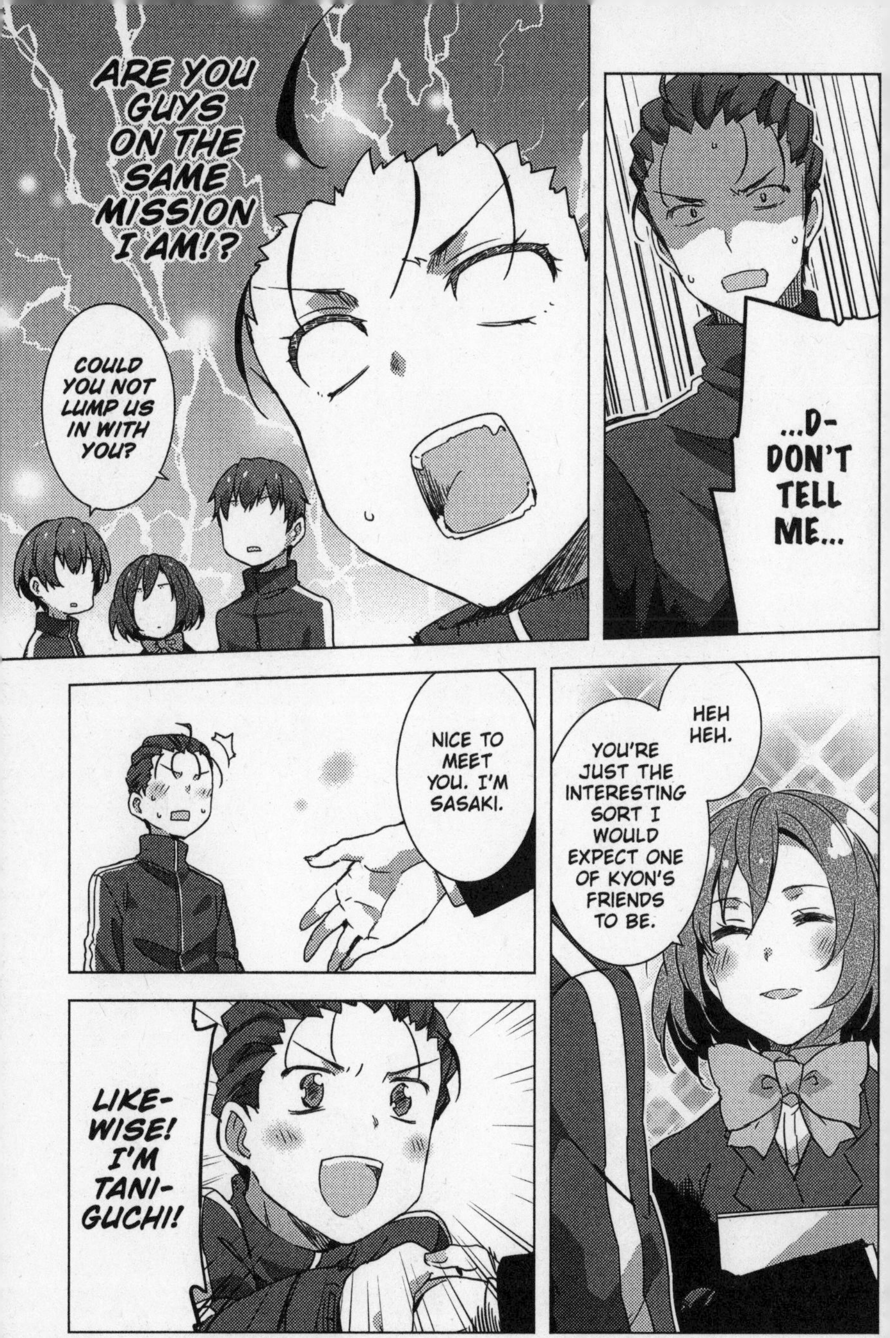
...D-DON'T TELL ME...
ARE YOU GUYS ON THE SAME MISSION I AM!?
COULD YOU NOT LUMP US IN WITH YOU?
HEH HEH.
YOU'RE JUST THE INTERESTING SORT I WOULD EXPECT ONE OF KYON'S FRIENDS TO BE.
NICE TO MEET YOU. I'M SASAKI.
LIKE-WISE! I'M TANI-GUCHI!

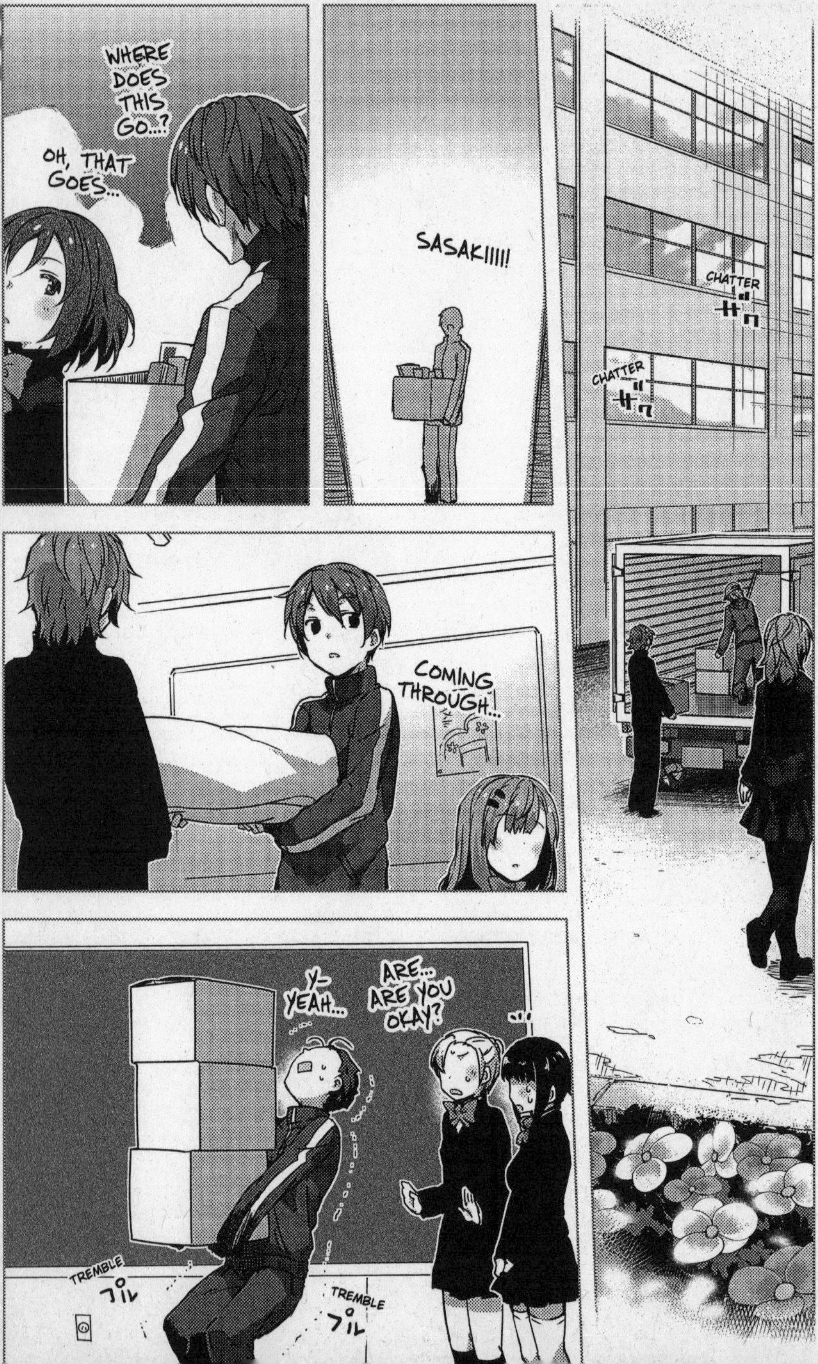

CHATTER
ザワ
CHATTER
ザワ
SASAKIIIII!
WHERE DOES THIS GO...?
OH, THAT GOES...
COMING THROUGH...
...
ARE... ARE YOU OKAY?
Y-YEAH...
TREMBLE
プル
TREMBLE
プル

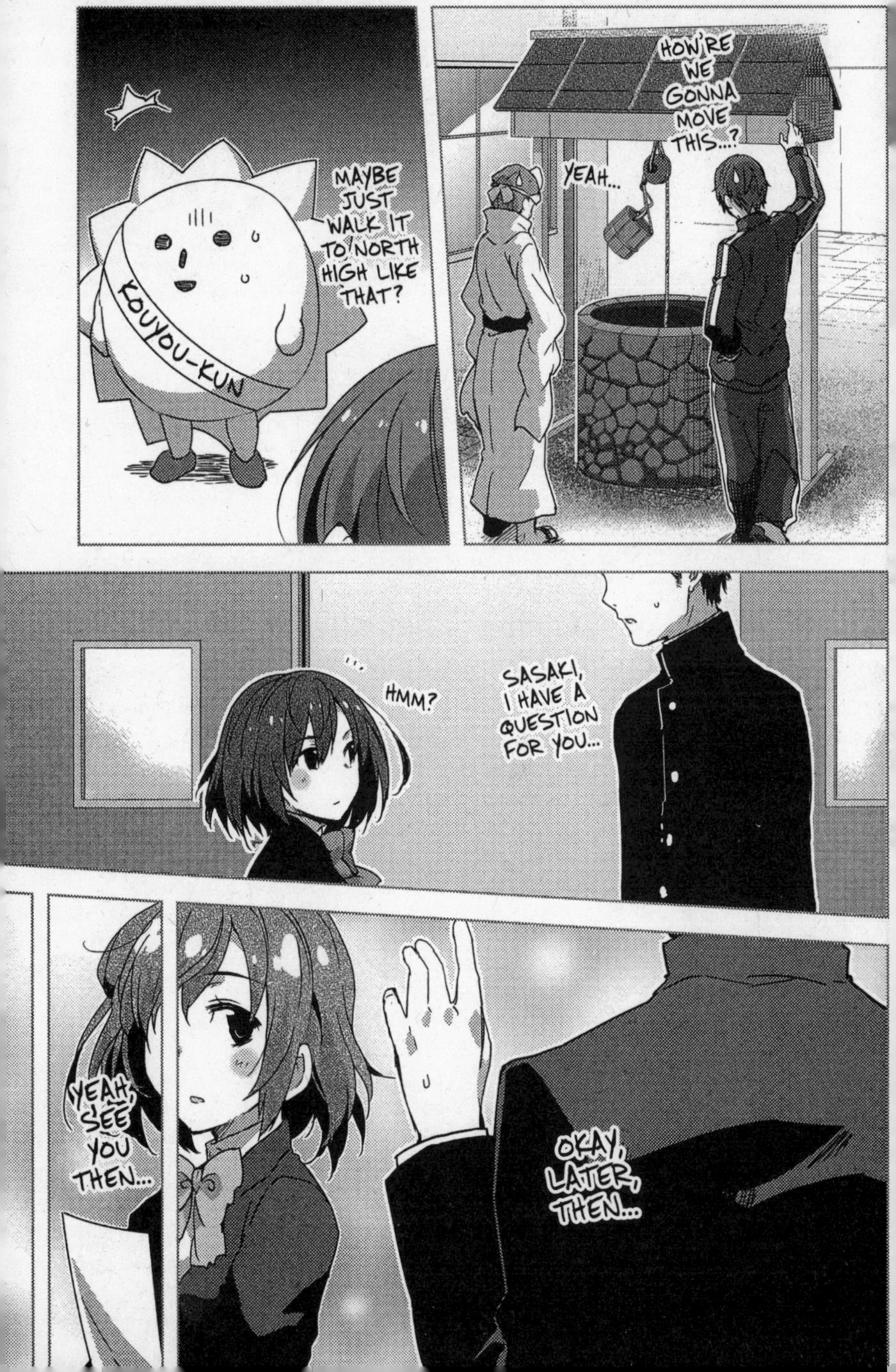
HOW'RE WE GONNA MOVE THIS...?
YEAH...
MAYBE JUST WALK IT TO NORTH HIGH LIKE THAT?
KOUYOU-KUN
SASAKI, I HAVE A QUESTION FOR YOU...
HMM?
OKAY, LATER, THEN...
YEAH, SEE YOU THEN...

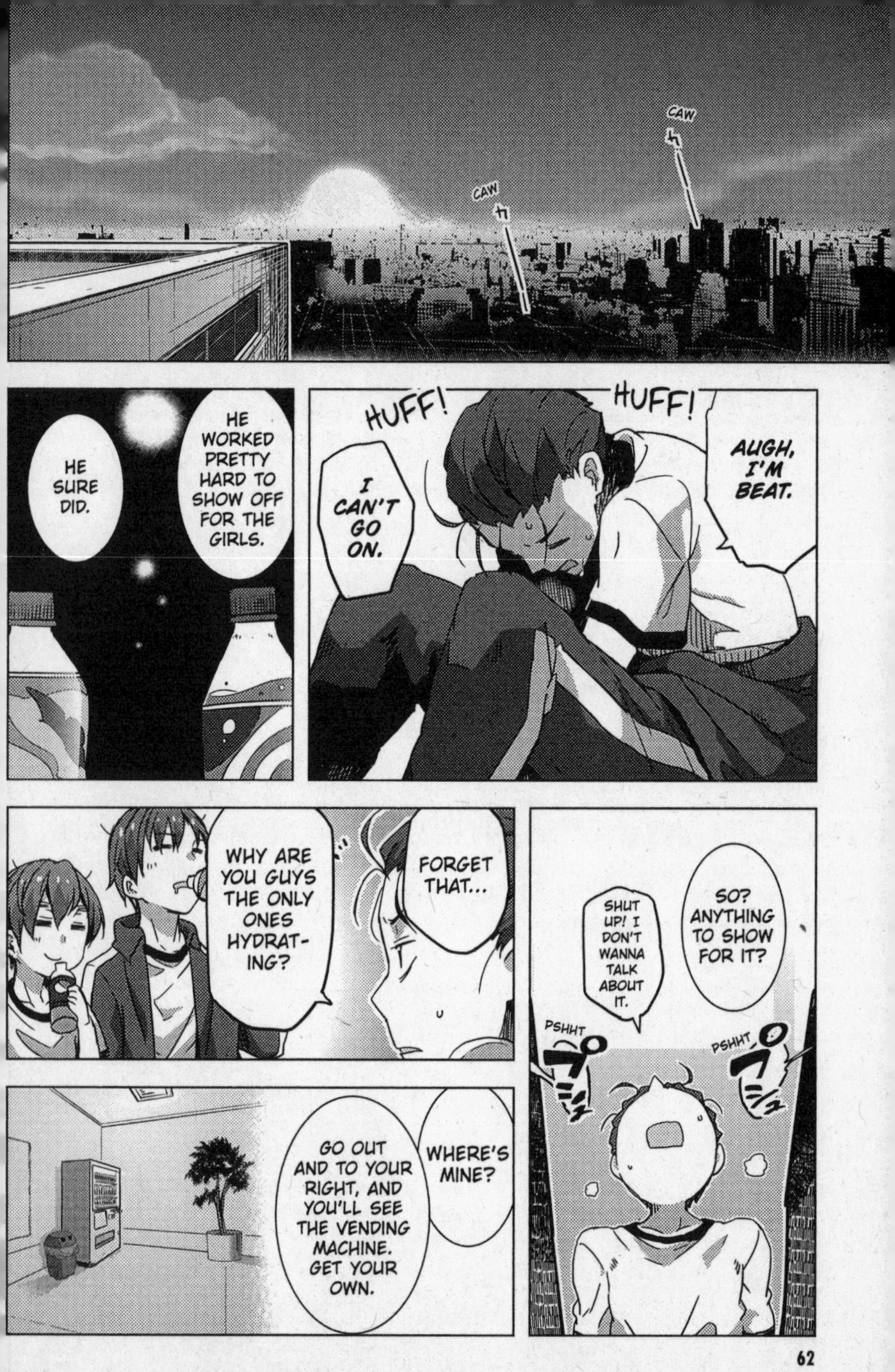
CAW
CAW
HUFF!
HUFF!
AUGH, I'M BEAT.
I CAN'T GO ON.
HE WORKED PRETTY HARD TO SHOW OFF FOR THE GIRLS.
HE SURE DID.
SO? ANYTHING TO SHOW FOR IT?
SHUT UP! I DON'T WANNA TALK ABOUT IT.
PSHHT
PSHHT
FORGET THAT...
WHY ARE YOU GUYS THE ONLY ONES HYDRAT-ING?
WHERE'S MINE?
GO OUT AND TO YOUR RIGHT, AND YOU'LL SEE THE VENDING MACHINE. GET YOUR OWN.

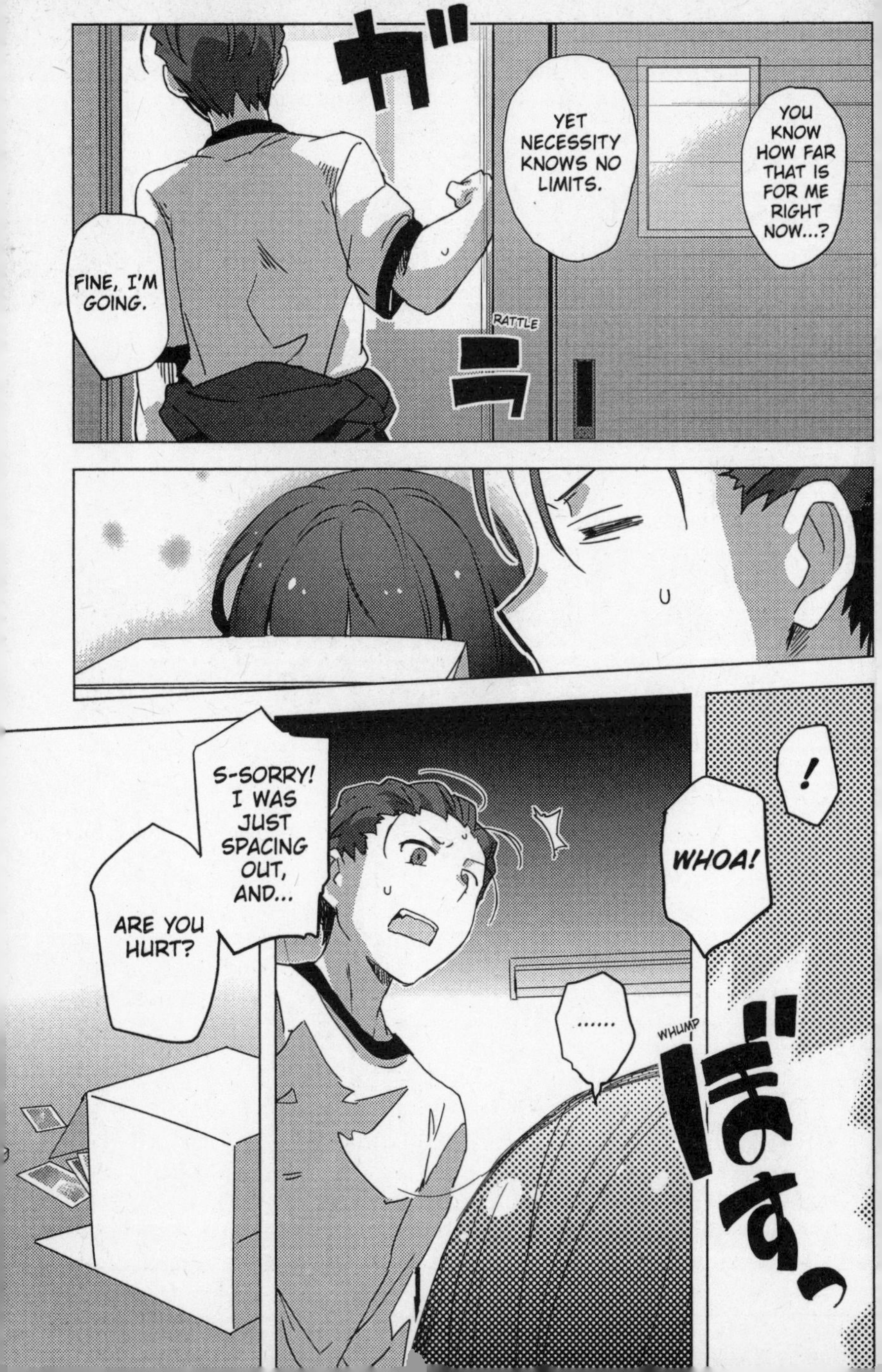
YOU KNOW HOW FAR THAT IS FOR ME RIGHT NOW...?
YET NECESSITY KNOWS NO LIMITS.
ガ
RATTLE
ラ
FINE, I'M GOING.
!
WHOA!
S-SORRY! I WAS JUST SPACING OUT, AND...
ARE YOU HURT?
......
WHUMP
ぼすっ

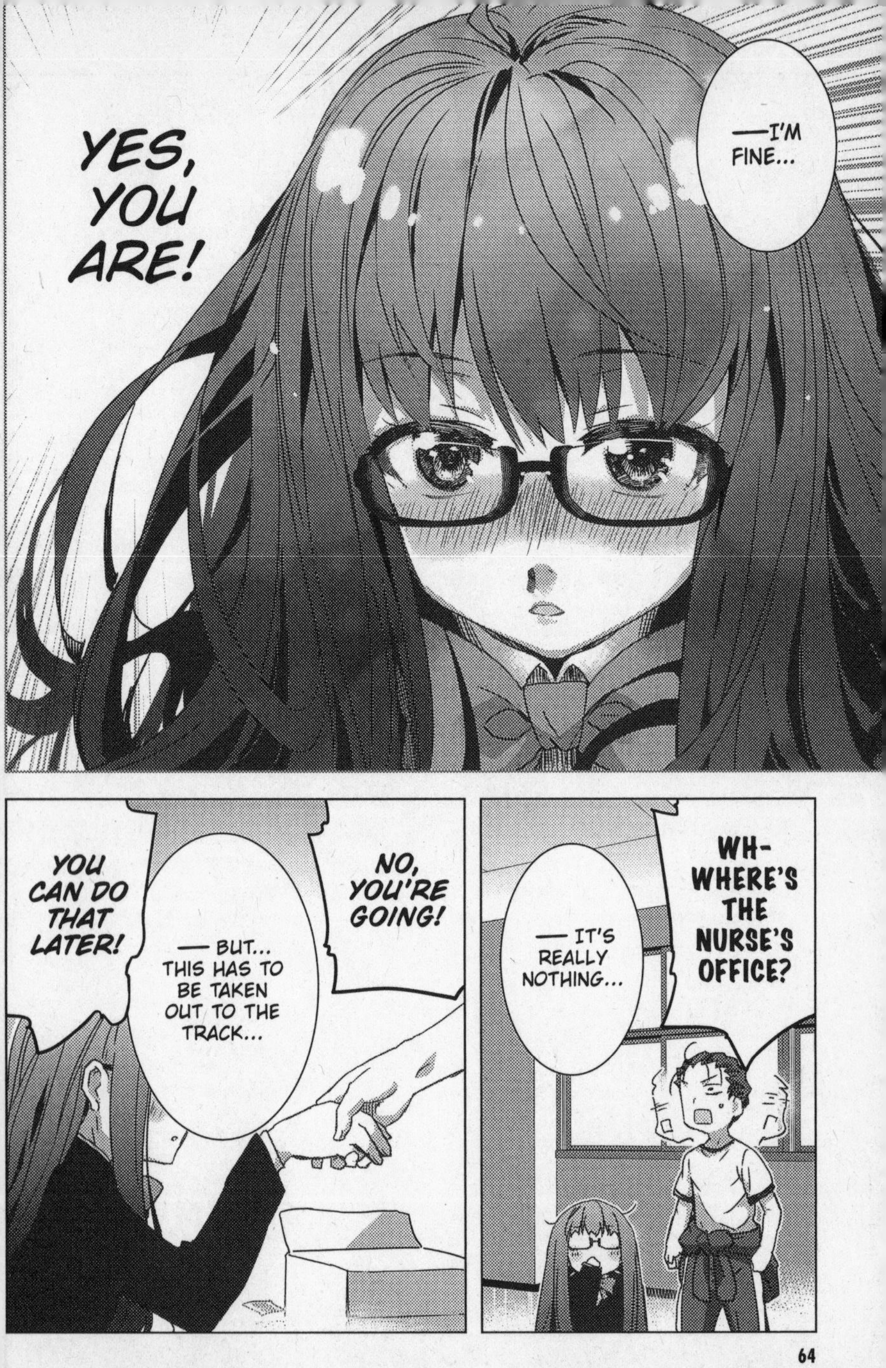
—I'M FINE...
YES, YOU ARE!
WH-WHERE'S THE NURSE'S OFFICE?
—IT'S REALLY NOTHING...
NO, YOU'RE GOING!
—BUT... THIS HAS TO BE TAKEN OUT TO THE TRACK...
YOU CAN DO THAT LATER!

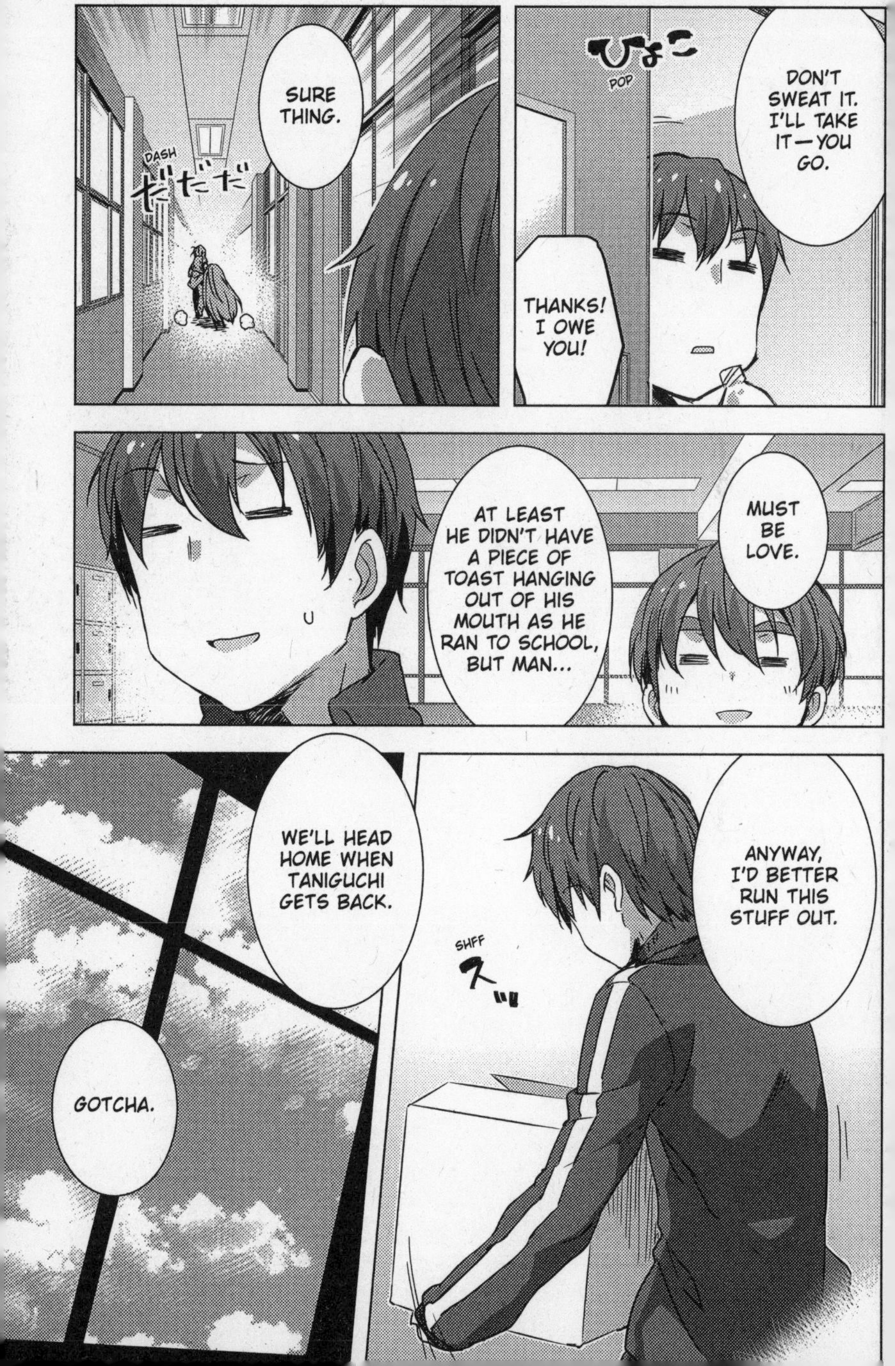
ひょこ
POP
DON'T SWEAT IT. I'LL TAKE IT—YOU GO.
THANKS! I OWE YOU!
SURE THING.
DASH
だだだ
MUST BE LOVE.
AT LEAST HE DIDN'T HAVE A PIECE OF TOAST HANGING OUT OF HIS MOUTH AS HE RAN TO SCHOOL, BUT MAN...
ANYWAY, I'D BETTER RUN THIS STUFF OUT.
SHFF
スッ
WE'LL HEAD HOME WHEN TANIGUCHI GETS BACK.
GOTCHA.

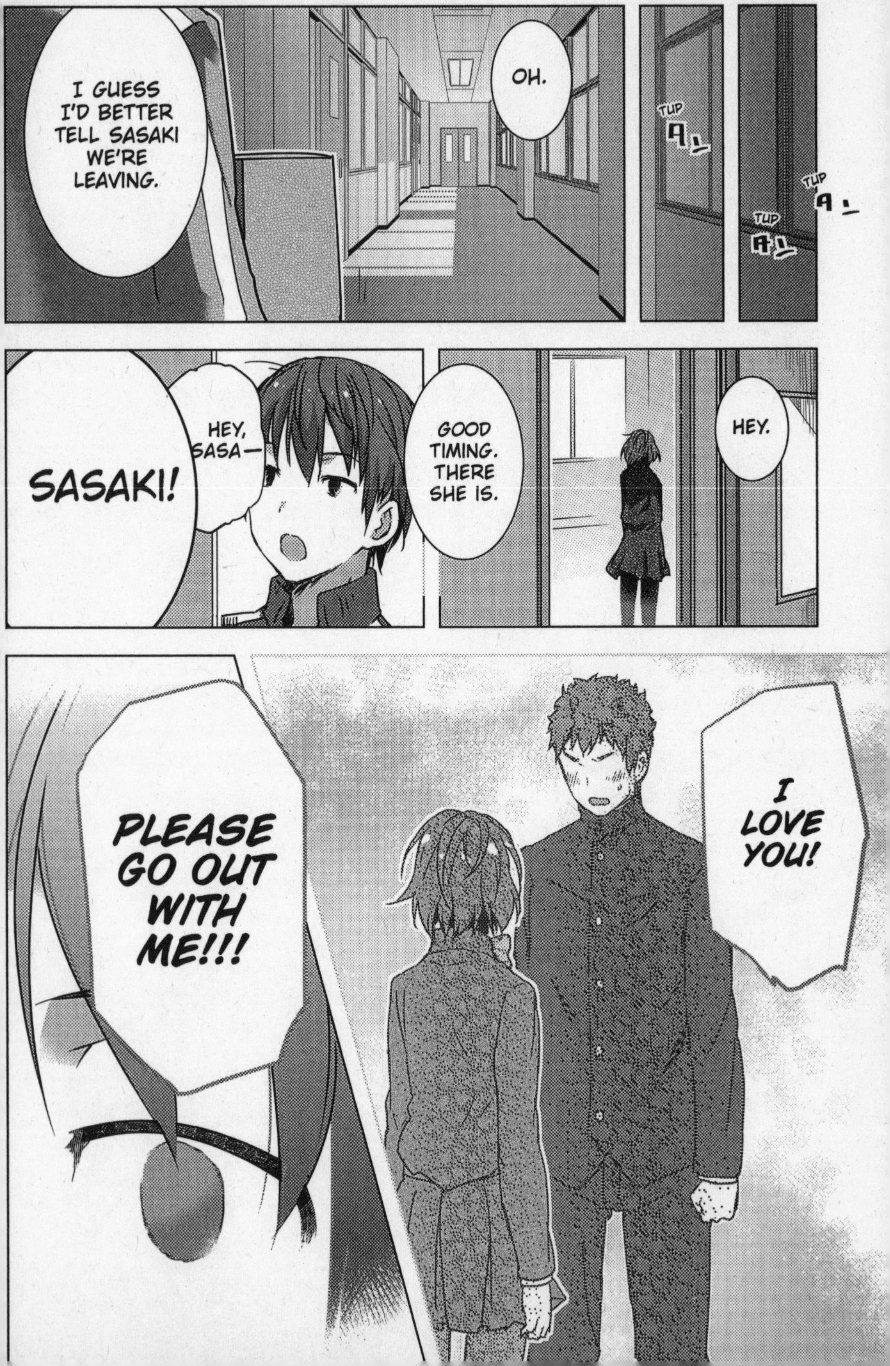
TUP
TUP
TUP
OH.
I GUESS I'D BETTER TELL SASAKI WE'RE LEAVING.
HEY.
GOOD TIMING. THERE SHE IS.
HEY, SASA—
SASAKI!
I LOVE YOU!
PLEASE GO OUT WITH ME!!!

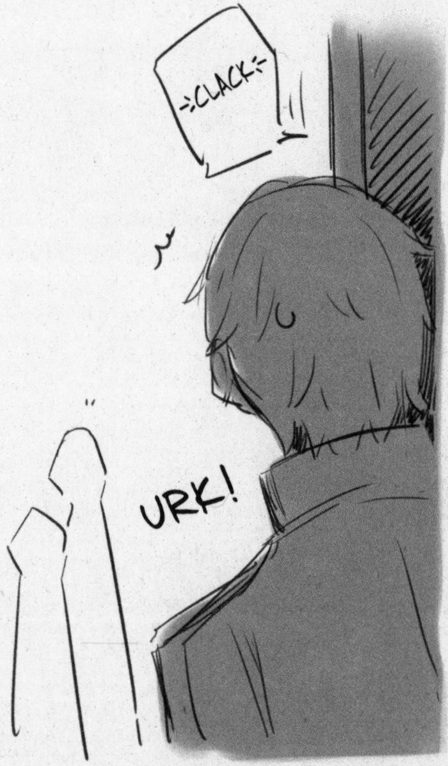
CLACK
URK!

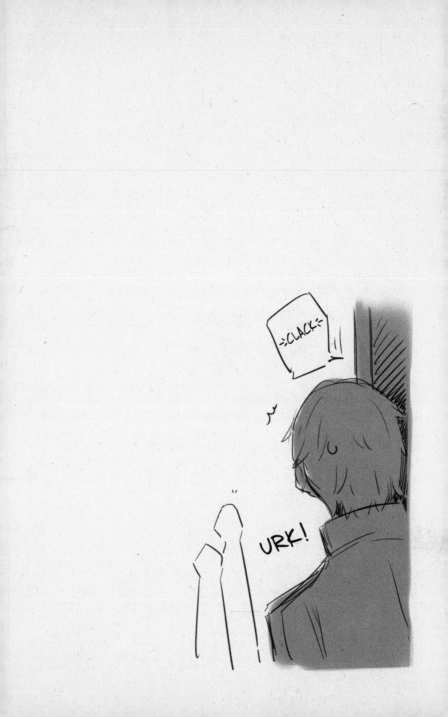

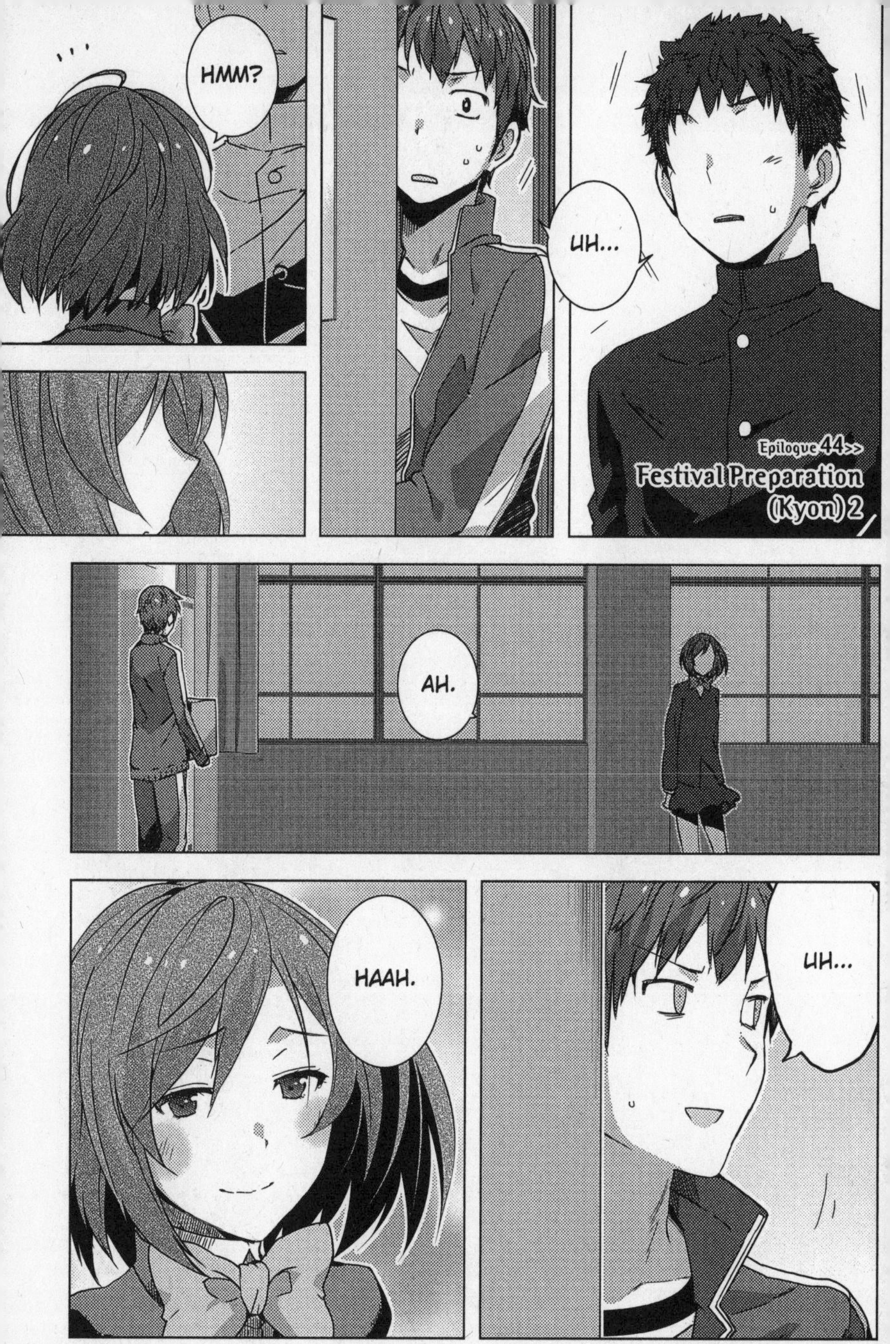
UH...
Epilogue 44>>
Festival Preparation (Kyon) 2
...
HMM?
AH.
UH...
HAAH.

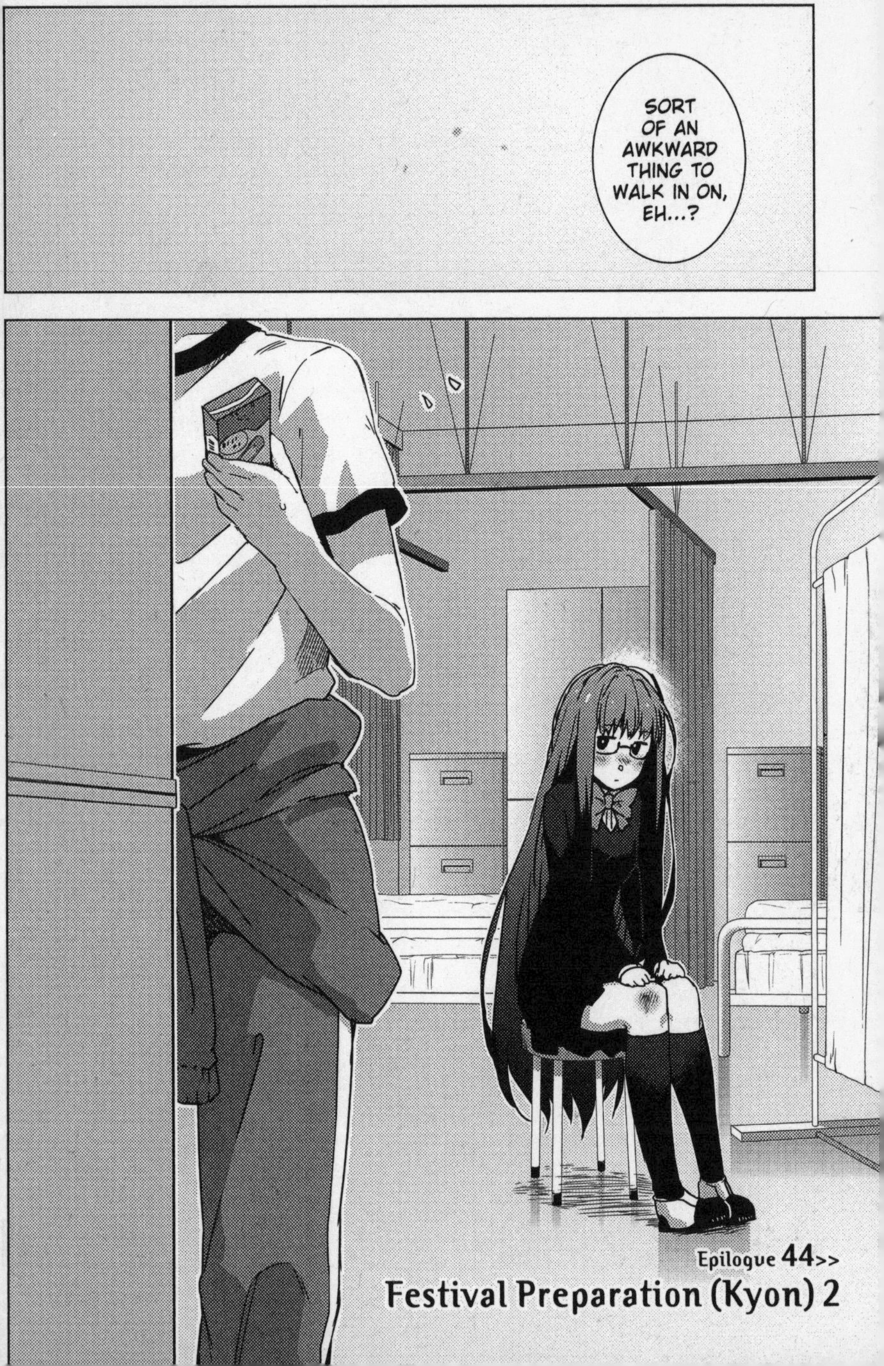
SORT OF AN AWKWARD THING TO WALK IN ON, EH...?
Epilogue 44>>
Festival Preparation (Kyon) 2

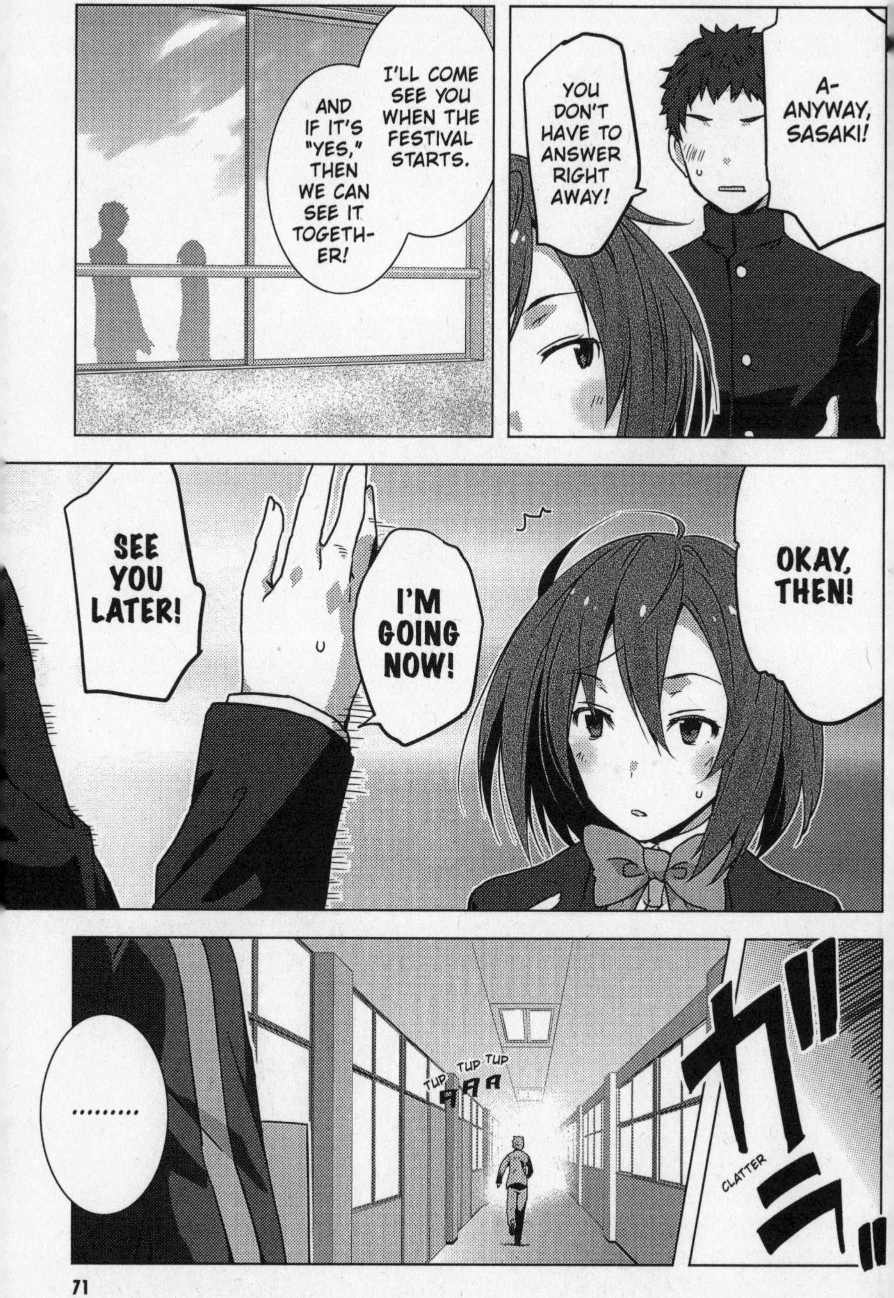
A- ANYWAY, SASAKI!
YOU DON'T HAVE TO ANSWER RIGHT AWAY!
I'LL COME SEE YOU WHEN THE FESTIVAL STARTS.
AND IF IT'S "YES," THEN WE CAN SEE IT TOGETH-ER!
OKAY, THEN!
I'M GOING NOW!
SEE YOU LATER!
CLATTER
TUP TUP TUP
....

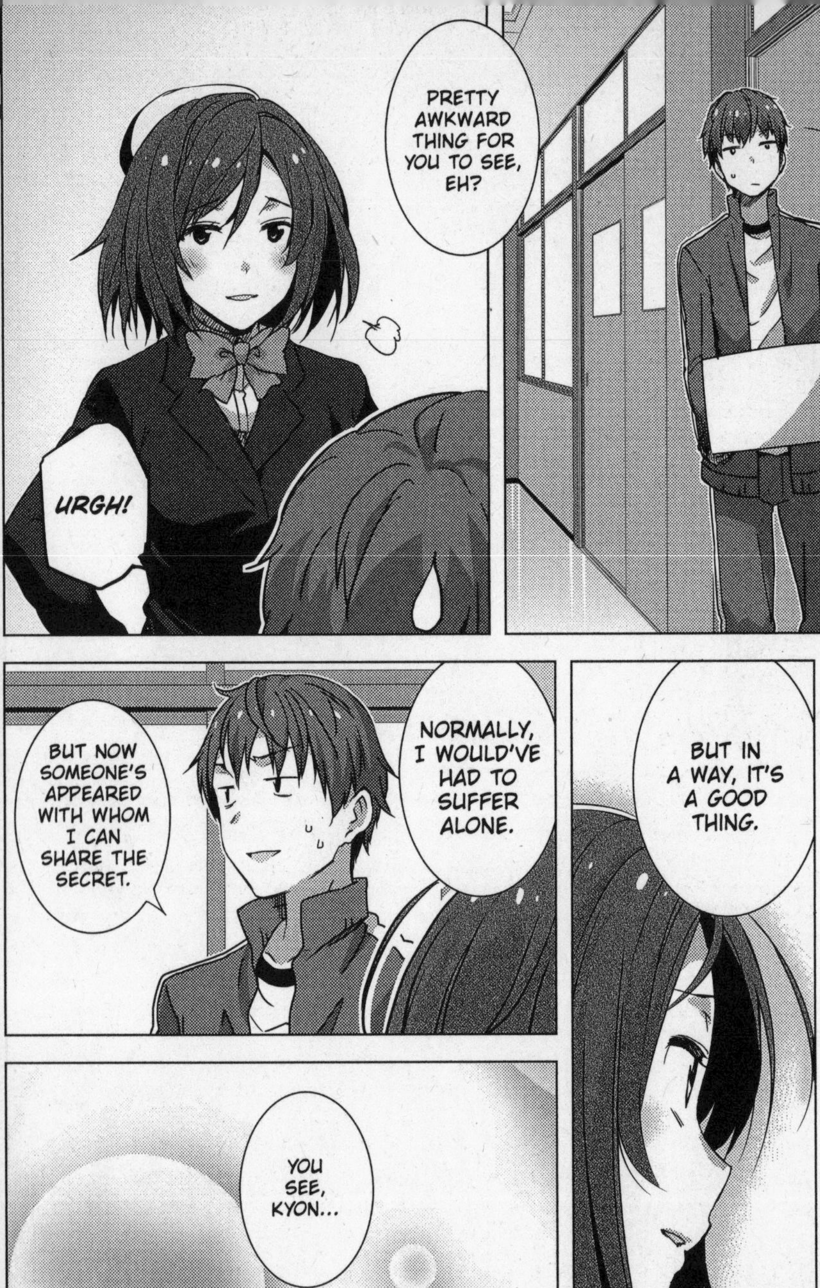
PRETTY AWKWARD THING FOR YOU TO SEE, EH?
URGH!
BUT IN A WAY, IT'S A GOOD THING.
NORMALLY, I WOULD'VE HAD TO SUFFER ALONE.
BUT NOW SOMEONE'S APPEARED WITH WHOM I CAN SHARE THE SECRET.
YOU SEE, KYON...

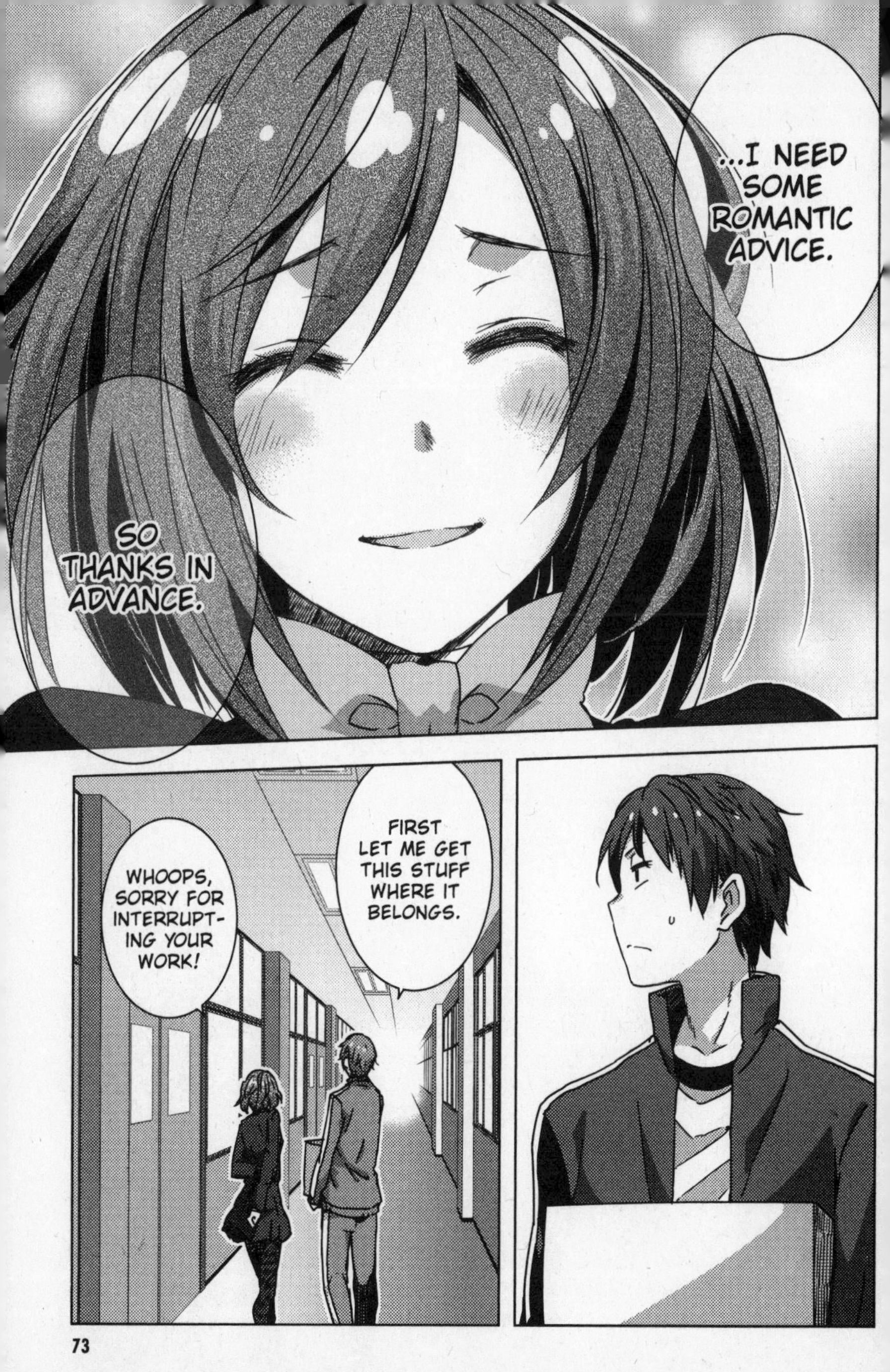
...I NEED SOME ROMANTIC ADVICE.
SO THANKS IN ADVANCE.
FIRST LET ME GET THIS STUFF WHERE IT BELONGS.
WHOOPS, SORRY FOR INTERRUPTING YOUR WORK!

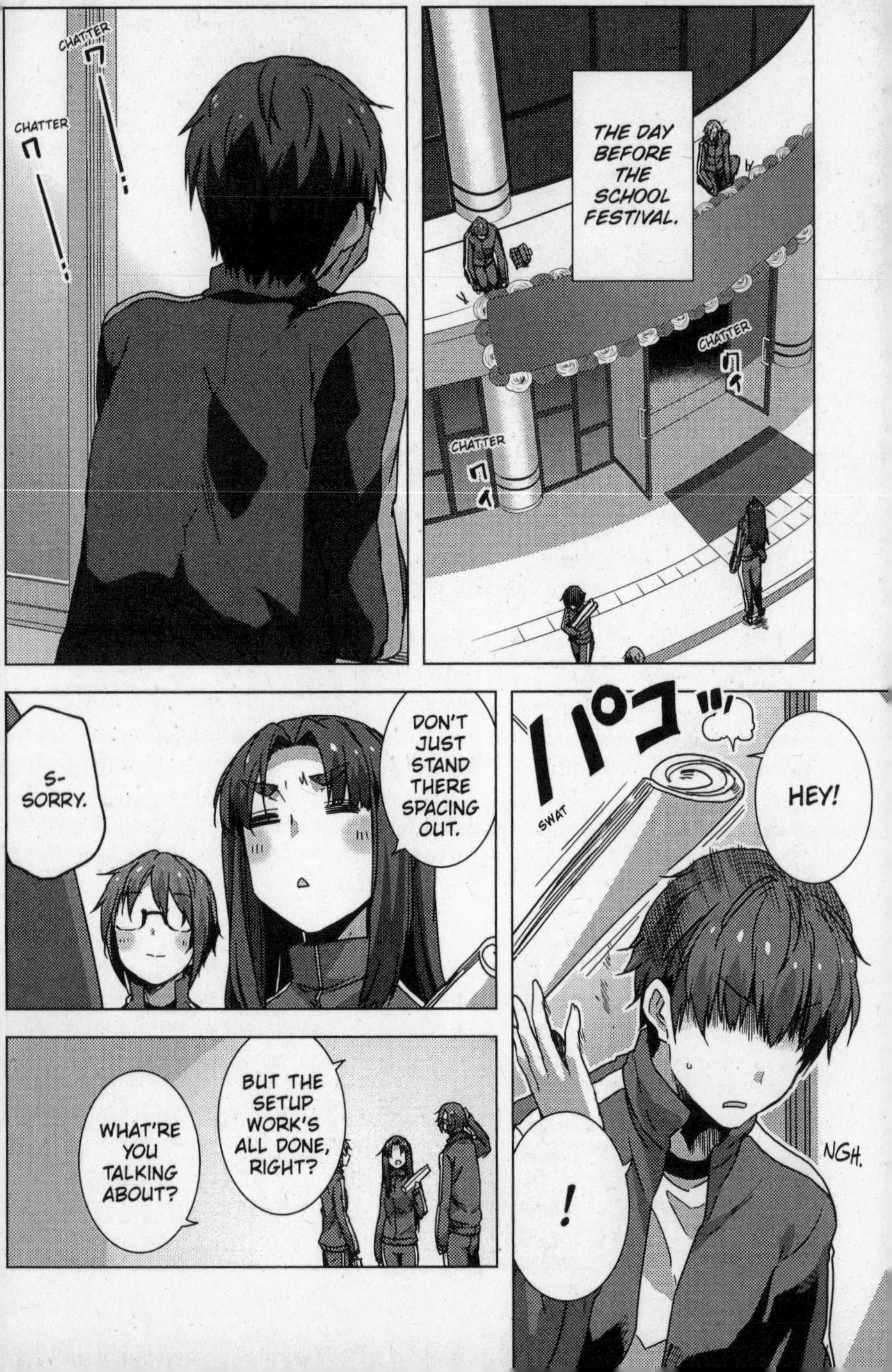
THE DAY BEFORE THE SCHOOL FESTIVAL.
CHATTER
CHATTER
CHATTER
CHATTER
HEY!
パコッ
SWAT
NGH.
!
DON'T JUST STAND THERE SPACING OUT.
S-SORRY.
BUT THE SETUP WORK'S ALL DONE, RIGHT?
WHAT'RE YOU TALKING ABOUT?

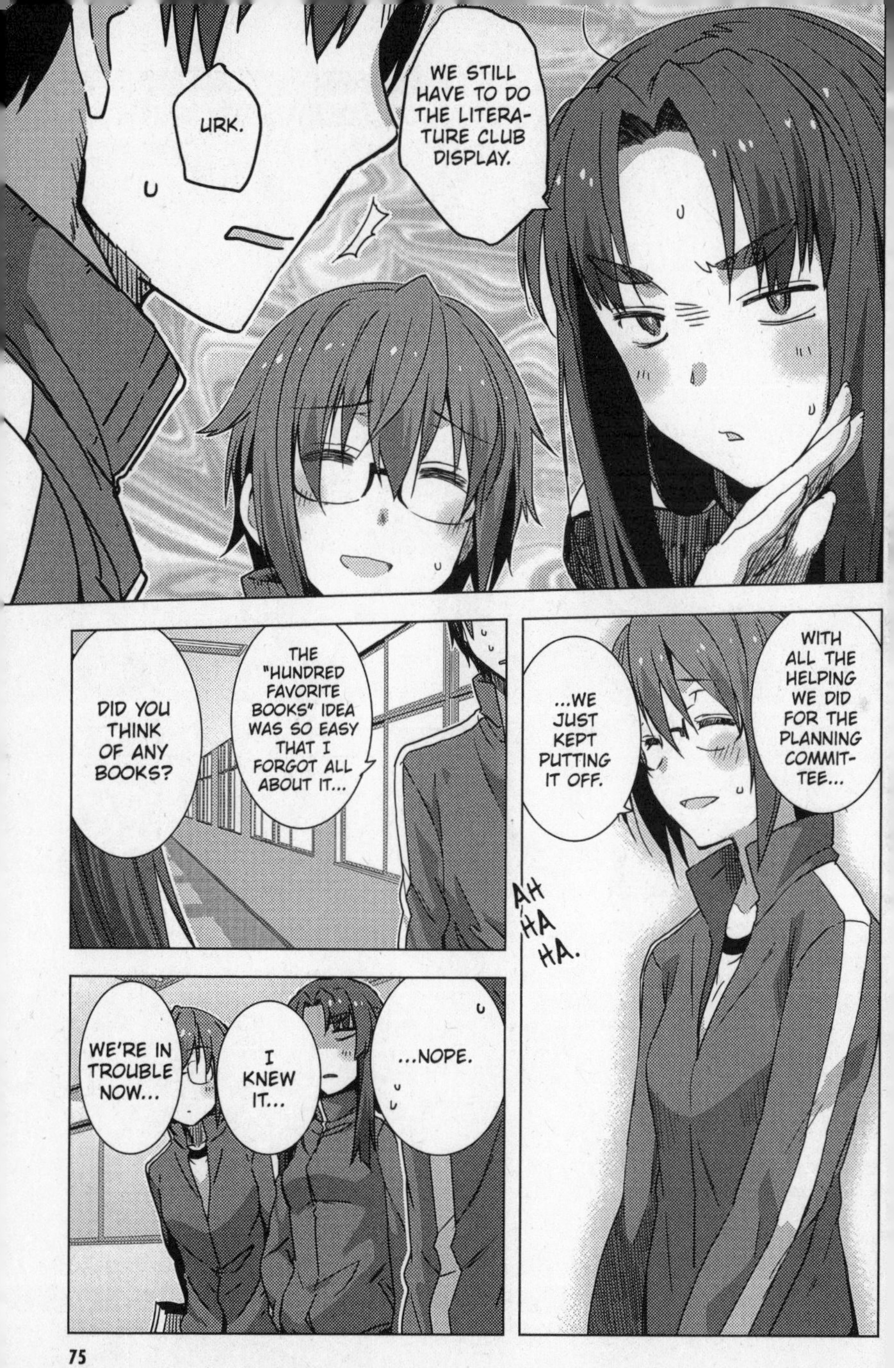
WE STILL HAVE TO DO THE LITERATURE CLUB DISPLAY.
URK.
WITH ALL THE HELPING WE DID FOR THE PLANNING COMMITTEE...
...WE JUST KEPT PUTTING IT OFF.
AH HA HA.
THE "HUNDRED FAVORITE BOOKS" IDEA WAS SO EASY THAT I FORGOT ALL ABOUT IT...
DID YOU THINK OF ANY BOOKS?
...NOPE.
I KNEW IT...
WE'RE IN TROUBLE NOW...

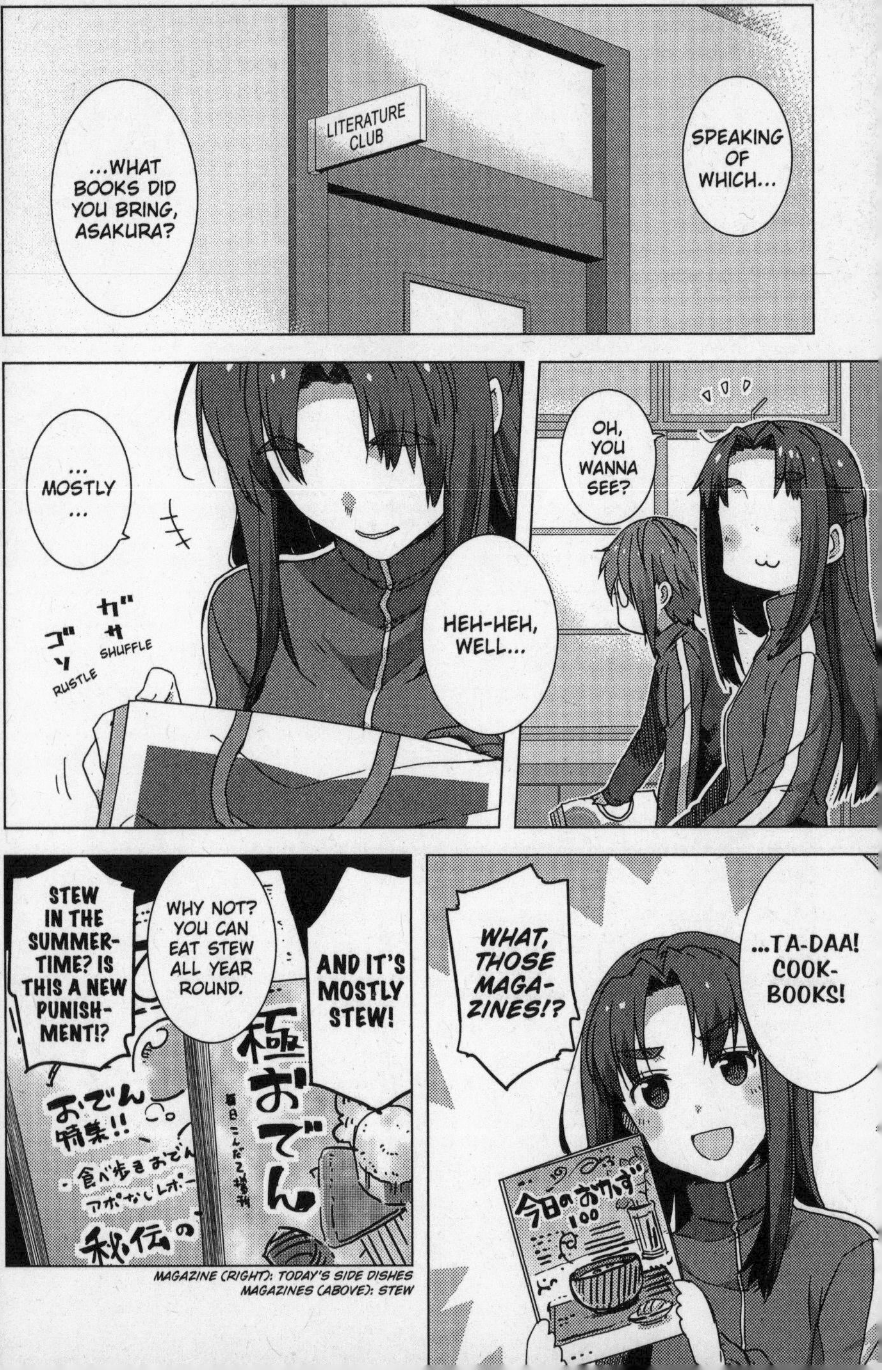
SPEAKING OF WHICH...
LITERATURE CLUB
...WHAT BOOKS DID YOU BRING, ASAKURA?
OH, YOU WANNA SEE?
HEH-HEH, WELL...
...MOSTLY...
ガサ SHUFFLE
ゴソ RUSTLE
...TA-DAA! COOKBOOKS!
今日のおかず 100
WHAT, THOSE MAGAZINES!?
AND IT'S MOSTLY STEW!
極おでん
毎日こんだて増刊
WHY NOT? YOU CAN EAT STEW ALL YEAR ROUND.
STEW IN THE SUMMERTIME? IS THIS A NEW PUNISHMENT!?
おでん特集!!
・食べ歩きおでん
アポなしレポー
秘伝の
MAGAZINE (RIGHT): TODAY'S SIDE DISHES
MAGAZINES (ABOVE): STEW

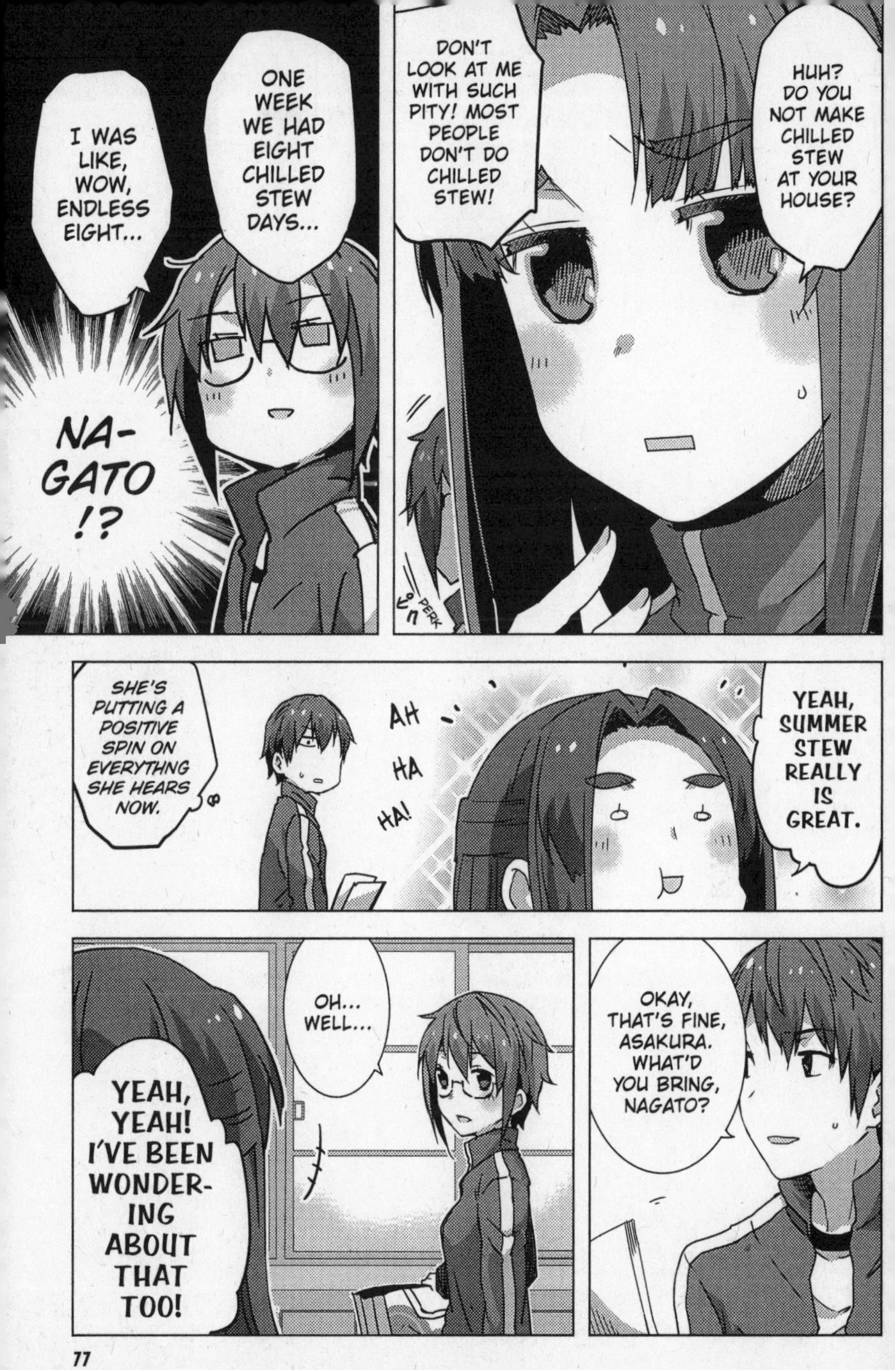
HUH? DO YOU NOT MAKE CHILLED STEW AT YOUR HOUSE?
DON'T LOOK AT ME WITH SUCH PITY! MOST PEOPLE DON'T DO CHILLED STEW!
PERK
ONE WEEK WE HAD EIGHT CHILLED STEW DAYS...
I WAS LIKE, WOW, ENDLESS EIGHT...
NA-GATO!?
YEAH, SUMMER STEW REALLY IS GREAT.
AH HA HA!
SHE'S PUTTING A POSITIVE SPIN ON EVERYTHNG SHE HEARS NOW.
OKAY, THAT'S FINE, ASAKURA. WHAT'D YOU BRING, NAGATO?
OH... WELL...
YEAH, YEAH! I'VE BEEN WONDER-ING ABOUT THAT TOO!

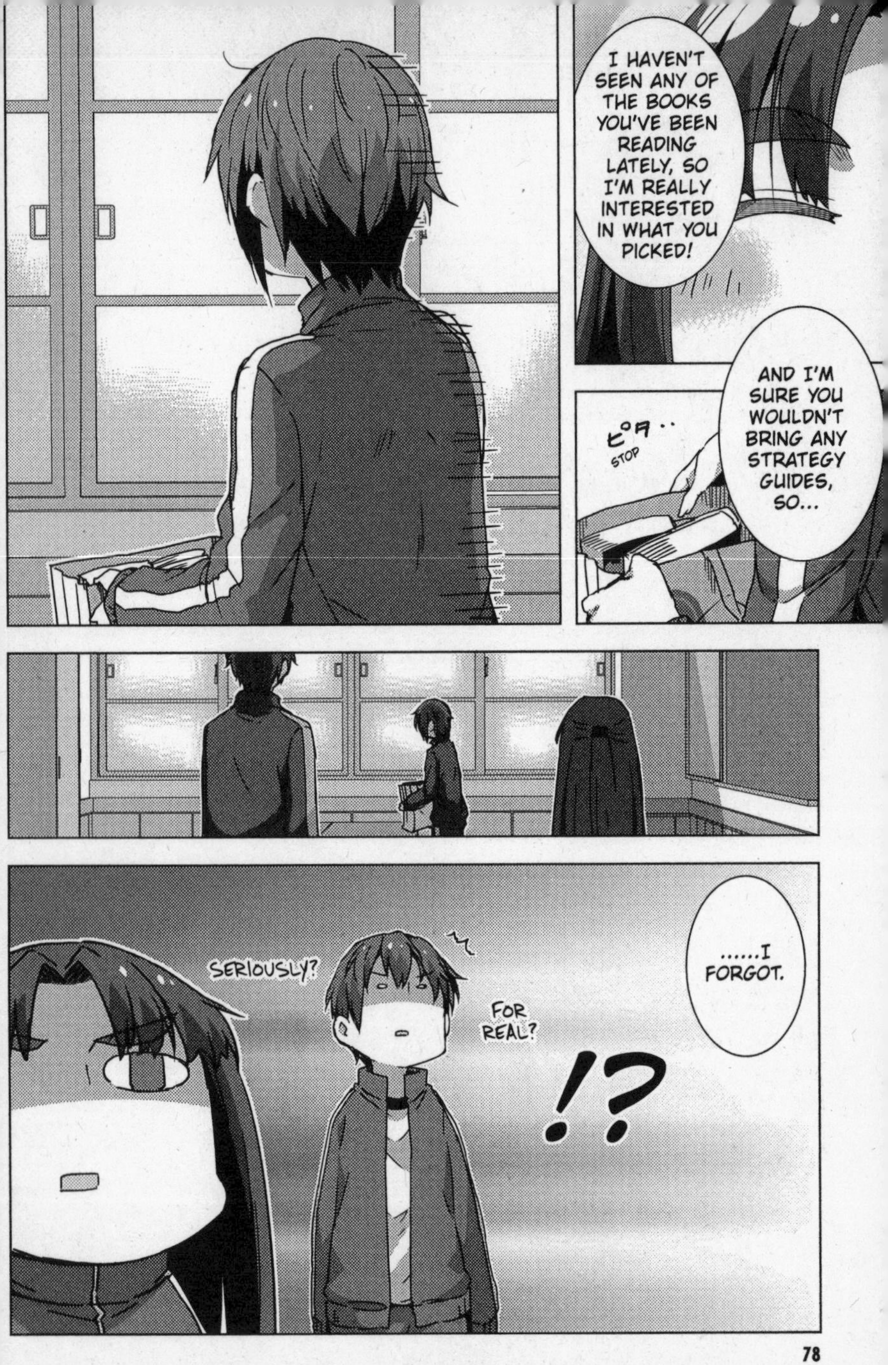
I HAVEN'T SEEN ANY OF THE BOOKS YOU'VE BEEN READING LATELY, SO I'M REALLY INTERESTED IN WHAT YOU PICKED!
AND I'M SURE YOU WOULDN'T BRING ANY STRATEGY GUIDES, SO...
ピタ‥
STOP
......I FORGOT.
!?
FOR REAL?
SERIOUSLY?

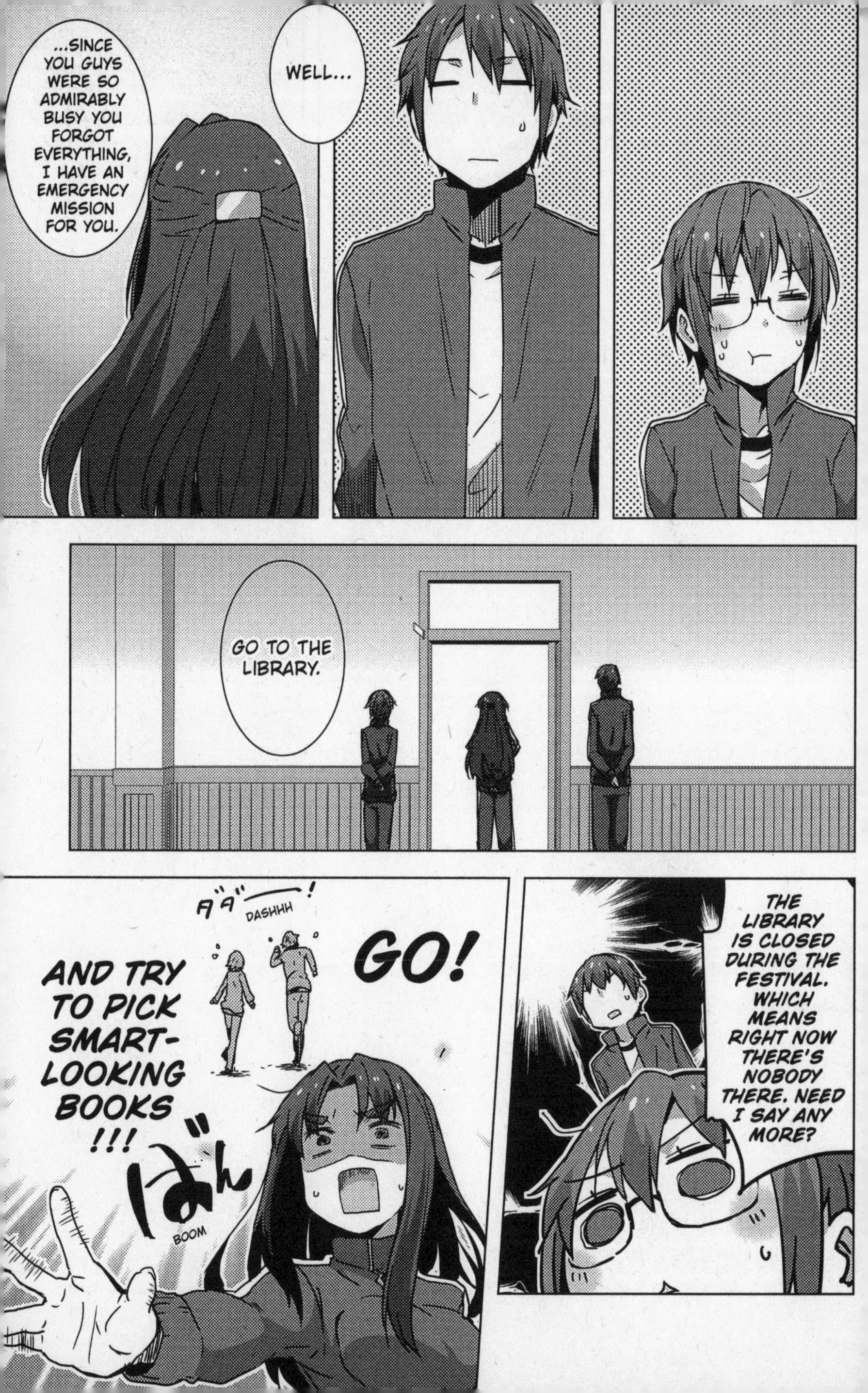
WELL...
...SINCE YOU GUYS WERE SO ADMIRABLY BUSY YOU FORGOT EVERYTHING, I HAVE AN EMERGENCY MISSION FOR YOU.
GO TO THE LIBRARY.
THE LIBRARY IS CLOSED DURING THE FESTIVAL. WHICH MEANS RIGHT NOW THERE'S NOBODY THERE. NEED I SAY ANY MORE?
GO!
ダダー!
DASHHH
AND TRY TO PICK SMART-LOOKING BOOKS!!!
ばん
BOOM

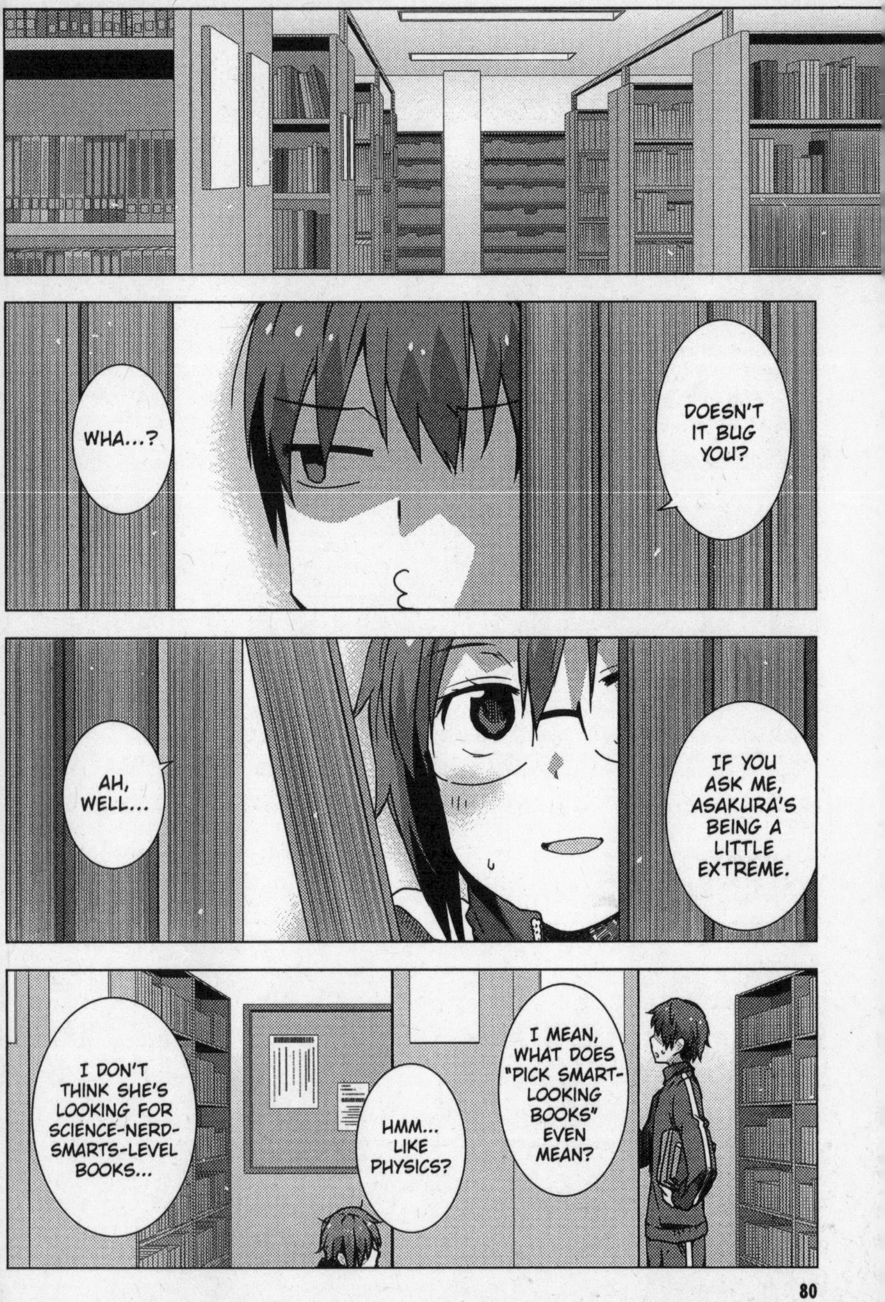
DOESN'T IT BUG YOU?
WHA...?
IF YOU ASK ME, ASAKURA'S BEING A LITTLE EXTREME.
AH, WELL...
I MEAN, WHAT DOES "PICK SMART-LOOKING BOOKS" EVEN MEAN?
HMM... LIKE PHYSICS?
I DON'T THINK SHE'S LOOKING FOR SCIENCE-NERD-SMARTS-LEVEL BOOKS...

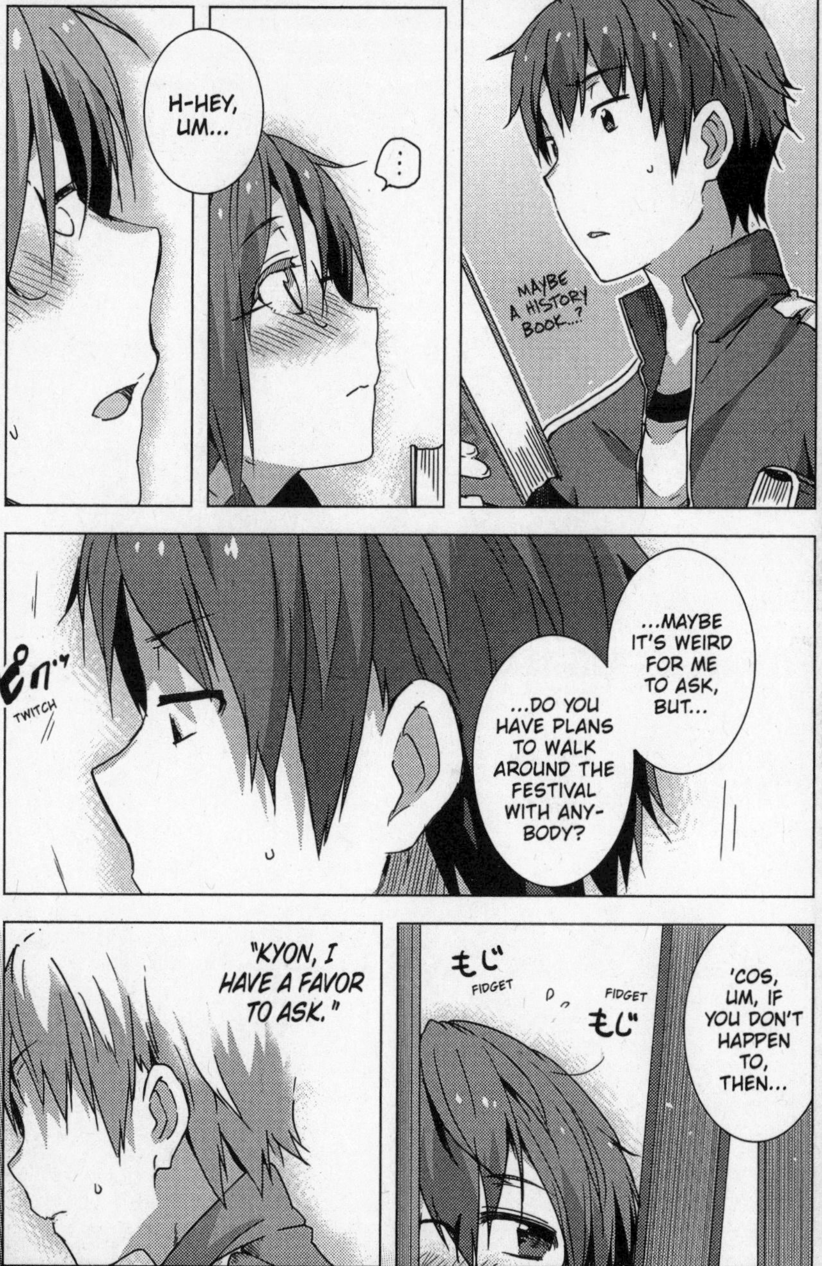
MAYBE A HISTORY BOOK...?
...
H-HEY, UM...
...MAYBE IT'S WEIRD FOR ME TO ASK, BUT...
...DO YOU HAVE PLANS TO WALK AROUND THE FESTIVAL WITH ANY-BODY?
ピクッ
TWITCH
'COS, UM, IF YOU DON'T HAPPEN TO, THEN...
もじ
FIDGET
もじ
FIDGET
"KYON, I HAVE A FAVOR TO ASK."

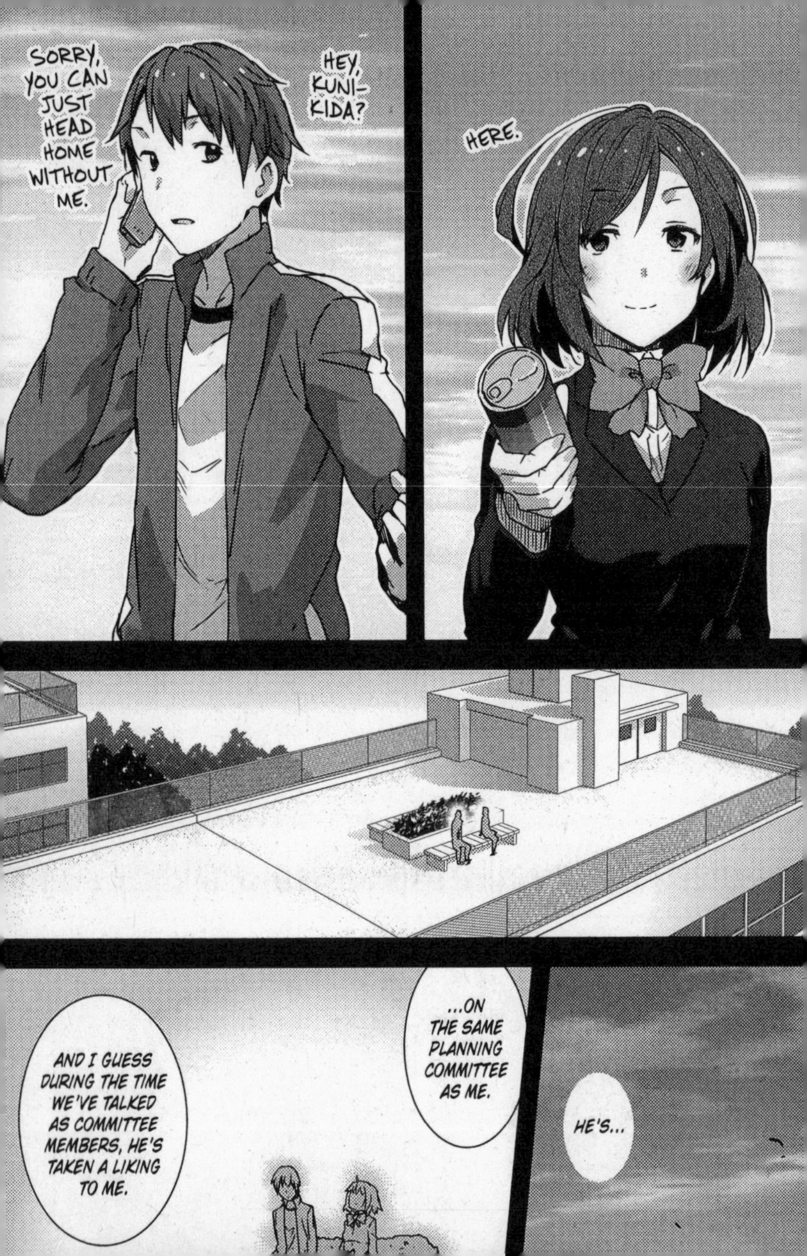
HERE.
HEY, KUNI-KIDA?
SORRY, YOU CAN JUST HEAD HOME WITHOUT ME.
HE'S...
...ON THE SAME PLANNING COMMITTEE AS ME.
AND I GUESS DURING THE TIME WE'VE TALKED AS COMMITTEE MEMBERS, HE'S TAKEN A LIKING TO ME.

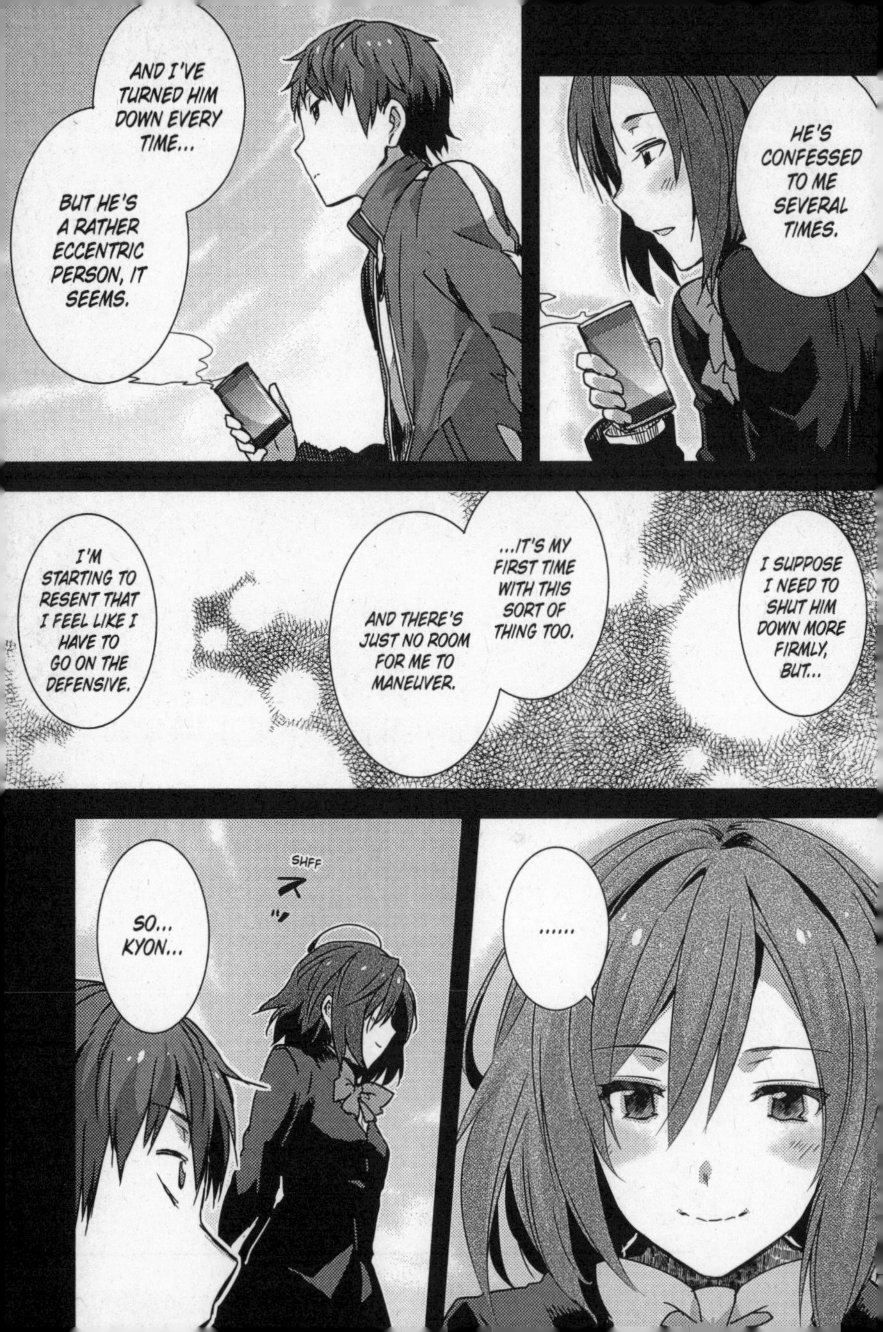
HE'S CONFESSED TO ME SEVERAL TIMES.
AND I'VE TURNED HIM DOWN EVERY TIME...
BUT HE'S A RATHER ECCENTRIC PERSON, IT SEEMS.
I SUPPOSE I NEED TO SHUT HIM DOWN MORE FIRMLY, BUT...
...IT'S MY FIRST TIME WITH THIS SORT OF THING TOO.
AND THERE'S JUST NO ROOM FOR ME TO MANEUVER.
I'M STARTING TO RESENT THAT I FEEL LIKE I HAVE TO GO ON THE DEFENSIVE.
......
SHFF
スッ
SO... KYON...

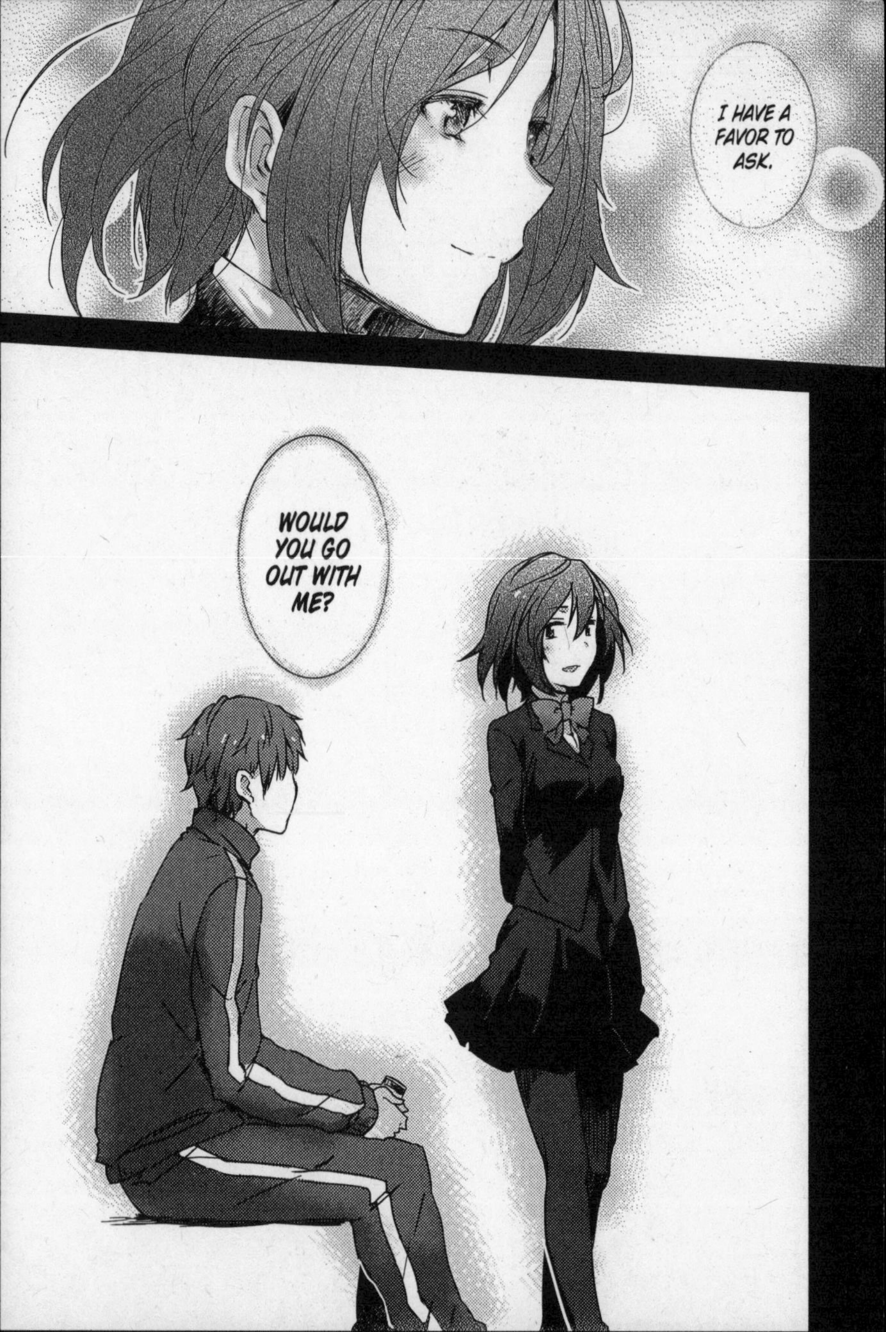
I HAVE A FAVOR TO ASK.
WOULD YOU GO OUT WITH ME?

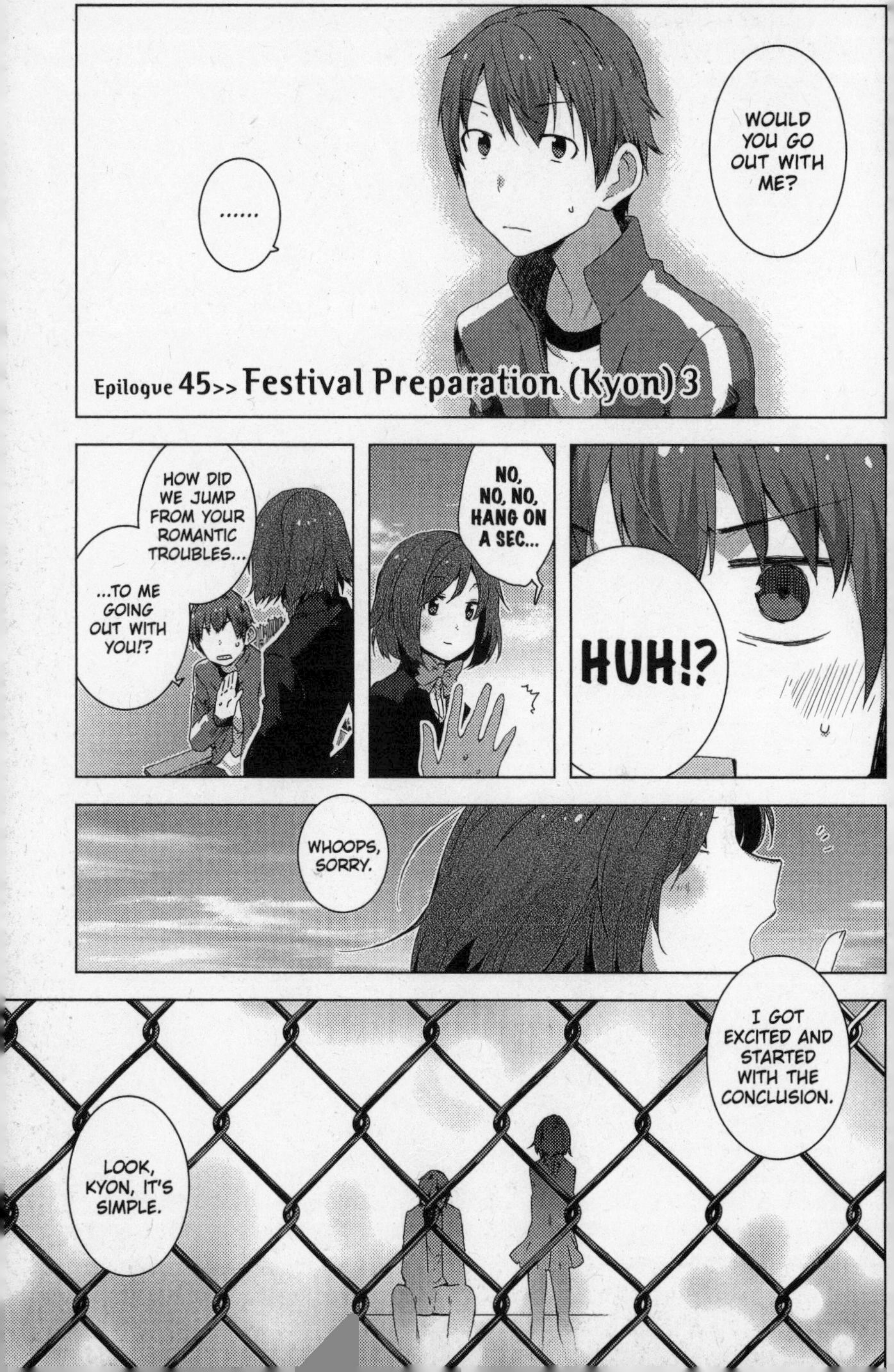
WOULD YOU GO OUT WITH ME?
......
Epilogue 45>> Festival Preparation (Kyon) 3
HUH!?
NO, NO, NO, HANG ON A SEC...
HOW DID WE JUMP FROM YOUR ROMANTIC TROUBLES...
...TO ME GOING OUT WITH YOU!?
WHOOPS, SORRY.
I GOT EXCITED AND STARTED WITH THE CONCLUSION.
LOOK, KYON, IT'S SIMPLE.

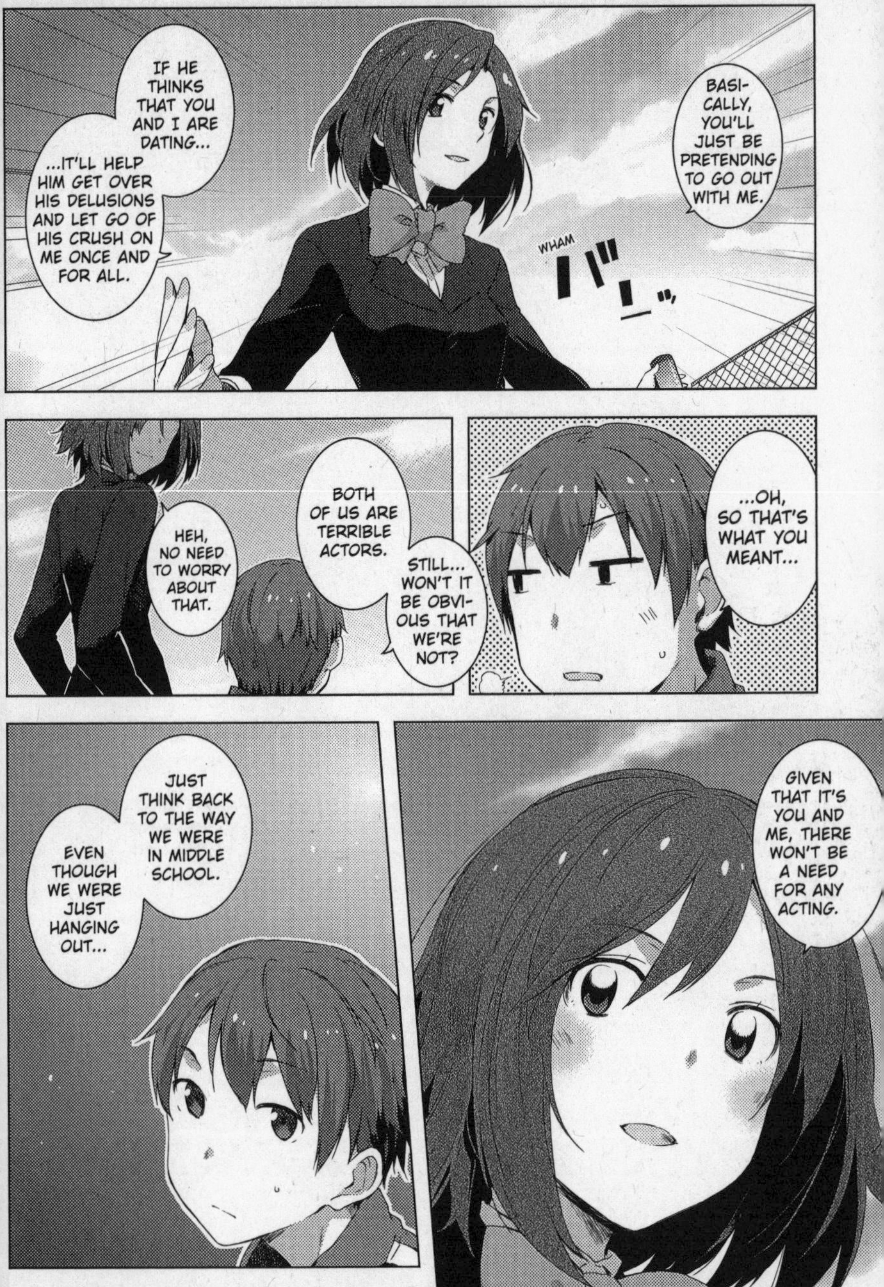
BASI-CALLY, YOU'LL JUST BE PRETENDING TO GO OUT WITH ME.
WHAM
バーッ
IF HE THINKS THAT YOU AND I ARE DATING...
...IT'LL HELP HIM GET OVER HIS DELUSIONS AND LET GO OF HIS CRUSH ON ME ONCE AND FOR ALL.
...OH, SO THAT'S WHAT YOU MEANT...
STILL... WON'T IT BE OBVI-OUS THAT WE'RE NOT?
BOTH OF US ARE TERRIBLE ACTORS.
HEH, NO NEED TO WORRY ABOUT THAT.
GIVEN THAT IT'S YOU AND ME, THERE WON'T BE A NEED FOR ANY ACTING.
JUST THINK BACK TO THE WAY WE WERE IN MIDDLE SCHOOL.
EVEN THOUGH WE WERE JUST HANGING OUT...

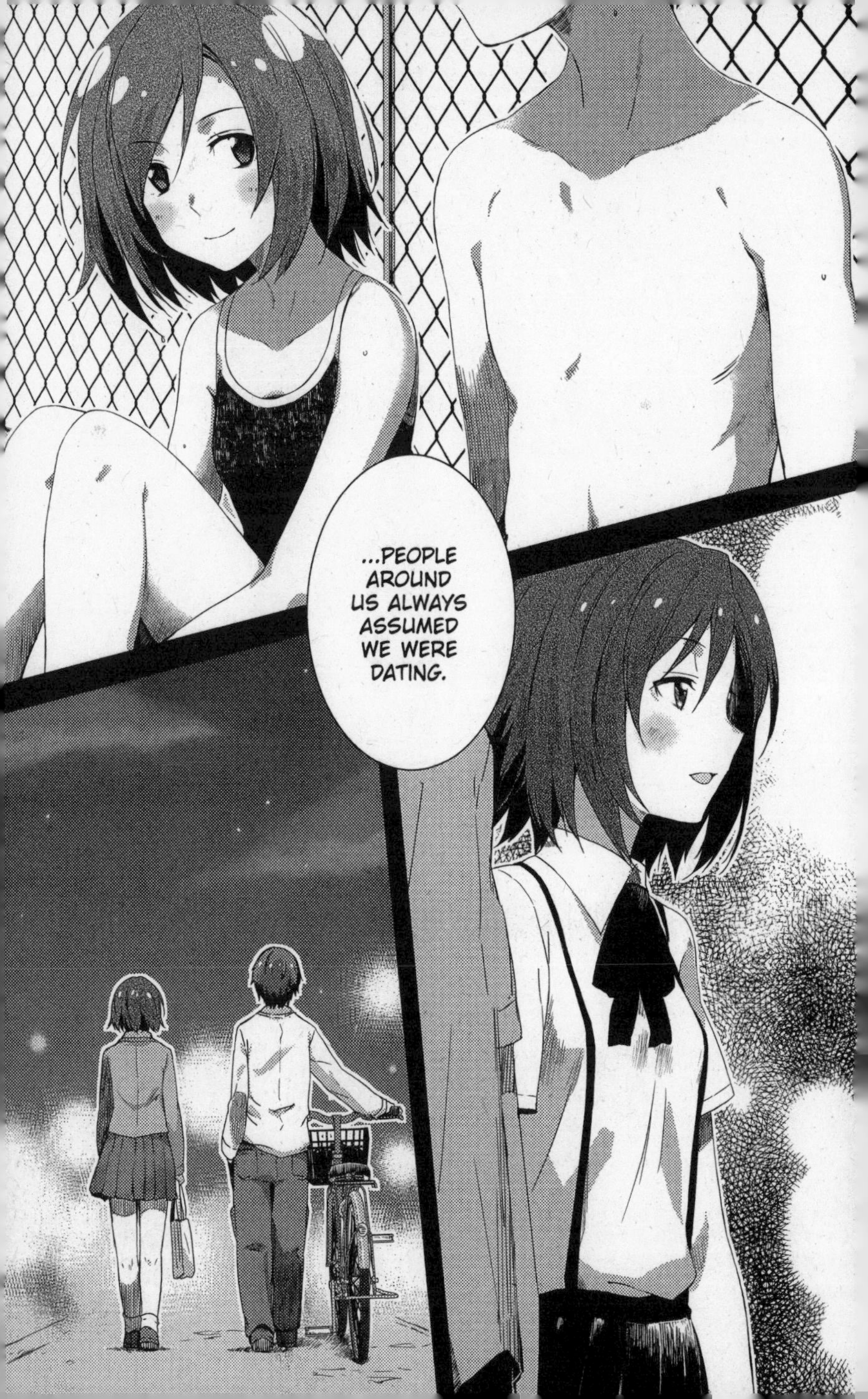
...PEOPLE AROUND US ALWAYS ASSUMED WE WERE DATING.

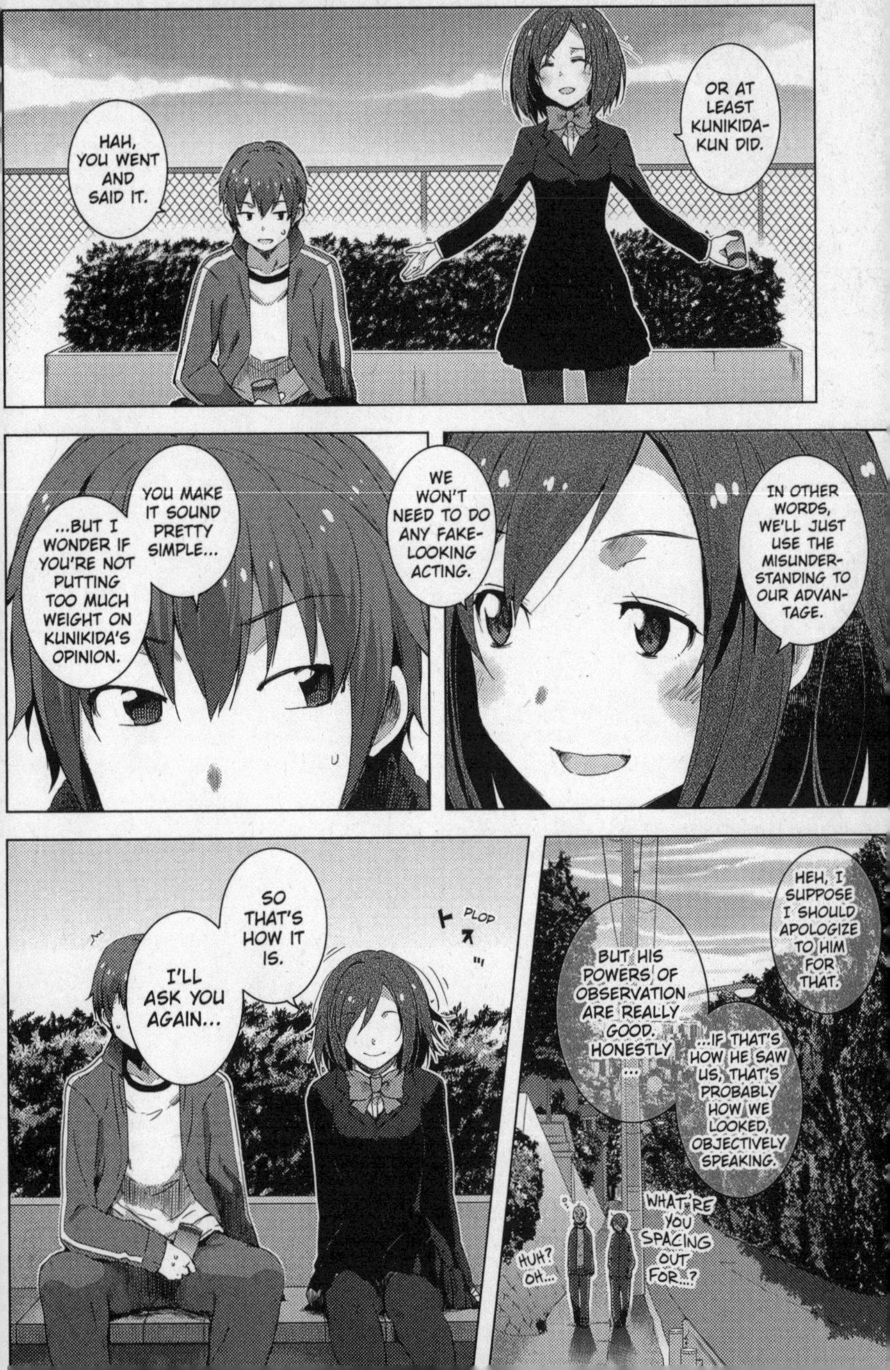
OR AT LEAST KUNIKIDA-KUN DID.
HAH, YOU WENT AND SAID IT.
IN OTHER WORDS, WE'LL JUST USE THE MISUNDERSTANDING TO OUR ADVANTAGE.
WE WON'T NEED TO DO ANY FAKE-LOOKING ACTING.
YOU MAKE IT SOUND PRETTY SIMPLE...
...BUT I WONDER IF YOU'RE NOT PUTTING TOO MUCH WEIGHT ON KUNIKIDA'S OPINION.
HEH, I SUPPOSE I SHOULD APOLOGIZE TO HIM FOR THAT.
BUT HIS POWERS OF OBSERVATION ARE REALLY GOOD. HONESTLY...
...IF THAT'S HOW HE SAW US, THAT'S PROBABLY HOW WE LOOKED, OBJECTIVELY SPEAKING.
WHAT'RE YOU SPACING OUT FOR...?
HUH? OH...
PLOP
SO THAT'S HOW IT IS.
I'LL ASK YOU AGAIN...

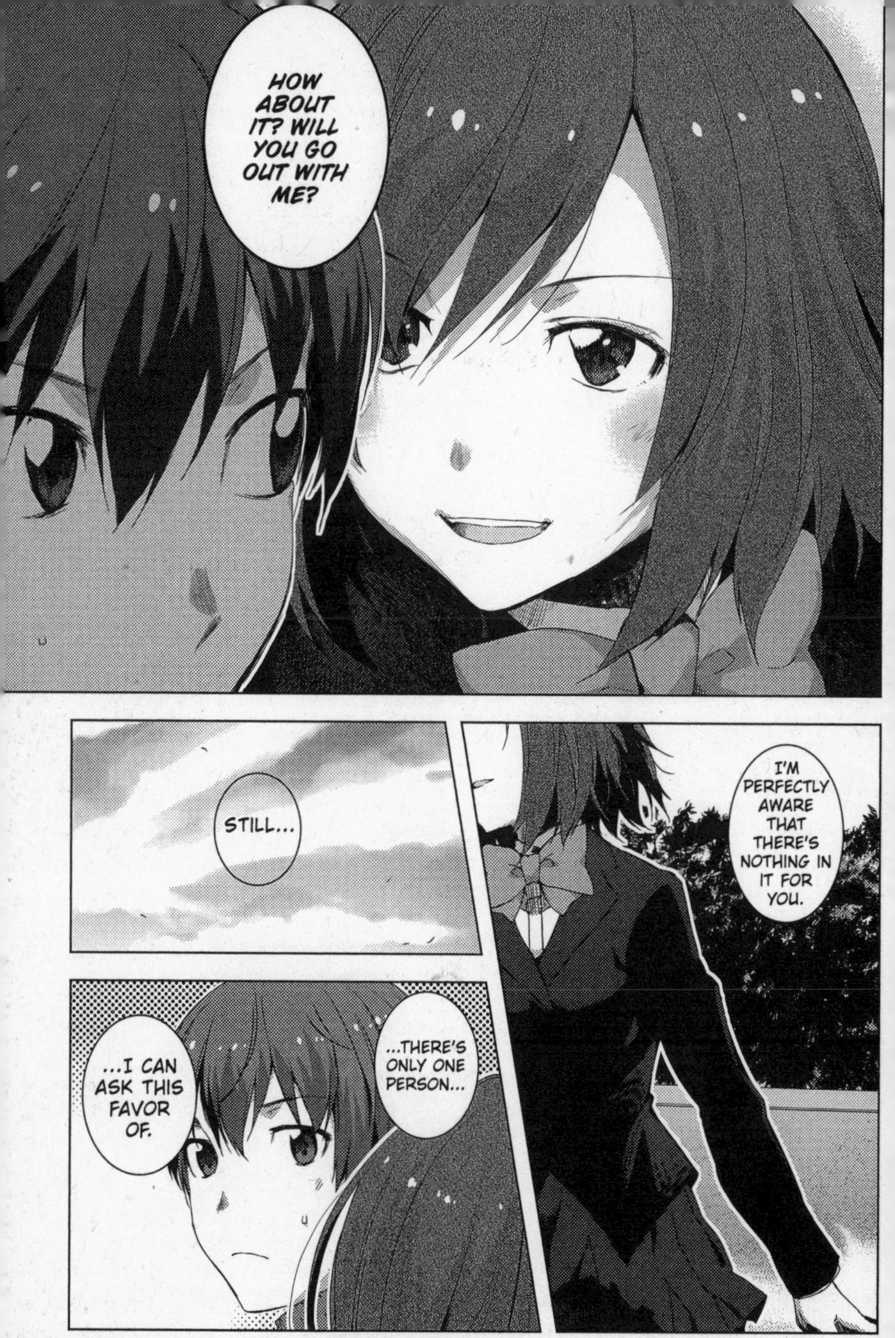
HOW ABOUT IT? WILL YOU GO OUT WITH ME?
I'M PERFECTLY AWARE THAT THERE'S NOTHING IN IT FOR YOU.
STILL...
...THERE'S ONLY ONE PERSON...
...I CAN ASK THIS FAVOR OF.

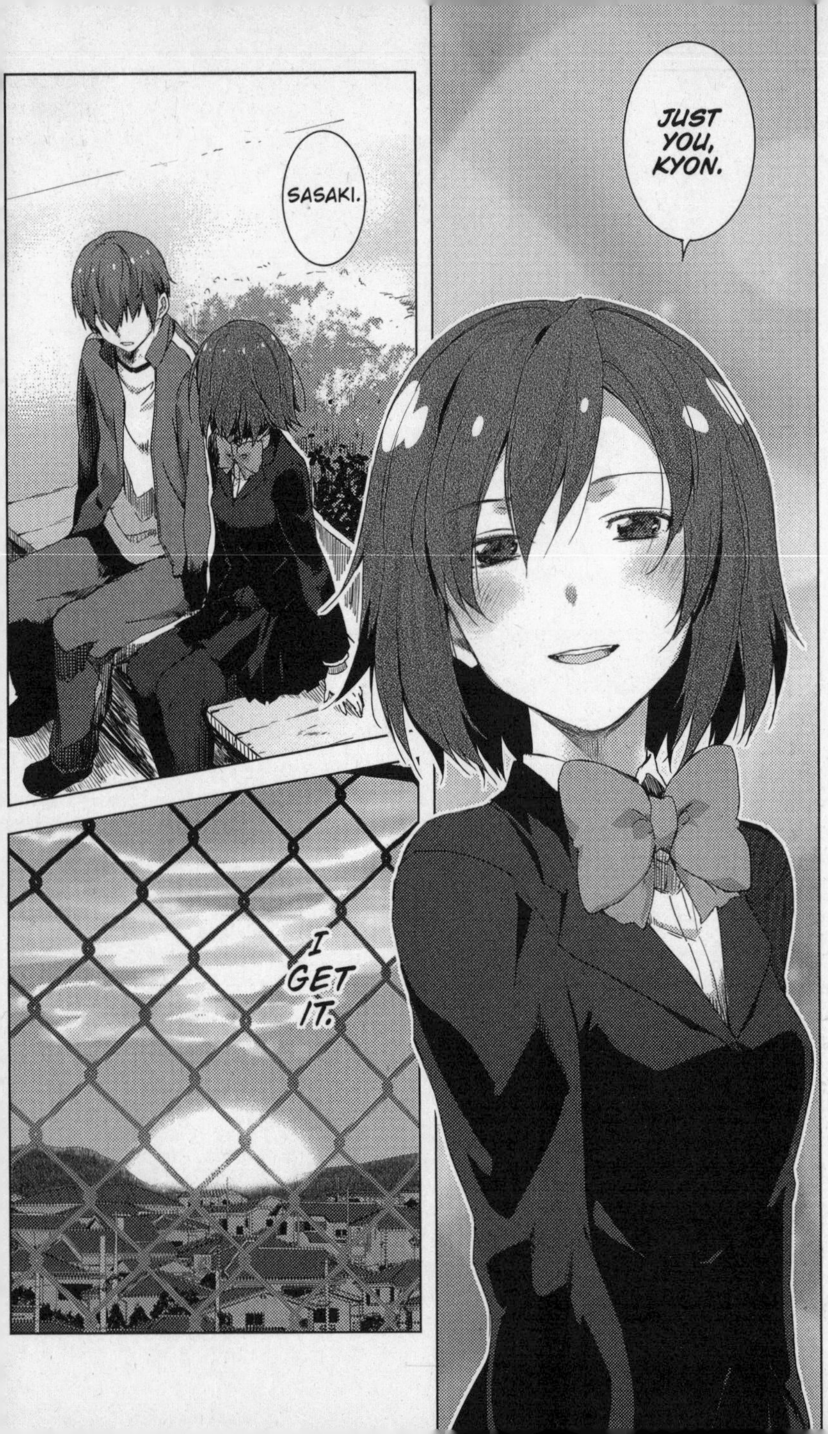
JUST YOU, KYON.
SASAKI.
I GET IT.

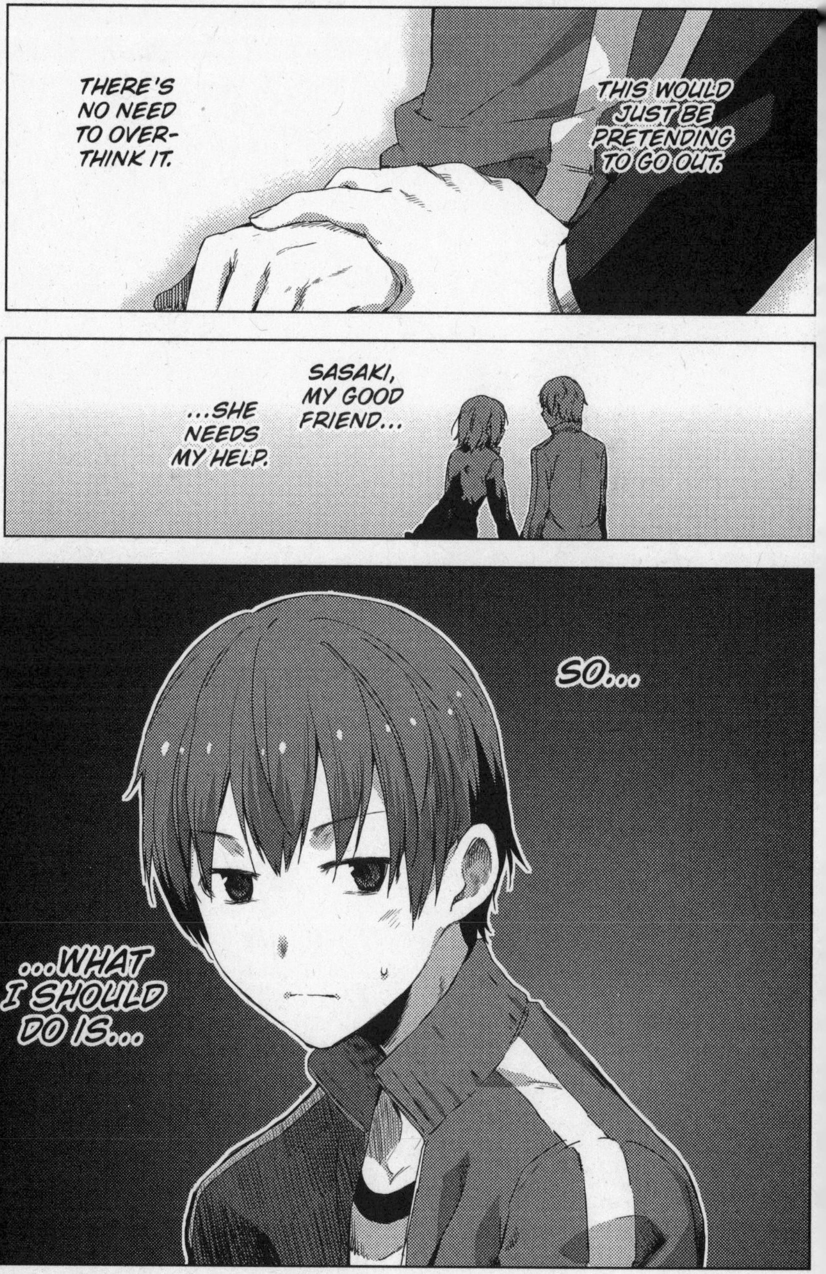
THIS WOULD JUST BE PRETENDING TO GO OUT.
THERE'S NO NEED TO OVER-THINK IT.
SASAKI, MY GOOD FRIEND...
...SHE NEEDS MY HELP.
SO...
...WHAT I SHOULD DO IS...

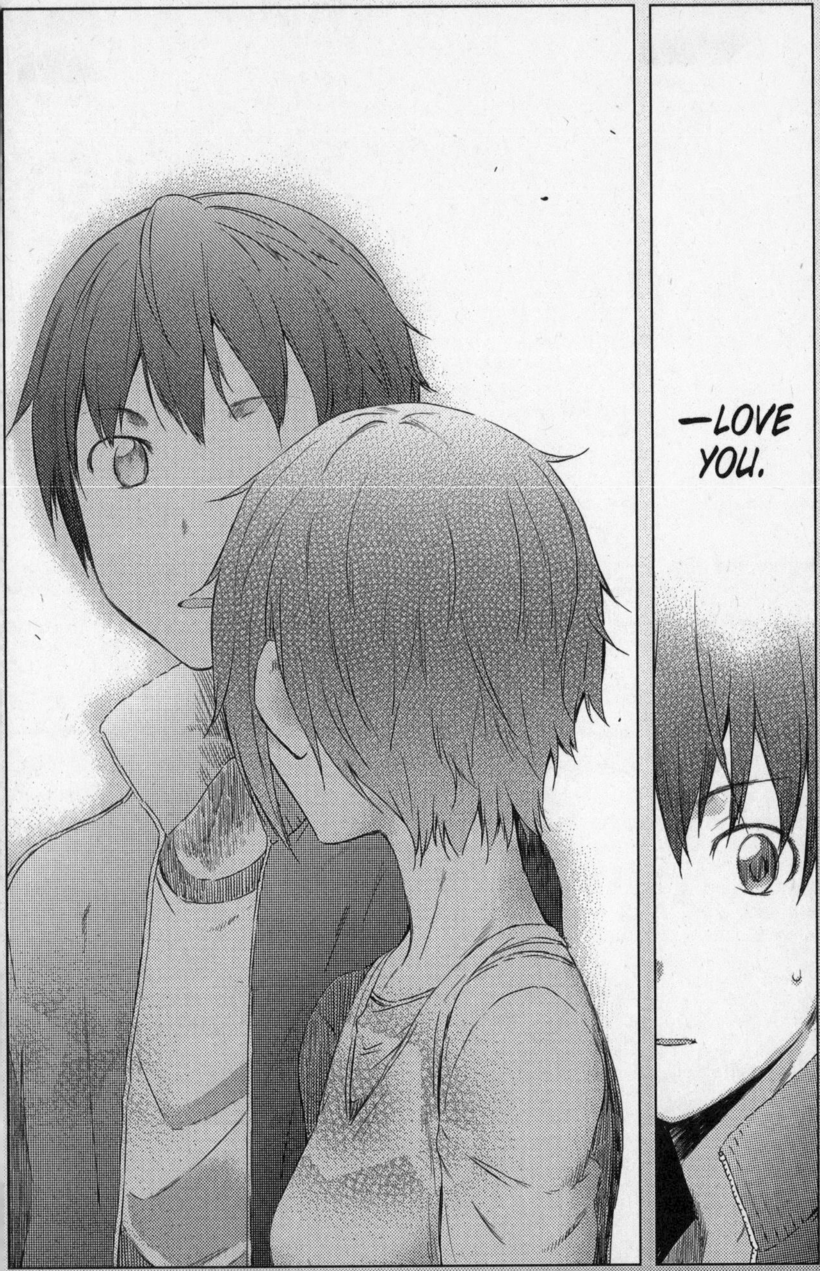
—LOVE YOU.

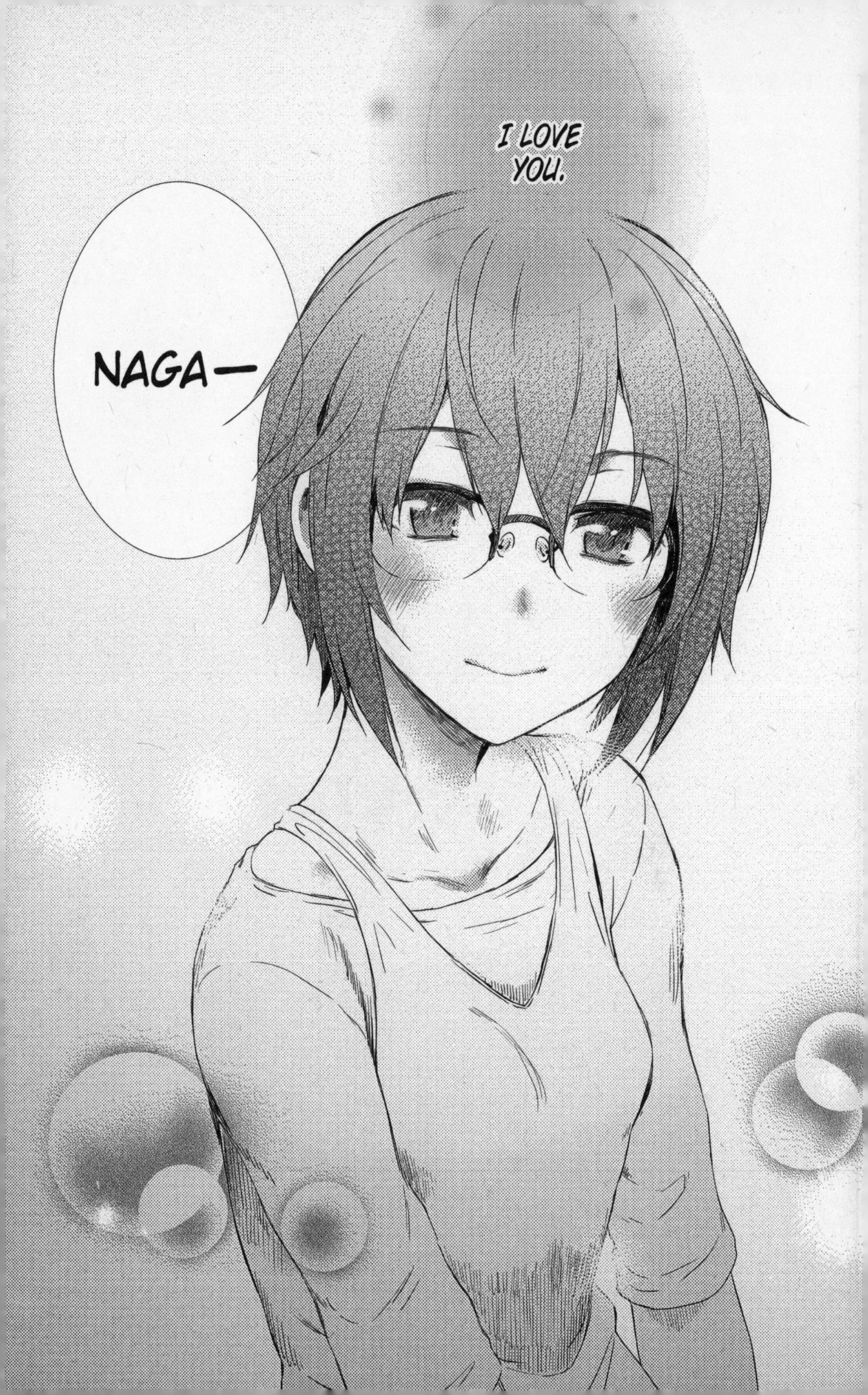
I LOVE YOU.
NAGA—

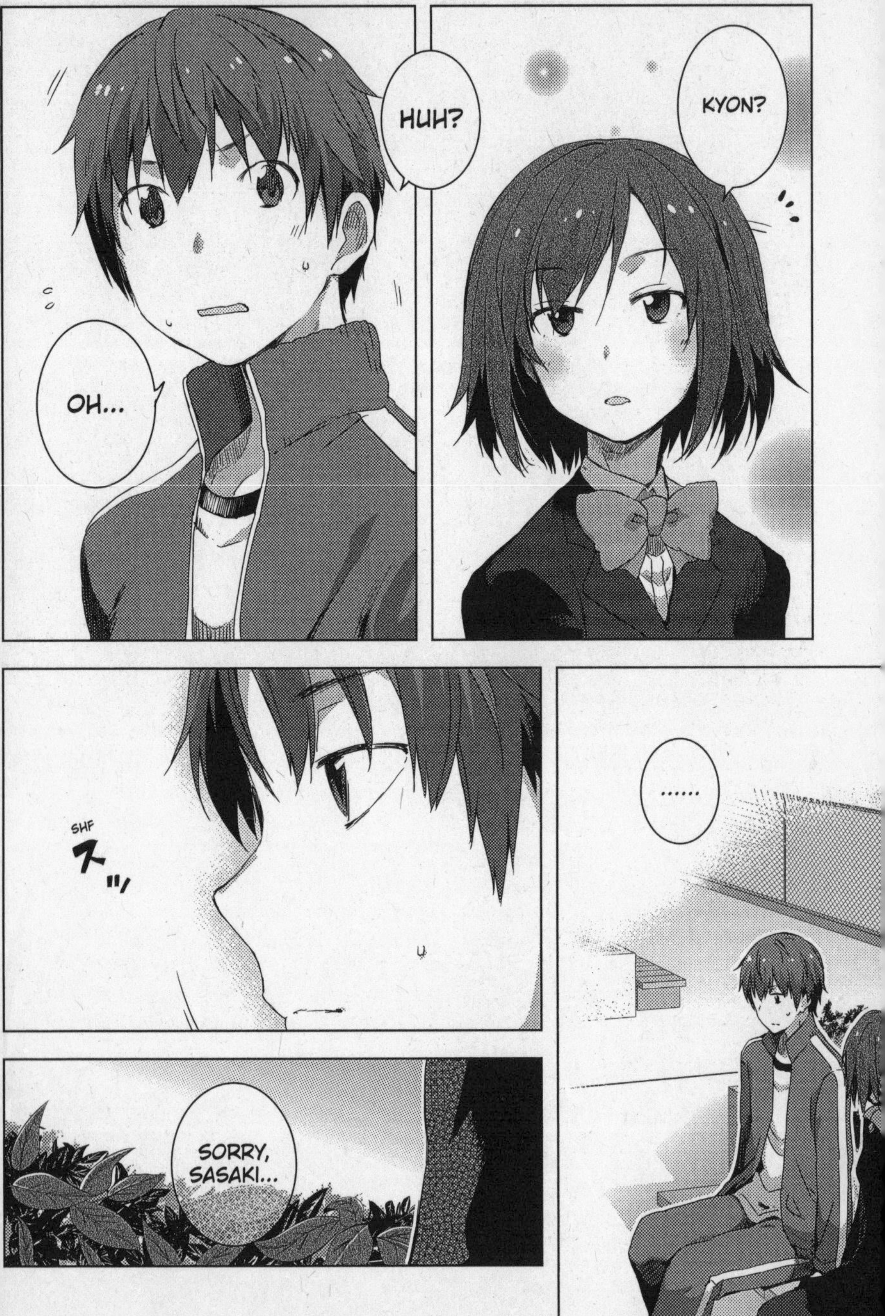
KYON?
HUH?
OH...
......
SHF
スッ
SORRY, SASAKI...

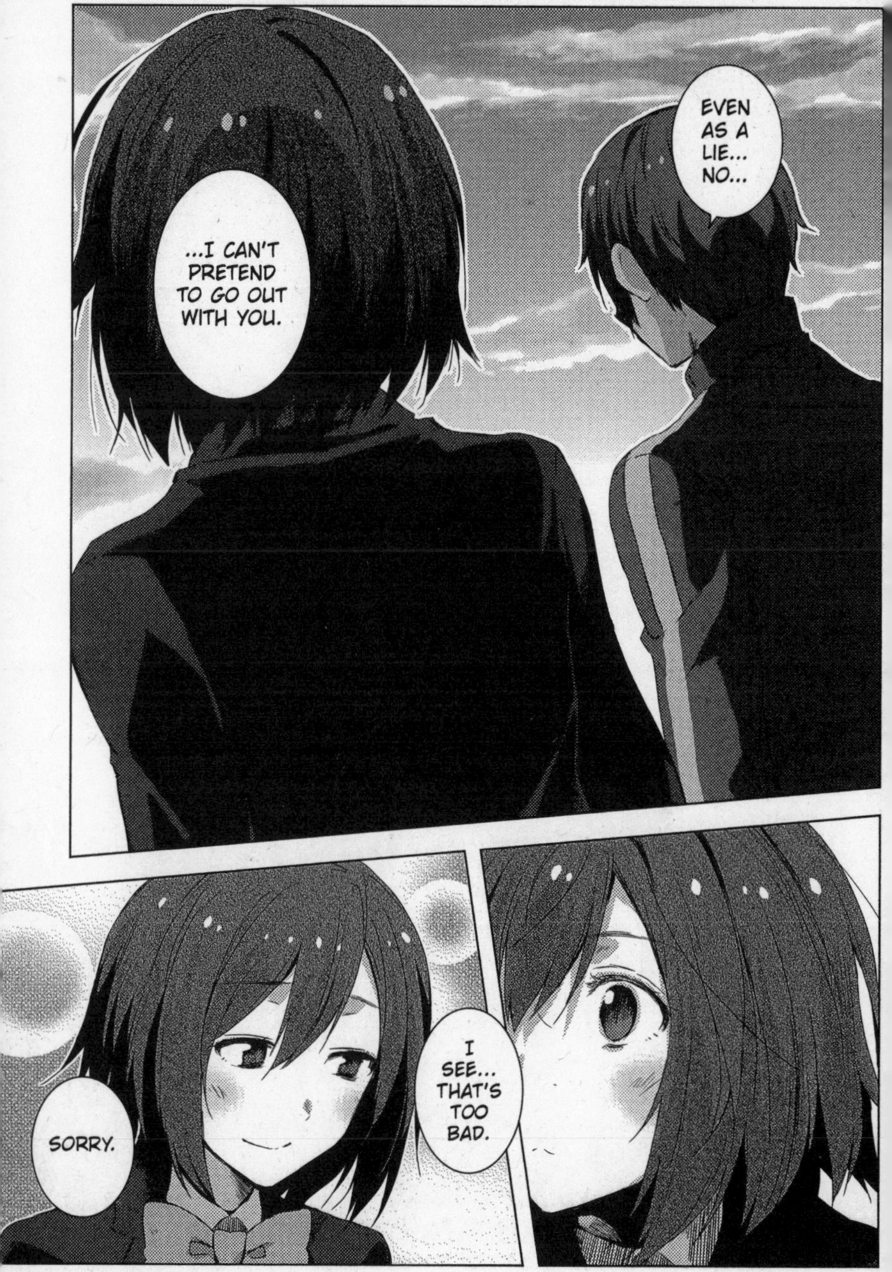
EVEN AS A LIE... NO...
...I CAN'T PRETEND TO GO OUT WITH YOU.
I SEE... THAT'S TOO BAD.
SORRY.

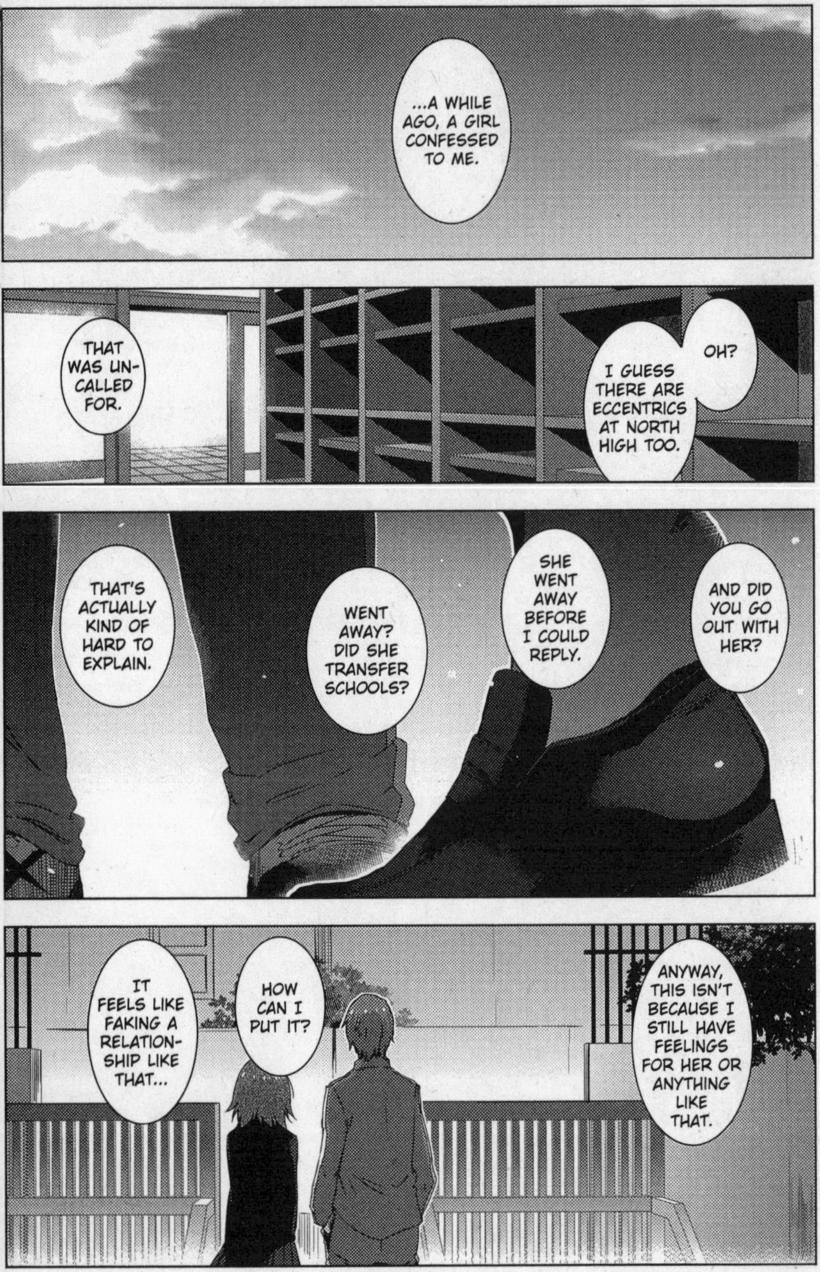
...A WHILE AGO, A GIRL CONFESSED TO ME.
OH?
I GUESS THERE ARE ECCENTRICS AT NORTH HIGH TOO.
THAT WAS UNCALLED FOR.
AND DID YOU GO OUT WITH HER?
SHE WENT AWAY BEFORE I COULD REPLY.
WENT AWAY? DID SHE TRANSFER SCHOOLS?
THAT'S ACTUALLY KIND OF HARD TO EXPLAIN.
ANYWAY, THIS ISN'T BECAUSE I STILL HAVE FEELINGS FOR HER OR ANYTHING LIKE THAT.
HOW CAN I PUT IT?
IT FEELS LIKE FAKING A RELATIONSHIP LIKE THAT...

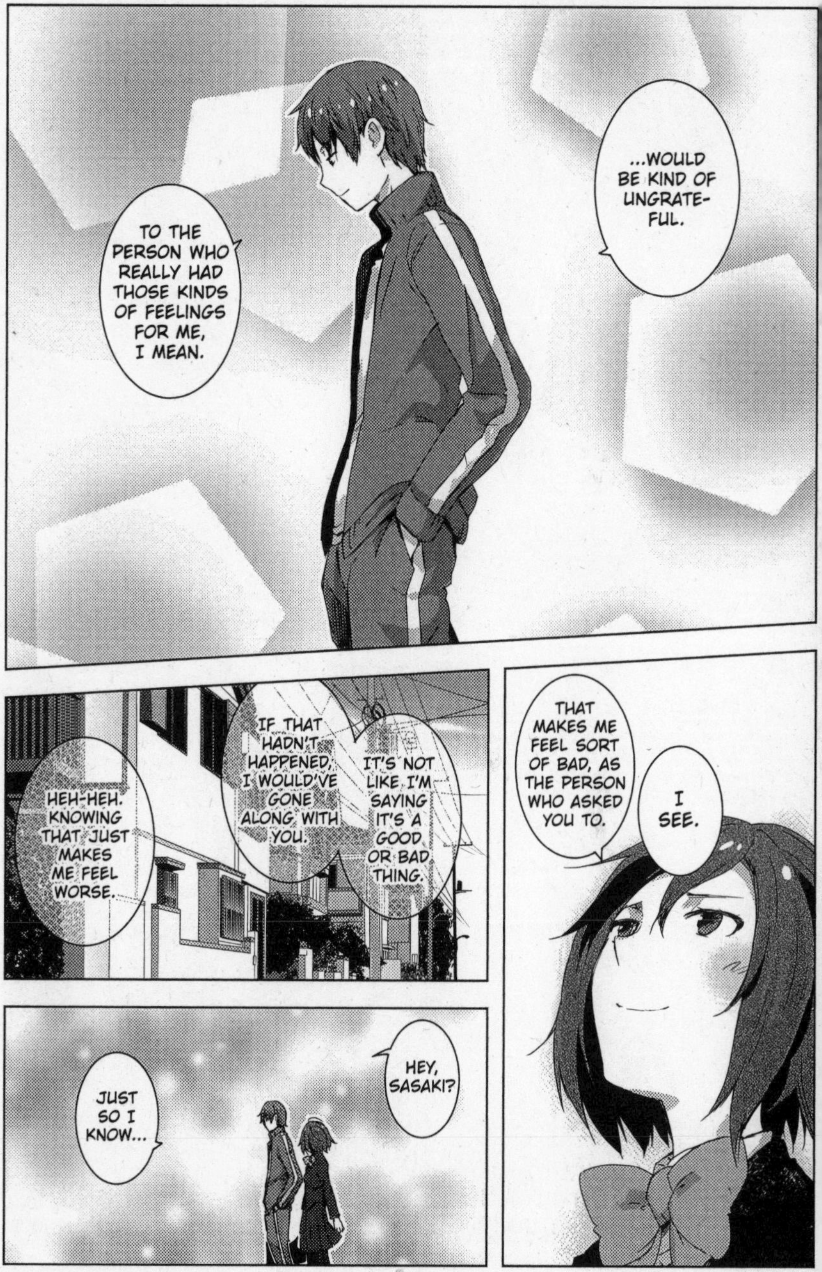
...WOULD BE KIND OF UNGRATE-FUL.
TO THE PERSON WHO REALLY HAD THOSE KINDS OF FEELINGS FOR ME, I MEAN.
I SEE.
THAT MAKES ME FEEL SORT OF BAD, AS THE PERSON WHO ASKED YOU TO.
IT'S NOT LIKE I'M SAYING IT'S A GOOD OR BAD THING.
IF THAT HADN'T HAPPENED, I WOULD'VE GONE ALONG WITH YOU.
HEH-HEH. KNOWING THAT JUST MAKES ME FEEL WORSE.
HEY, SASAKI?
JUST SO I KNOW...

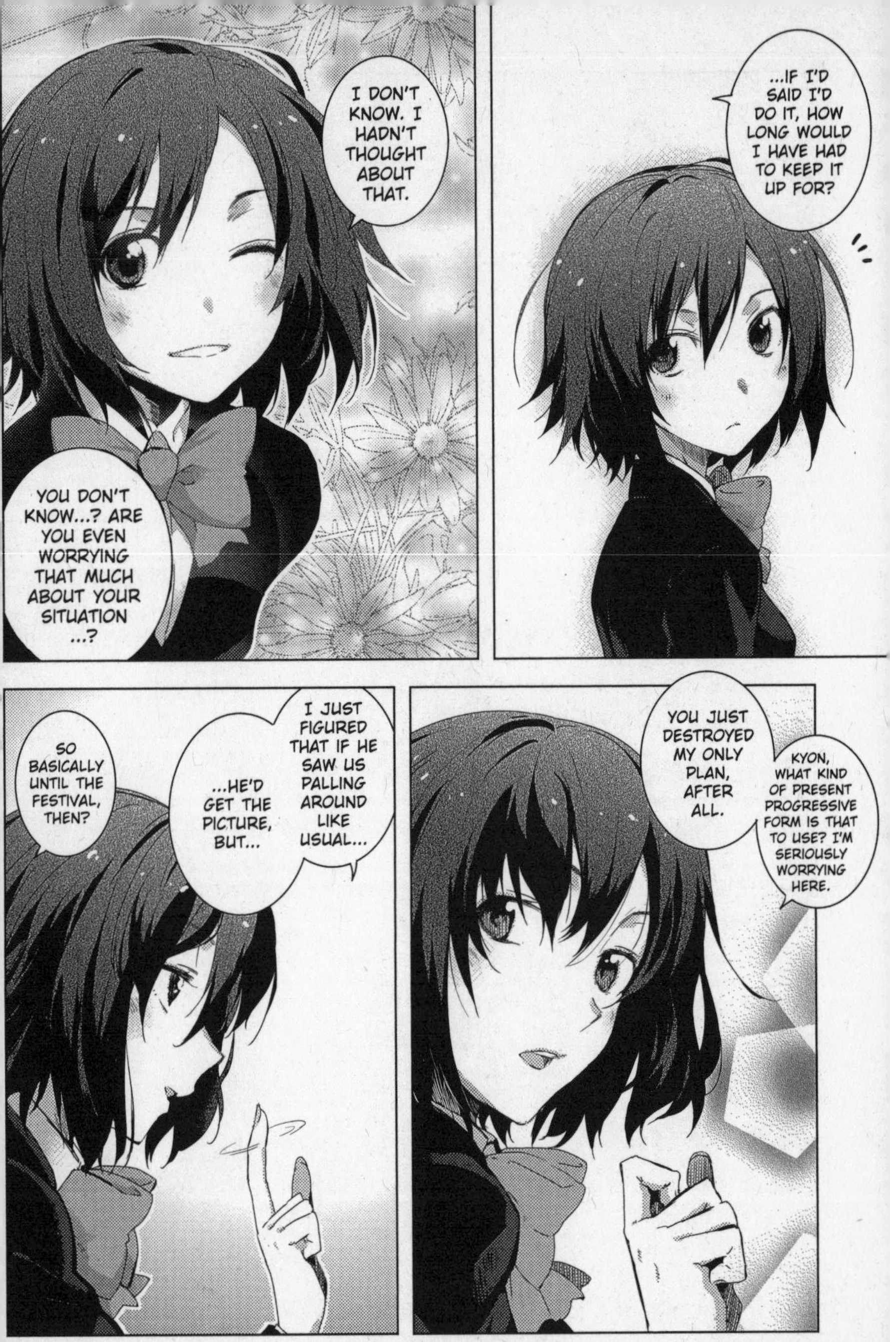
...IF I'D SAID I'D DO IT, HOW LONG WOULD I HAVE HAD TO KEEP IT UP FOR?
I DON'T KNOW. I HADN'T THOUGHT ABOUT THAT.
YOU DON'T KNOW...? ARE YOU EVEN WORRYING THAT MUCH ABOUT YOUR SITUATION ...?
KYON, WHAT KIND OF PRESENT PROGRESSIVE FORM IS THAT TO USE? I'M SERIOUSLY WORRYING HERE.
YOU JUST DESTROYED MY ONLY PLAN, AFTER ALL.
I JUST FIGURED THAT IF HE SAW US PALLING AROUND LIKE USUAL...
...HE'D GET THE PICTURE, BUT...
SO BASICALLY UNTIL THE FESTIVAL, THEN?

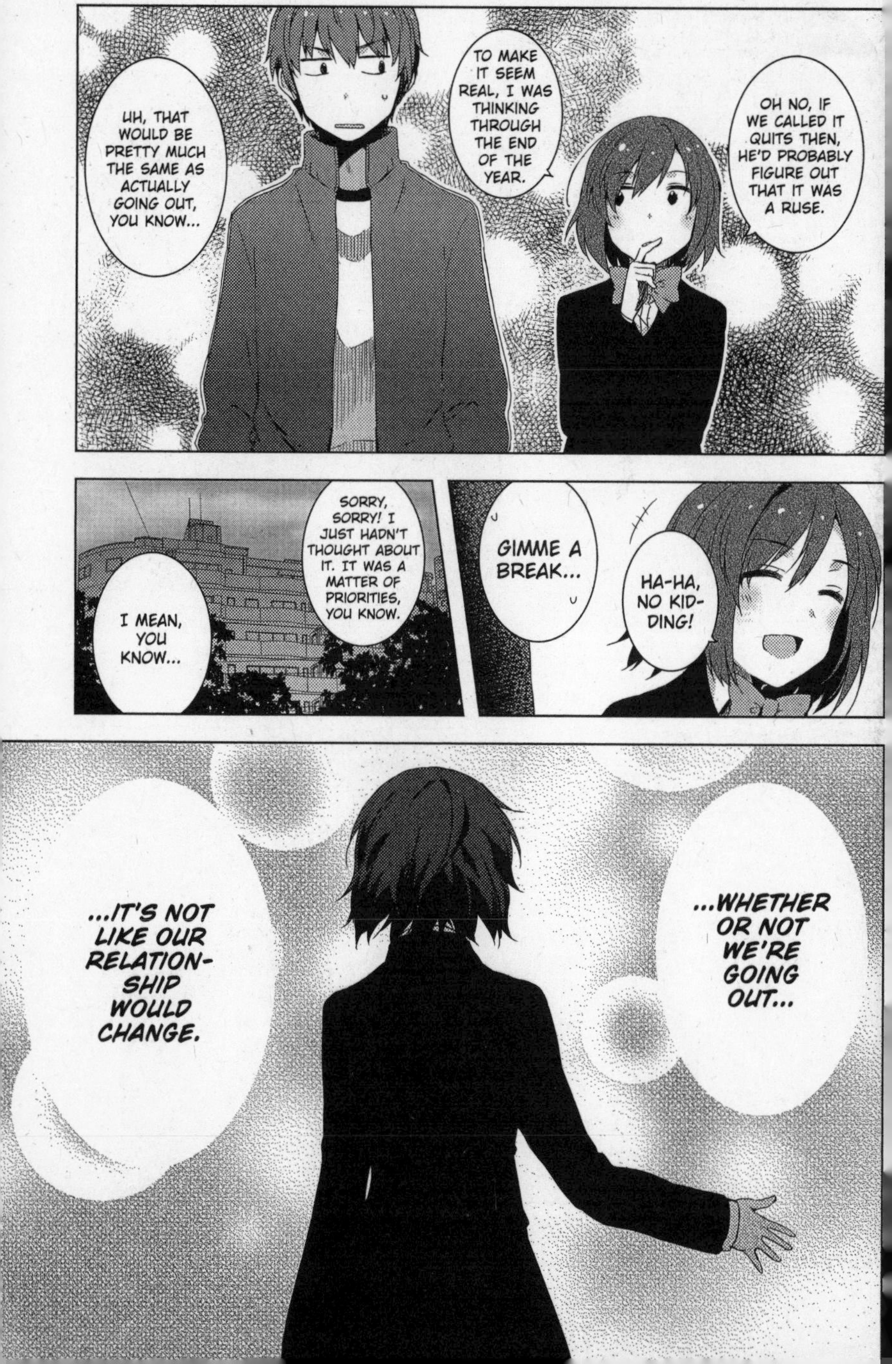
OH NO, IF WE CALLED IT QUITS THEN, HE'D PROBABLY FIGURE OUT THAT IT WAS A RUSE.
TO MAKE IT SEEM REAL, I WAS THINKING THROUGH THE END OF THE YEAR.
UH, THAT WOULD BE PRETTY MUCH THE SAME AS ACTUALLY GOING OUT, YOU KNOW...
HA-HA, NO KID-DING!
GIMME A BREAK...
SORRY, SORRY! I JUST HADN'T THOUGHT ABOUT IT. IT WAS A MATTER OF PRIORITIES, YOU KNOW.
I MEAN, YOU KNOW...
...WHETHER OR NOT WE'RE GOING OUT...
...IT'S NOT LIKE OUR RELATION-SHIP WOULD CHANGE.

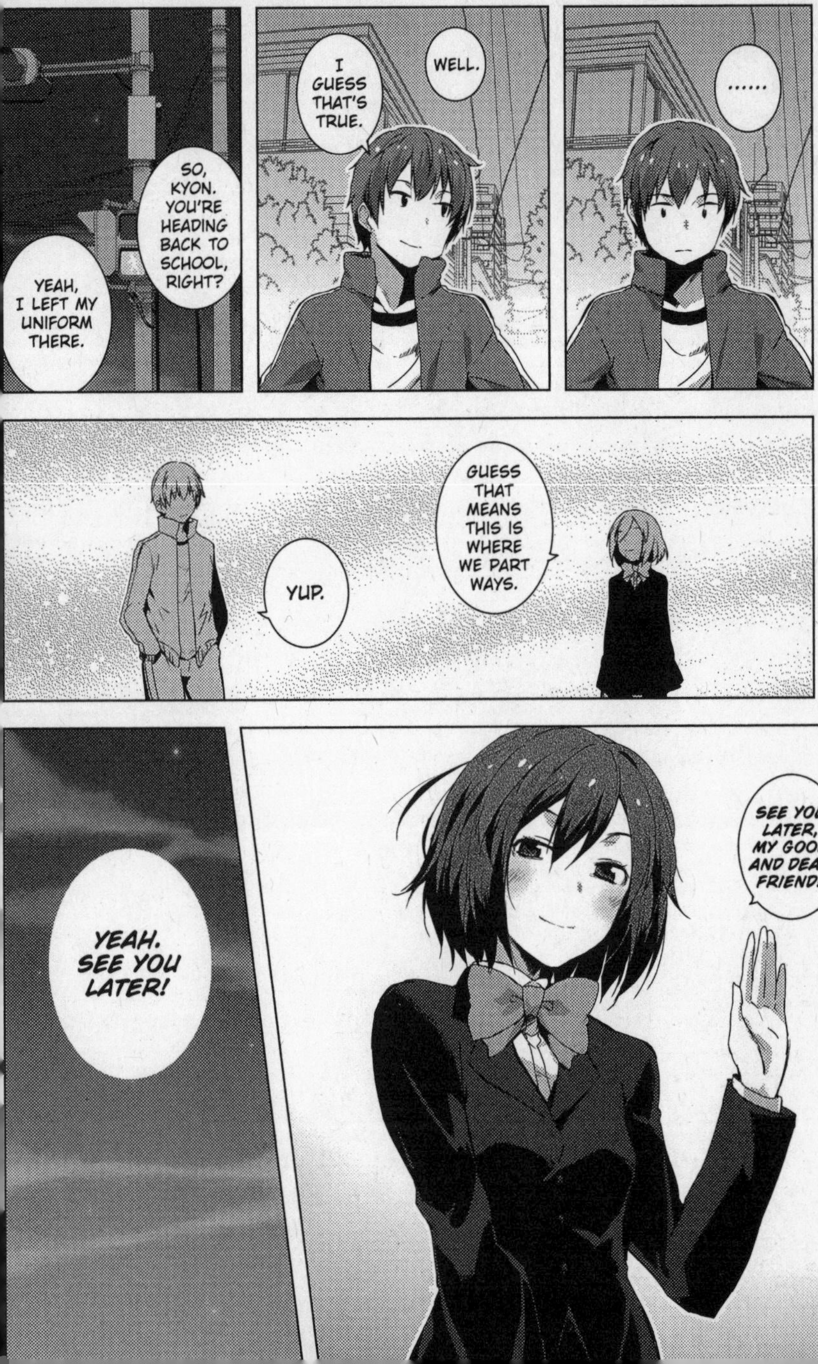
......
WELL.
I GUESS THAT'S TRUE.
SO, KYON. YOU'RE HEADING BACK TO SCHOOL, RIGHT?
YEAH, I LEFT MY UNIFORM THERE.
GUESS THAT MEANS THIS IS WHERE WE PART WAYS.
YUP.
SEE YOU LATER, MY GOOD AND DEAR FRIEND!
YEAH. SEE YOU LATER!

LATER...

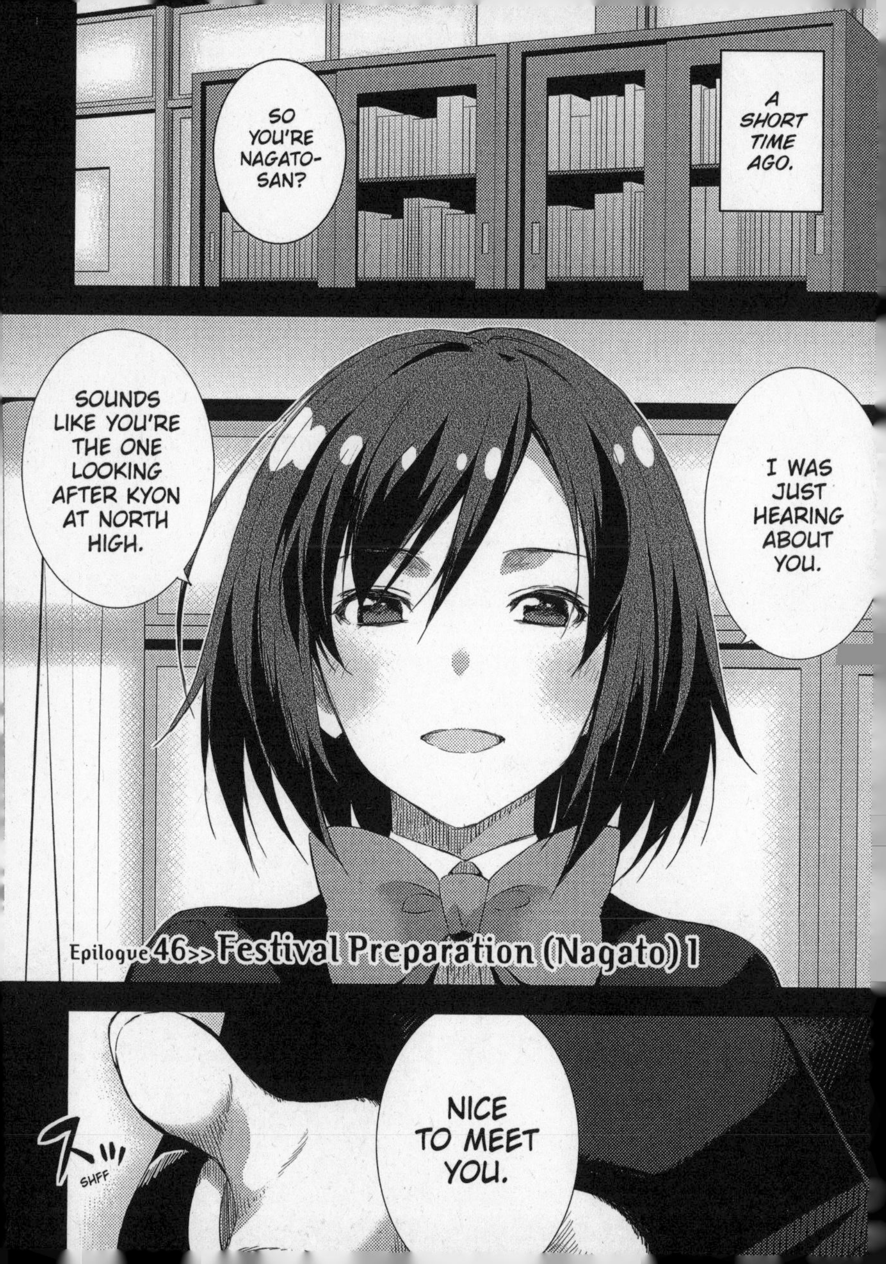
A SHORT TIME AGO.
SO YOU'RE NAGATO-SAN?
I WAS JUST HEARING ABOUT YOU.
SOUNDS LIKE YOU'RE THE ONE LOOKING AFTER KYON AT NORTH HIGH.
Epilogue 46>> Festival Preparation (Nagato) 1
NICE TO MEET YOU.
SHFF

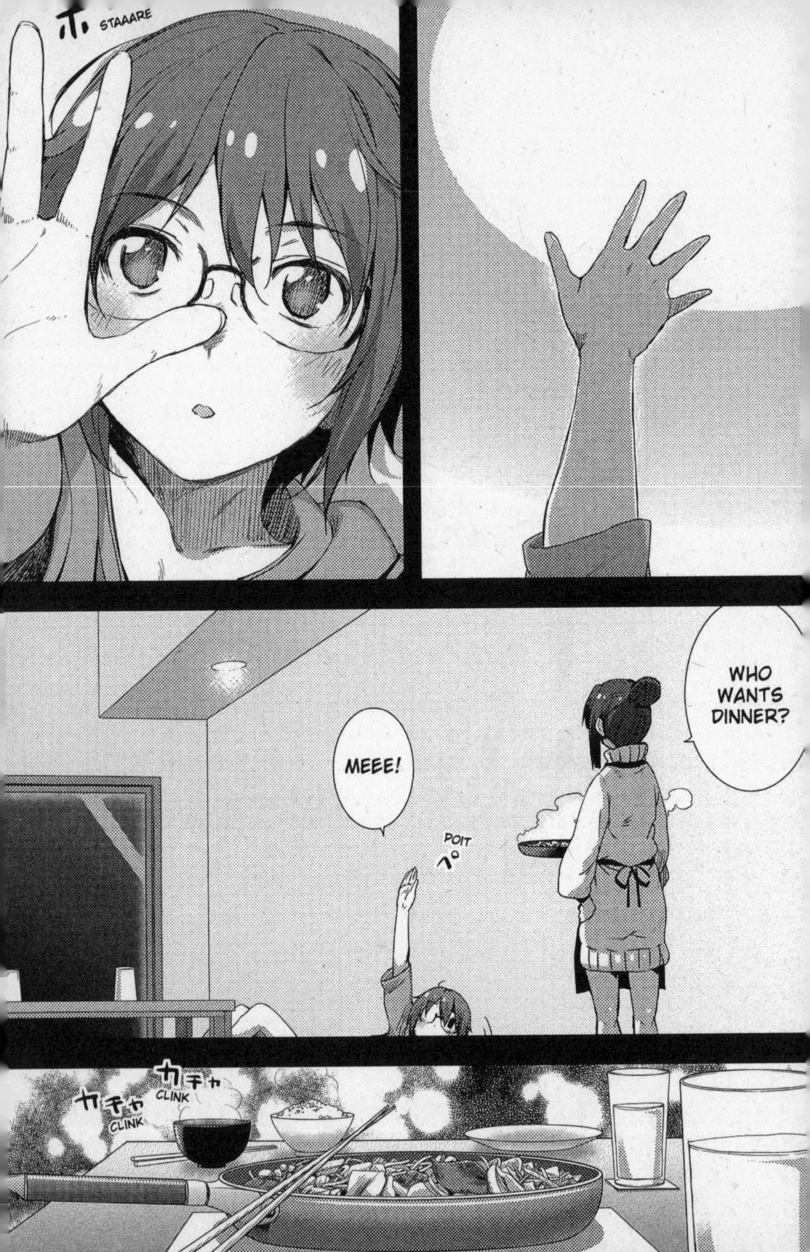
STAARE
WHO WANTS DINNER?
MEEE!
POIT
カチャ
CLINK
カチャ
CLINK

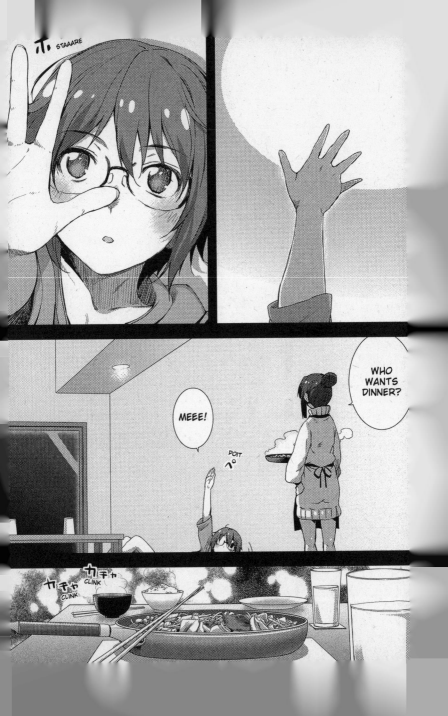

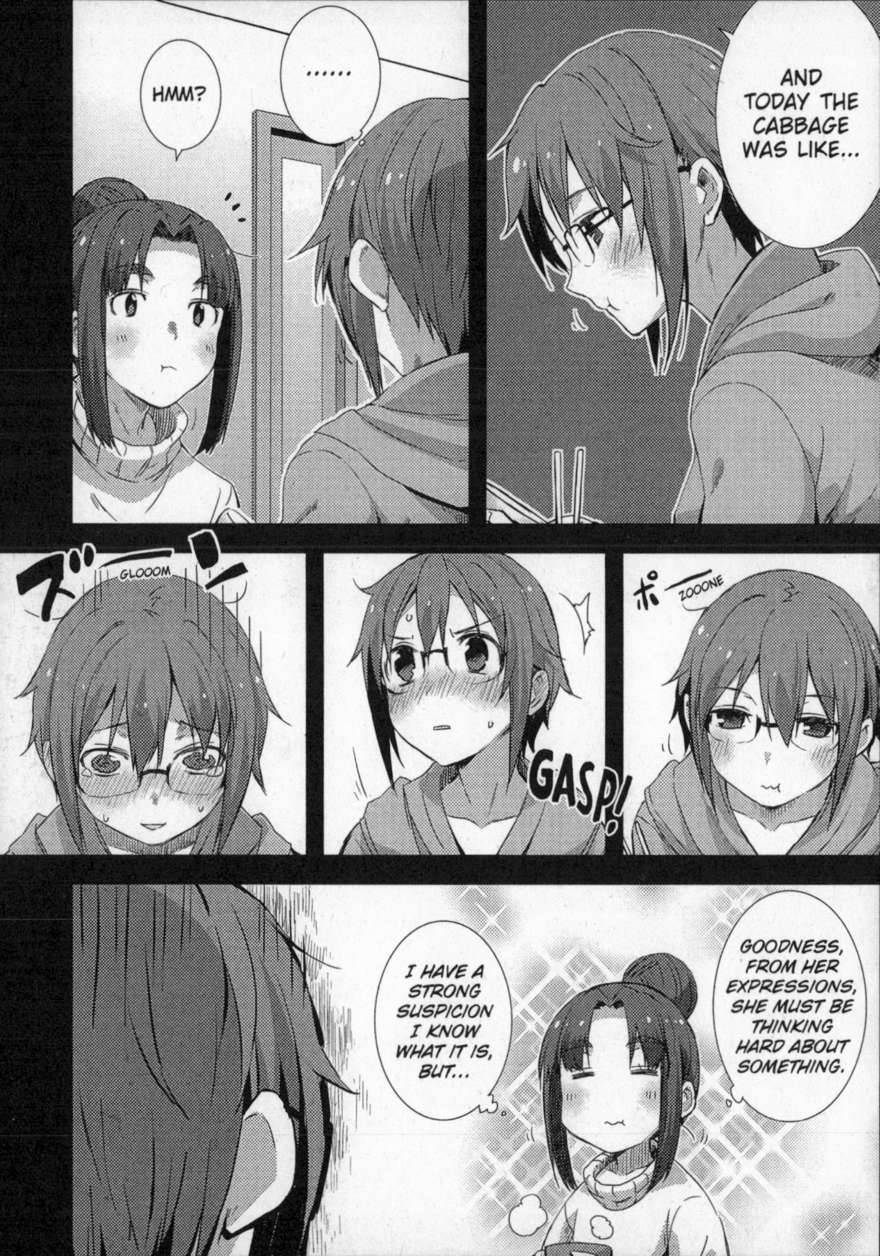
AND TODAY THE CABBAGE WAS LIKE...
......
HMM?
ポー
ZOOONE
GASP!
ズーン
GLOOOM
GOODNESS, FROM HER EXPRESSIONS, SHE MUST BE THINKING HARD ABOUT SOMETHING.
I HAVE A STRONG SUSPICION I KNOW WHAT IT IS, BUT...

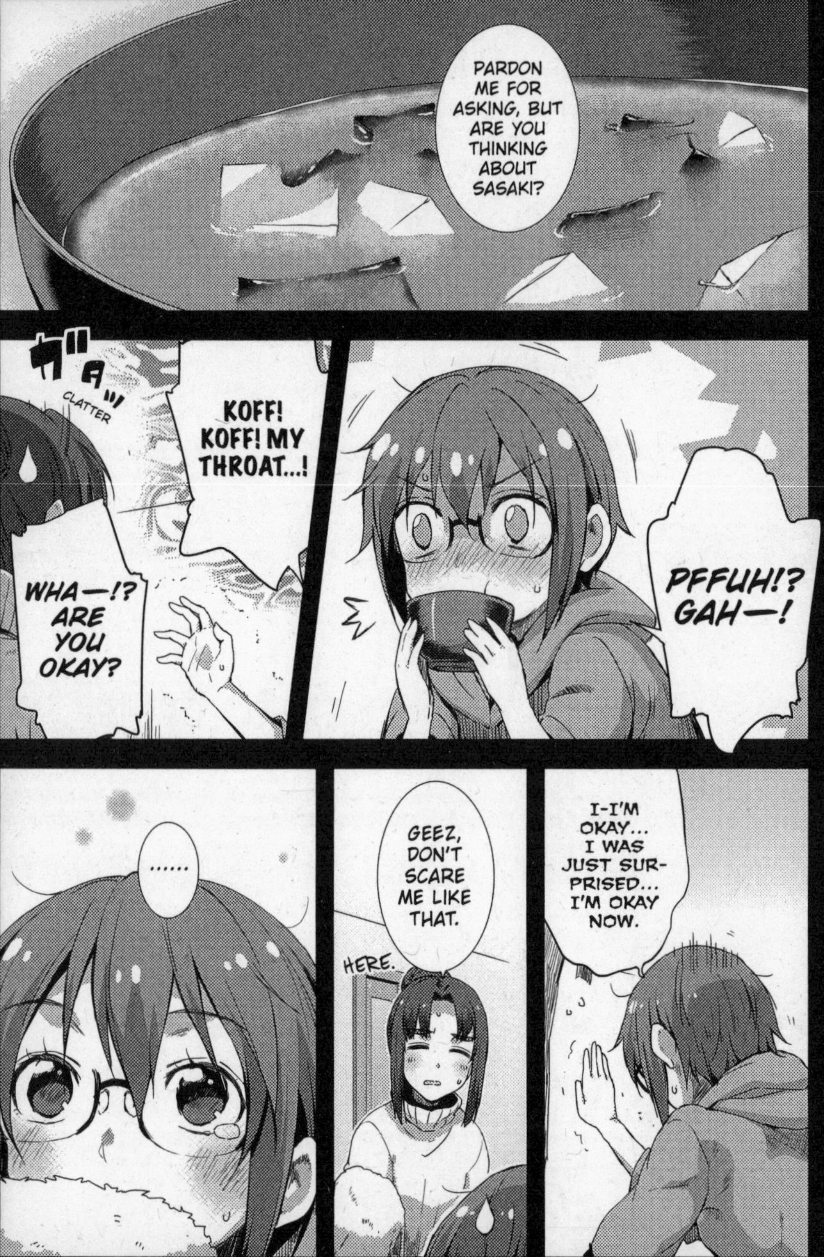
PARDON ME FOR ASKING, BUT ARE YOU THINKING ABOUT SASAKI?
PFFUH!? GAH—!
KOFF! KOFF! MY THROAT...!
ガタッ
CLATTER
WHA—!? ARE YOU OKAY?
I-I'M OKAY... I WAS JUST SUR-PRISED... I'M OKAY NOW.
GEEZ, DON'T SCARE ME LIKE THAT.
HERE.
......

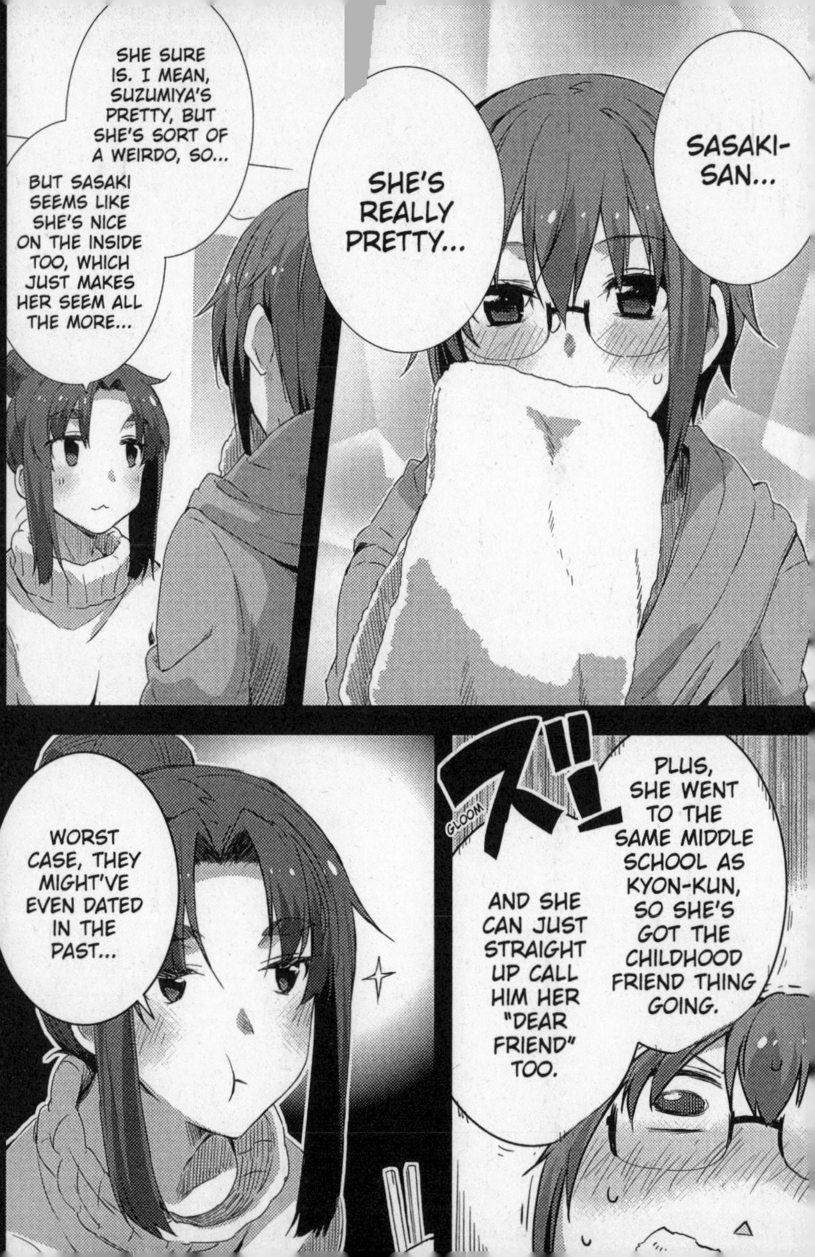
SASAKI-SAN...
SHE'S REALLY PRETTY...
SHE SURE IS. I MEAN, SUZUMIYA'S PRETTY, BUT SHE'S SORT OF A WEIRDO, SO...
BUT SASAKI SEEMS LIKE SHE'S NICE ON THE INSIDE TOO, WHICH JUST MAKES HER SEEM ALL THE MORE...
ズ!
GLOOM
PLUS, SHE WENT TO THE SAME MIDDLE SCHOOL AS KYON-KUN, SO SHE'S GOT THE CHILDHOOD FRIEND THING GOING.
AND SHE CAN JUST STRAIGHT UP CALL HIM HER "DEAR FRIEND" TOO.
WORST CASE, THEY MIGHT'VE EVEN DATED IN THE PAST...

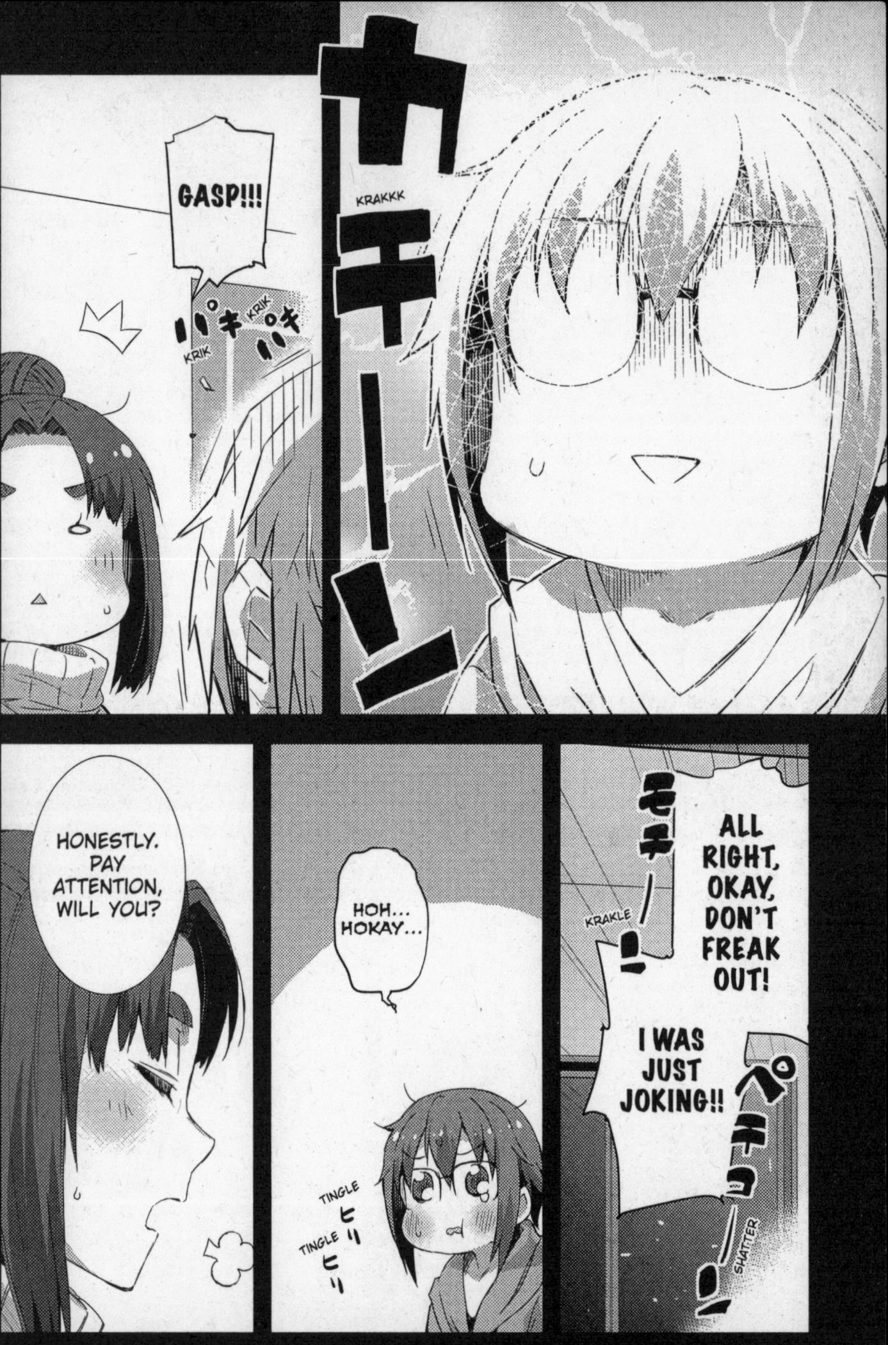
カチーン
KRAKKK
GASP!!!
パキ
KRIK
パキ
KRIK
ALL RIGHT, OKAY, DON'T FREAK OUT!
KRAKLE
I WAS JUST JOKING!!
SHATTER
HOH... HOKAY...
TINGLE
ヒリ
TINGLE
ヒリ
HONESTLY. PAY ATTENTION, WILL YOU?

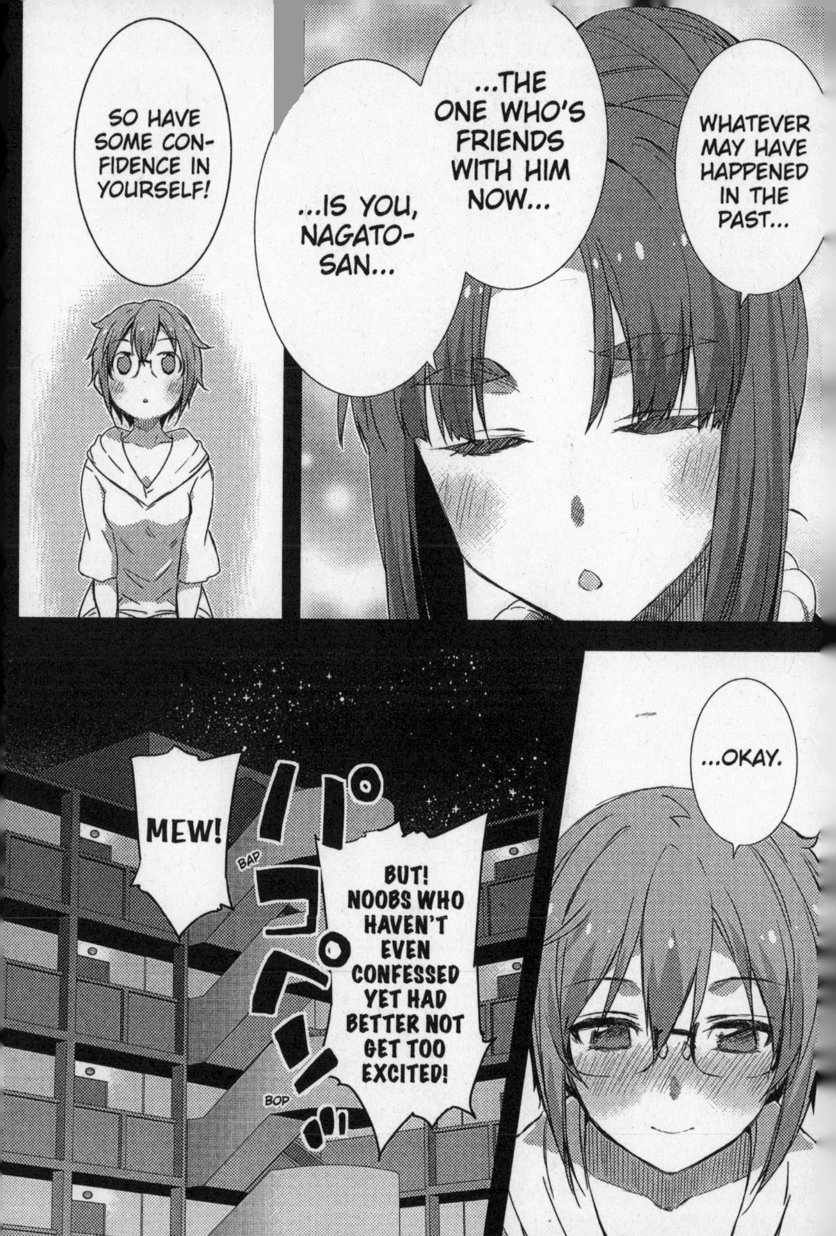
WHATEVER MAY HAVE HAPPENED IN THE PAST...
...THE ONE WHO'S FRIENDS WITH HIM NOW...
...IS YOU, NAGATO-SAN...
SO HAVE SOME CON-FIDENCE IN YOURSELF!
...OKAY.
BUT! NOOBS WHO HAVEN'T EVEN CONFESSED YET HAD BETTER NOT GET TOO EXCITED!
MEW!
BAP
BOP

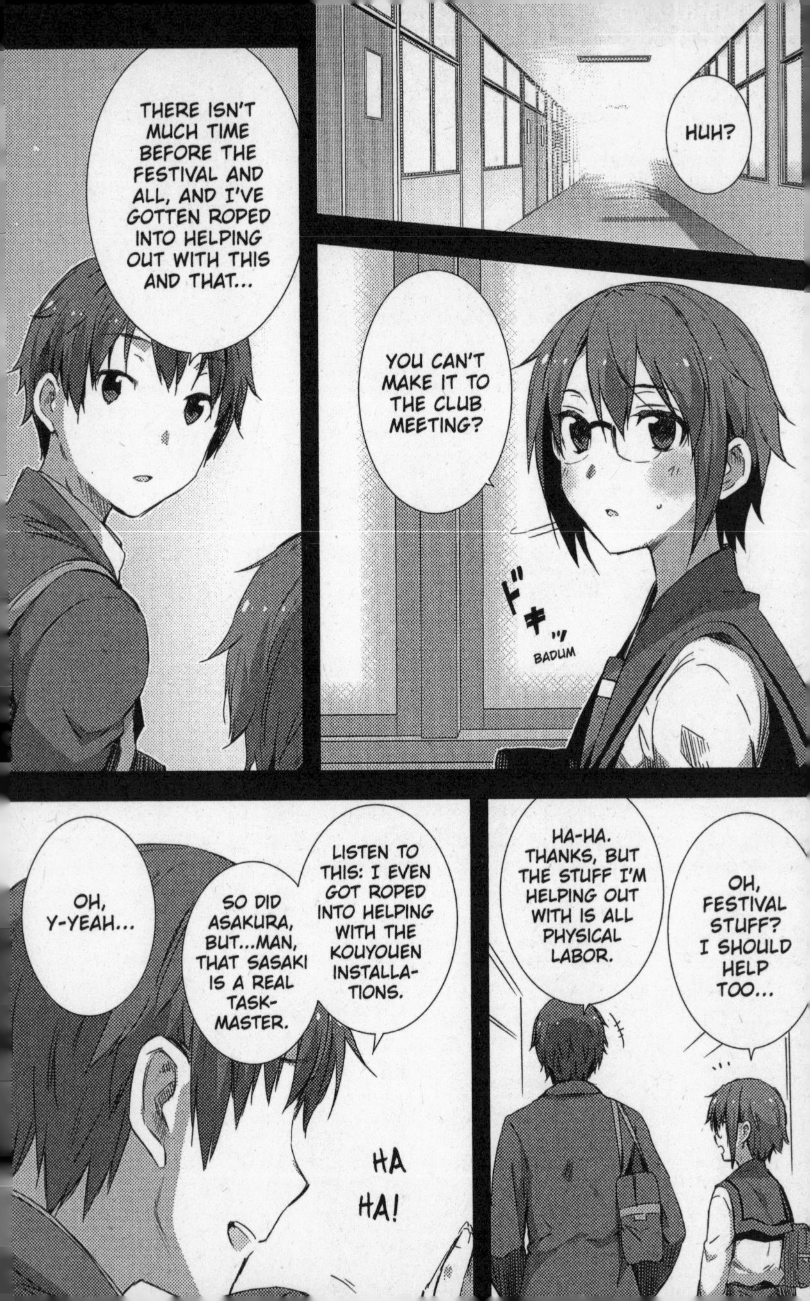
HUH?
YOU CAN'T MAKE IT TO THE CLUB MEETING?
ドキッ
BADUM
THERE ISN'T MUCH TIME BEFORE THE FESTIVAL AND ALL, AND I'VE GOTTEN ROPED INTO HELPING OUT WITH THIS AND THAT...
OH, FESTIVAL STUFF? I SHOULD HELP TOO...
HA-HA. THANKS, BUT THE STUFF I'M HELPING OUT WITH IS ALL PHYSICAL LABOR.
LISTEN TO THIS: I EVEN GOT ROPED INTO HELPING WITH THE KOUYOUEN INSTALLA-TIONS.
SO DID ASAKURA, BUT...MAN, THAT SASAKI IS A REAL TASK-MASTER.
HA HA!
OH, Y-YEAH...

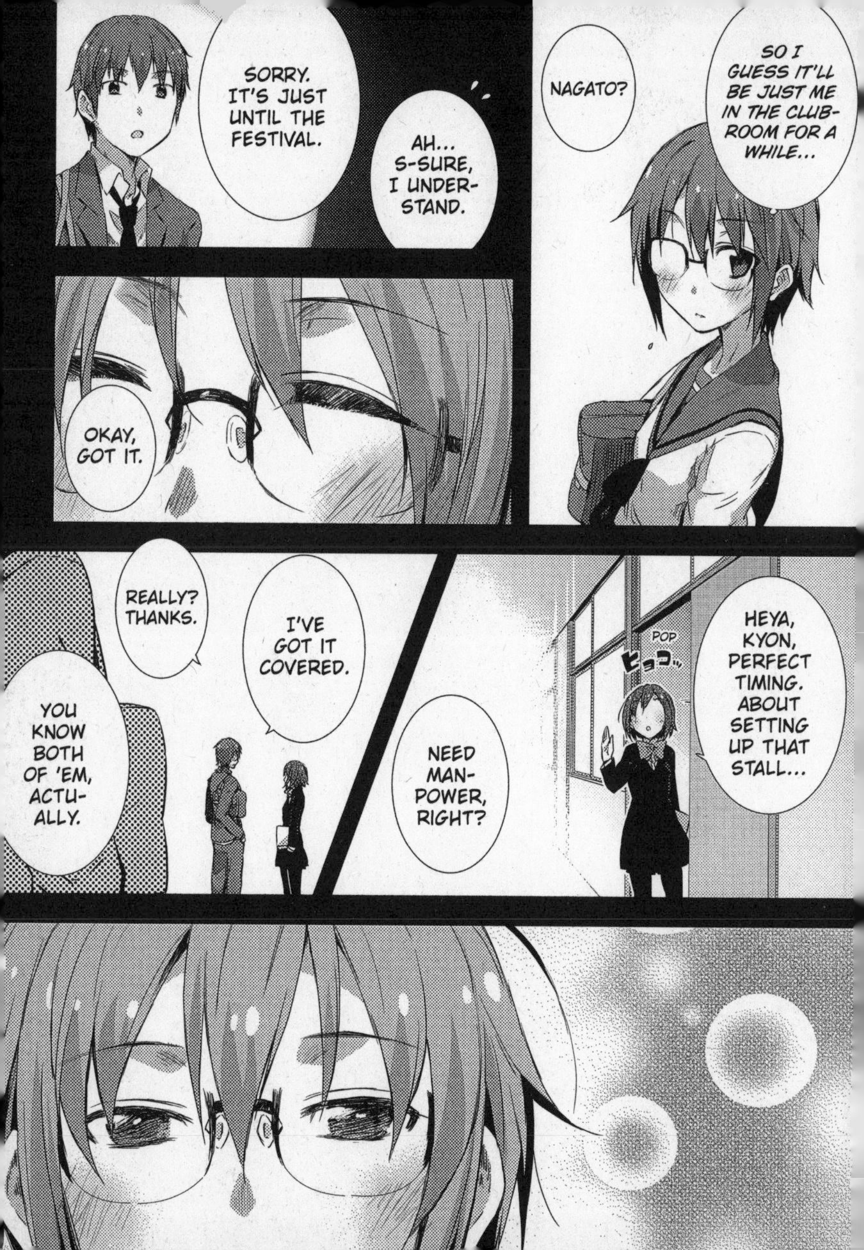
SO I GUESS IT'LL BE JUST ME IN THE CLUB-ROOM FOR A WHILE...
NAGATO?
SORRY. IT'S JUST UNTIL THE FESTIVAL.
AH... S-SURE, I UNDER-STAND.
OKAY, GOT IT.
HEYA, KYON, PERFECT TIMING. ABOUT SETTING UP THAT STALL...
POP
ヒョコ
NEED MAN-POWER, RIGHT?
I'VE GOT IT COVERED.
REALLY? THANKS.
YOU KNOW BOTH OF 'EM, ACTU-ALLY.

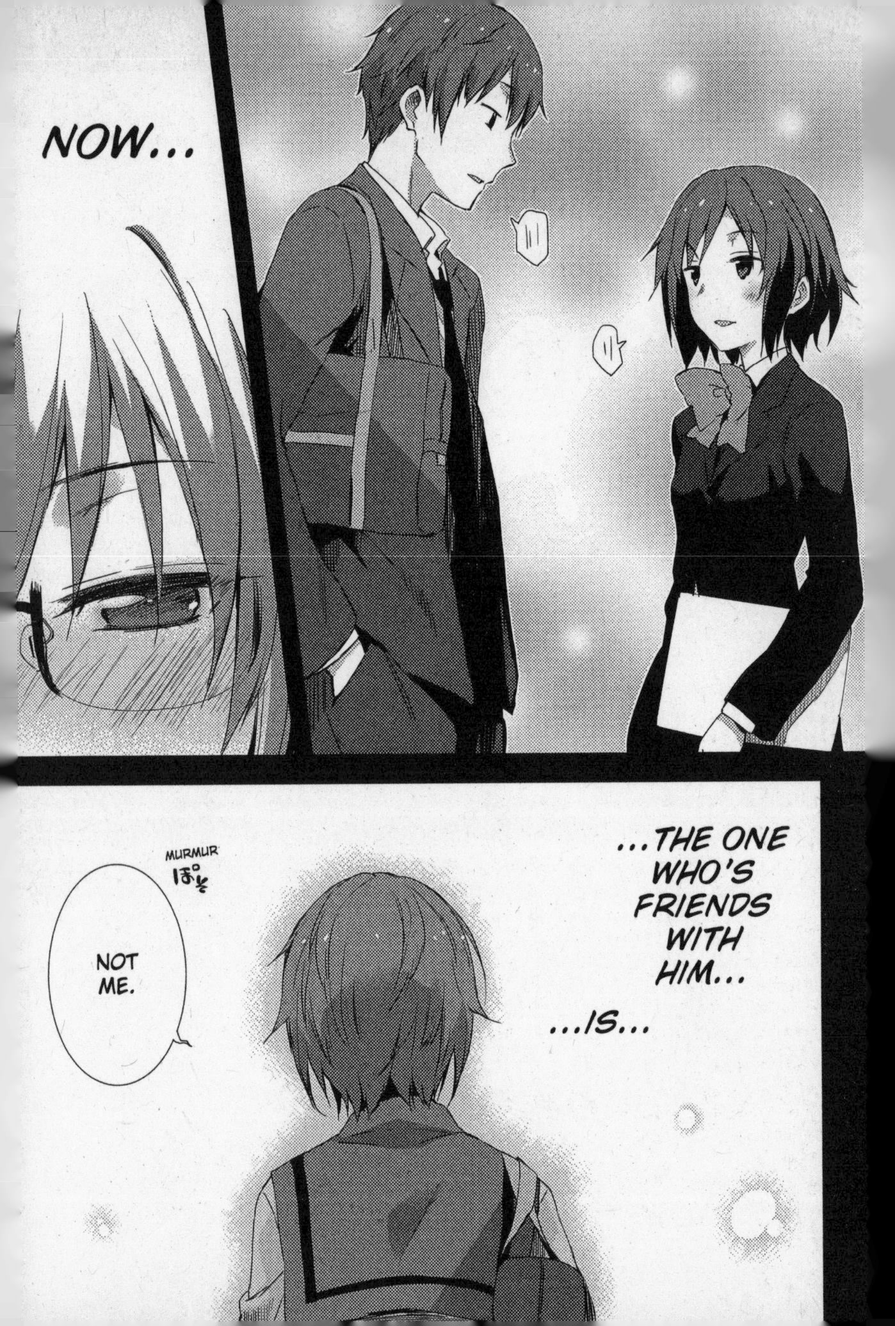
NOW...
...THE ONE WHO'S FRIENDS WITH HIM...
...IS...
MURMUR
NOT ME.

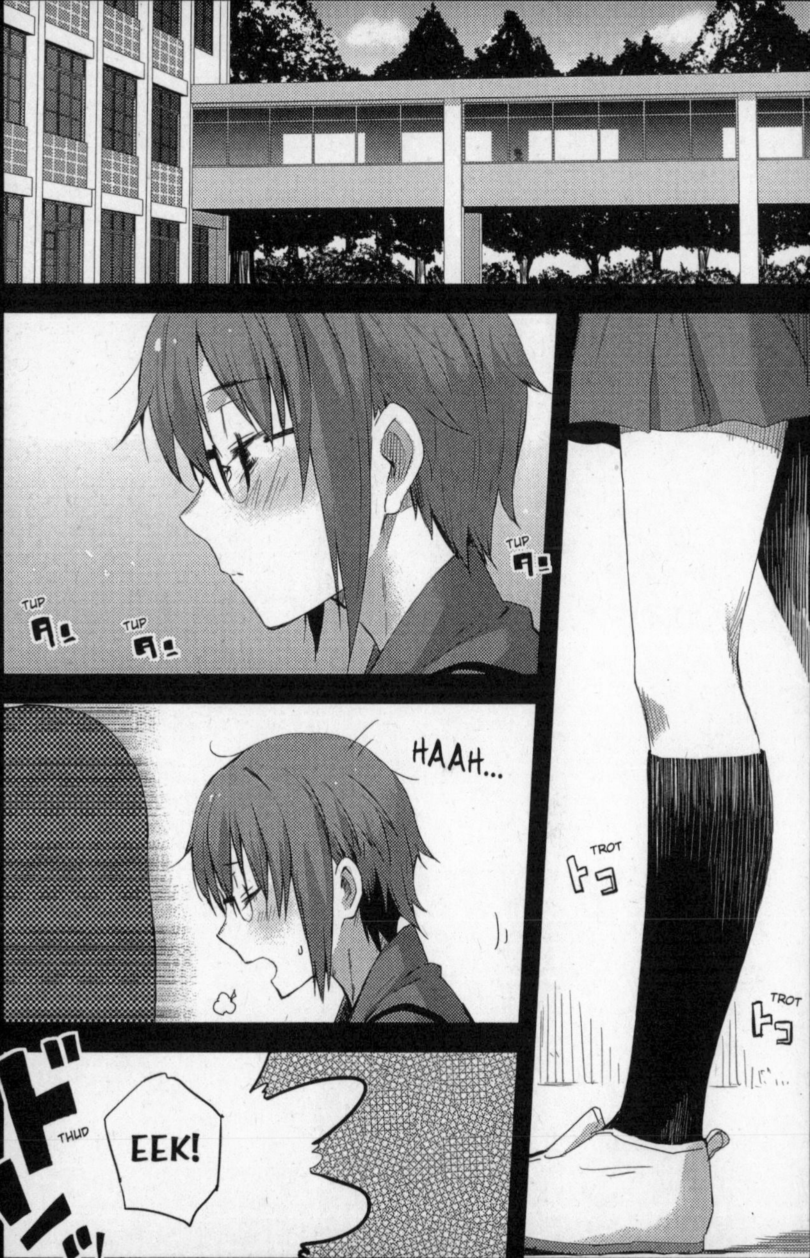
TROT
トコ
TROT
トコ
TUP
TUP
TUP
HAAH...
THUD
EEK!

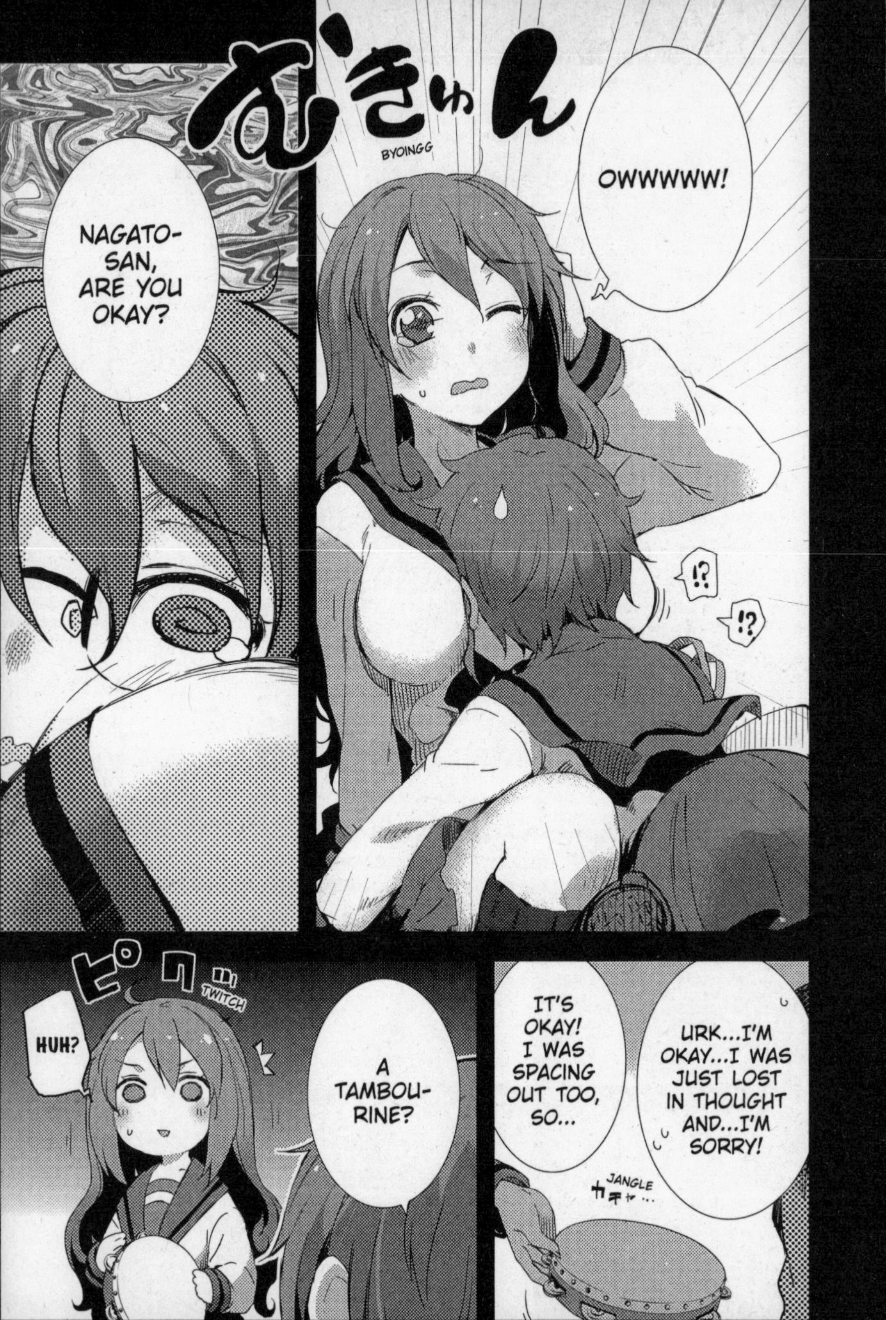
BYOINGG
OWWWWW!
!?
!?
NAGATO-SAN, ARE YOU OKAY?
URK...I'M OKAY...I WAS JUST LOST IN THOUGHT AND...I'M SORRY!
IT'S OKAY! I WAS SPACING OUT TOO, SO...
JANGLE
TWITCH
A TAMBOURINE?
HUH?

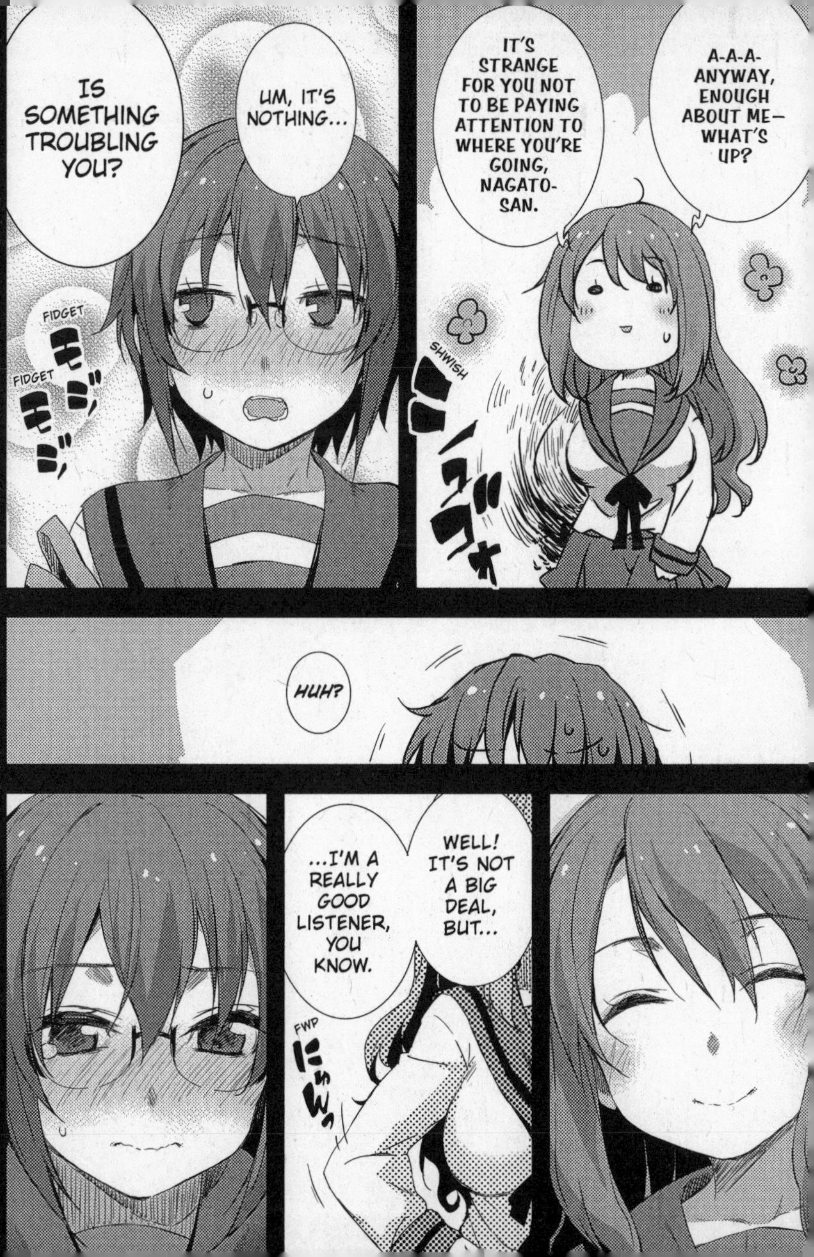
A-A-A-ANYWAY, ENOUGH ABOUT ME— WHAT'S UP?
IT'S STRANGE FOR YOU NOT TO BE PAYING ATTENTION TO WHERE YOU'RE GOING, NAGATO-SAN.
SHWISH
UM, IT'S NOTHING...
IS SOMETHING TROUBLING YOU?
FIDGET
FIDGET
HUH?
WELL! IT'S NOT A BIG DEAL, BUT...
...I'M A REALLY GOOD LISTENER, YOU KNOW.
FWP

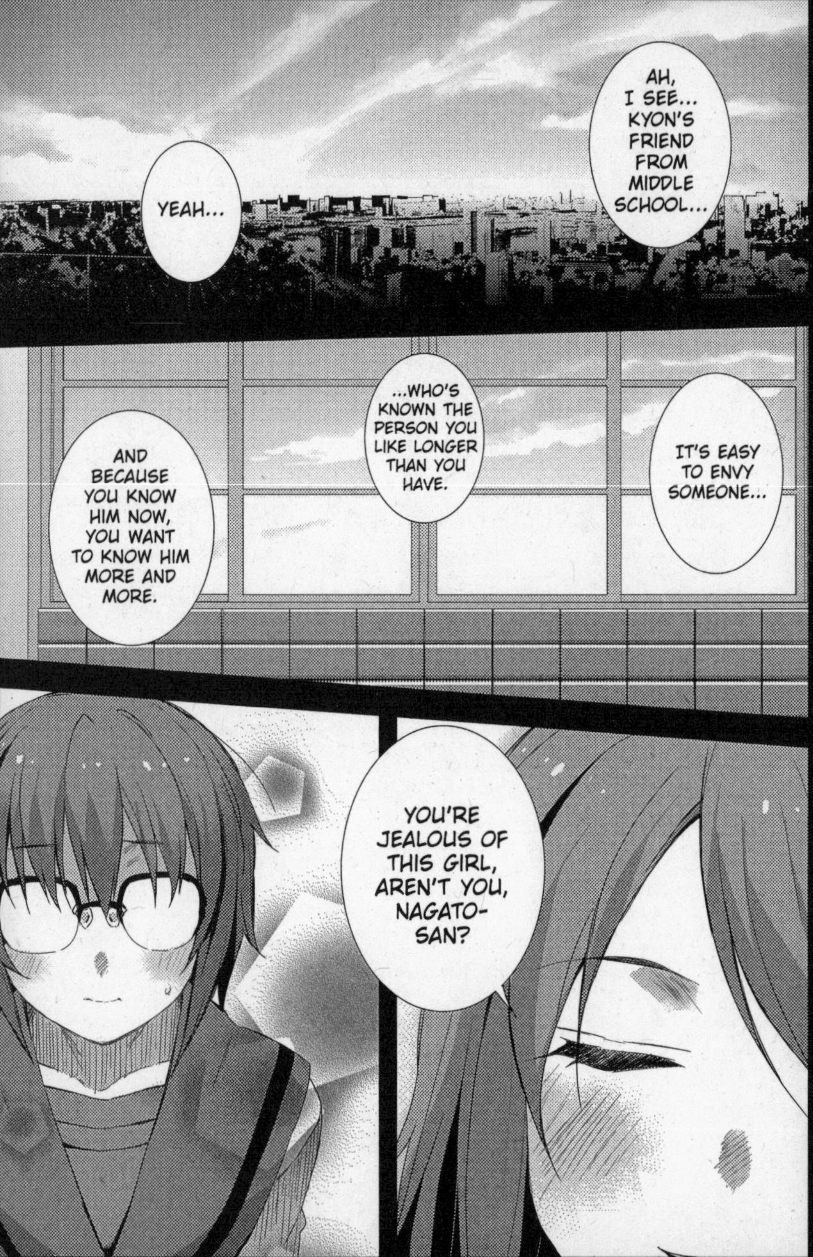
AH, I SEE... KYON'S FRIEND FROM MIDDLE SCHOOL...
YEAH...
IT'S EASY TO ENVY SOMEONE...
...WHO'S KNOWN THE PERSON YOU LIKE LONGER THAN YOU HAVE.
AND BECAUSE YOU KNOW HIM NOW, YOU WANT TO KNOW HIM MORE AND MORE.
YOU'RE JEALOUS OF THIS GIRL, AREN'T YOU, NAGATO-SAN?

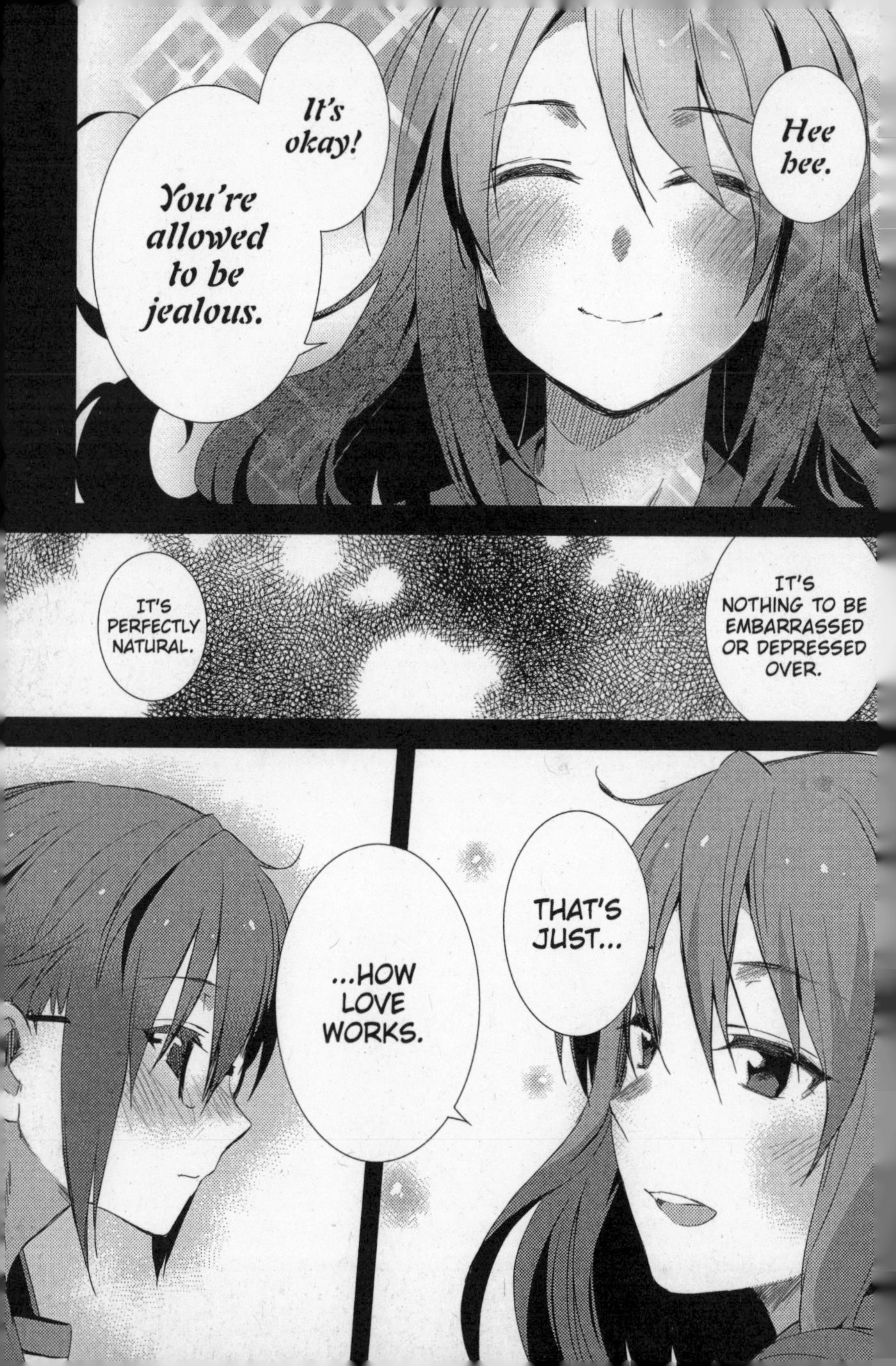
Hee hee.
It's okay!
You're allowed to be jealous.
IT'S NOTHING TO BE EMBARRASSED OR DEPRESSED OVER.
IT'S PERFECTLY NATURAL.
THAT'S JUST...
...HOW LOVE WORKS.

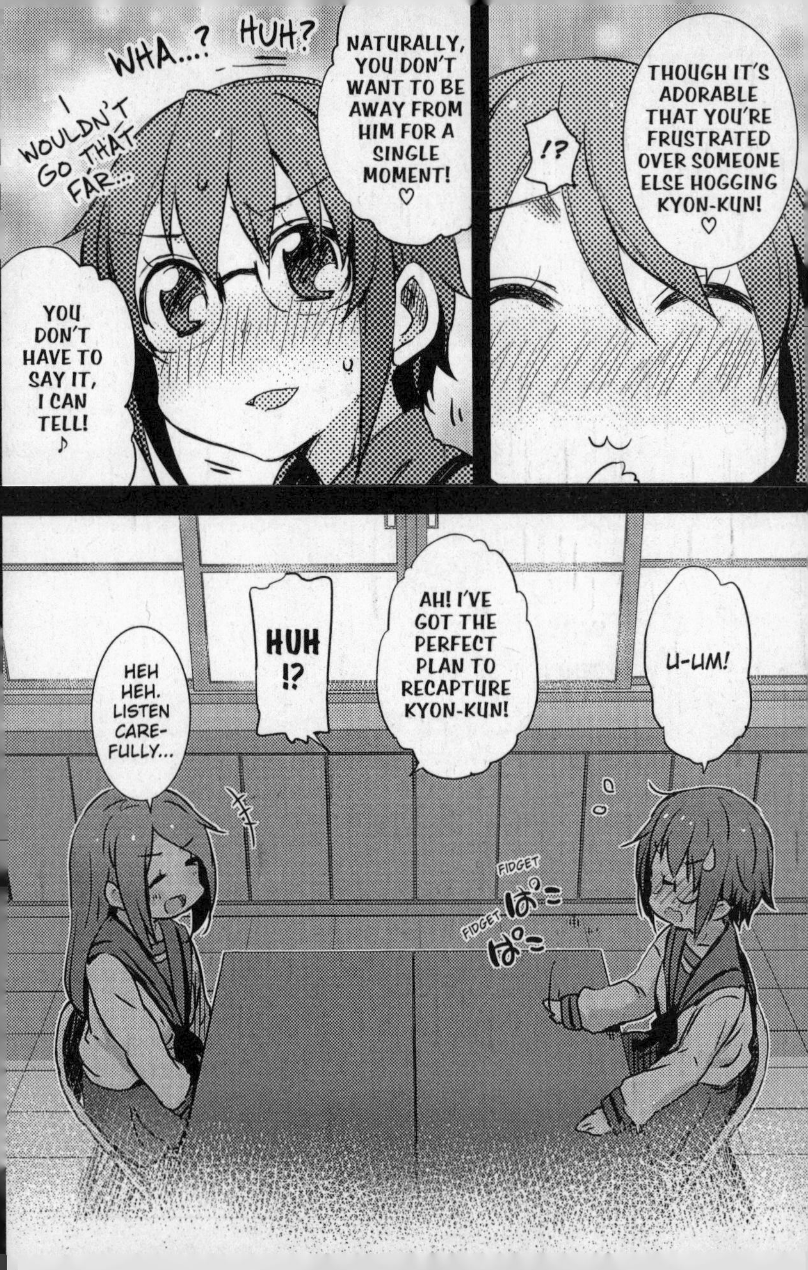
!?
THOUGH IT'S ADORABLE THAT YOU'RE FRUSTRATED OVER SOMEONE ELSE HOGGING KYON-KUN! ♡
NATURALLY, YOU DON'T WANT TO BE AWAY FROM HIM FOR A SINGLE MOMENT! ♡
HUH?
WHA...?
I WOULDN'T GO THAT FAR...
YOU DON'T HAVE TO SAY IT, I CAN TELL! ♪
U-UM!
AH! I'VE GOT THE PERFECT PLAN TO RECAPTURE KYON-KUN!
HUH!?
HEH HEH. LISTEN CARE-FULLY...
FIDGET ぱこ
FIDGET ぱこ

Epilogue 47 >> Festival Preparation (Nagato) 2

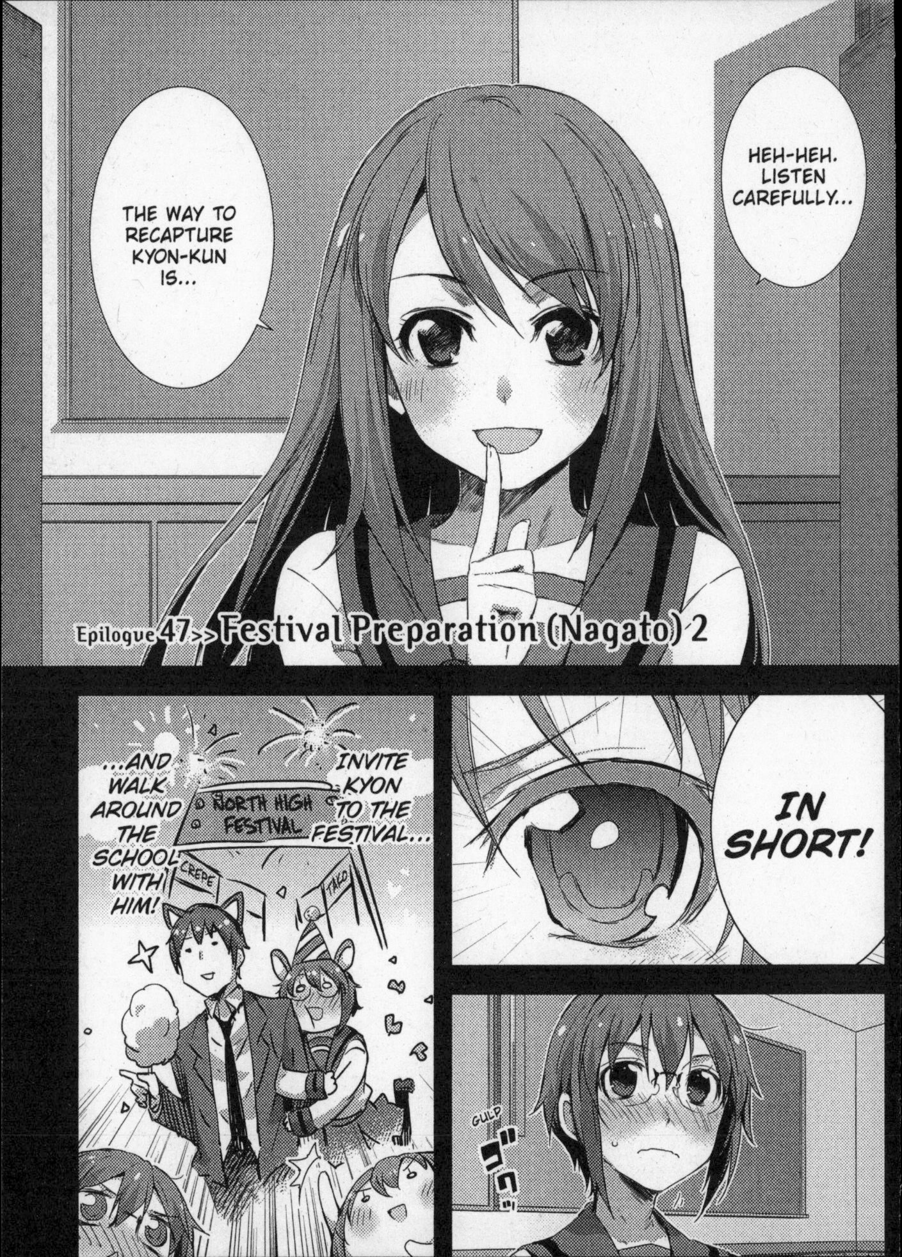
HEH-HEH. LISTEN CAREFULLY...
THE WAY TO RECAPTURE KYON-KUN IS...
Epilogue 47 >> Festival Preparation (Nagato) 2
IN SHORT!
GULP
INVITE KYON TO THE FESTIVAL...
...AND WALK AROUND THE SCHOOL WITH HIM!
NORTH HIGH FESTIVAL
CREPE
TAKO

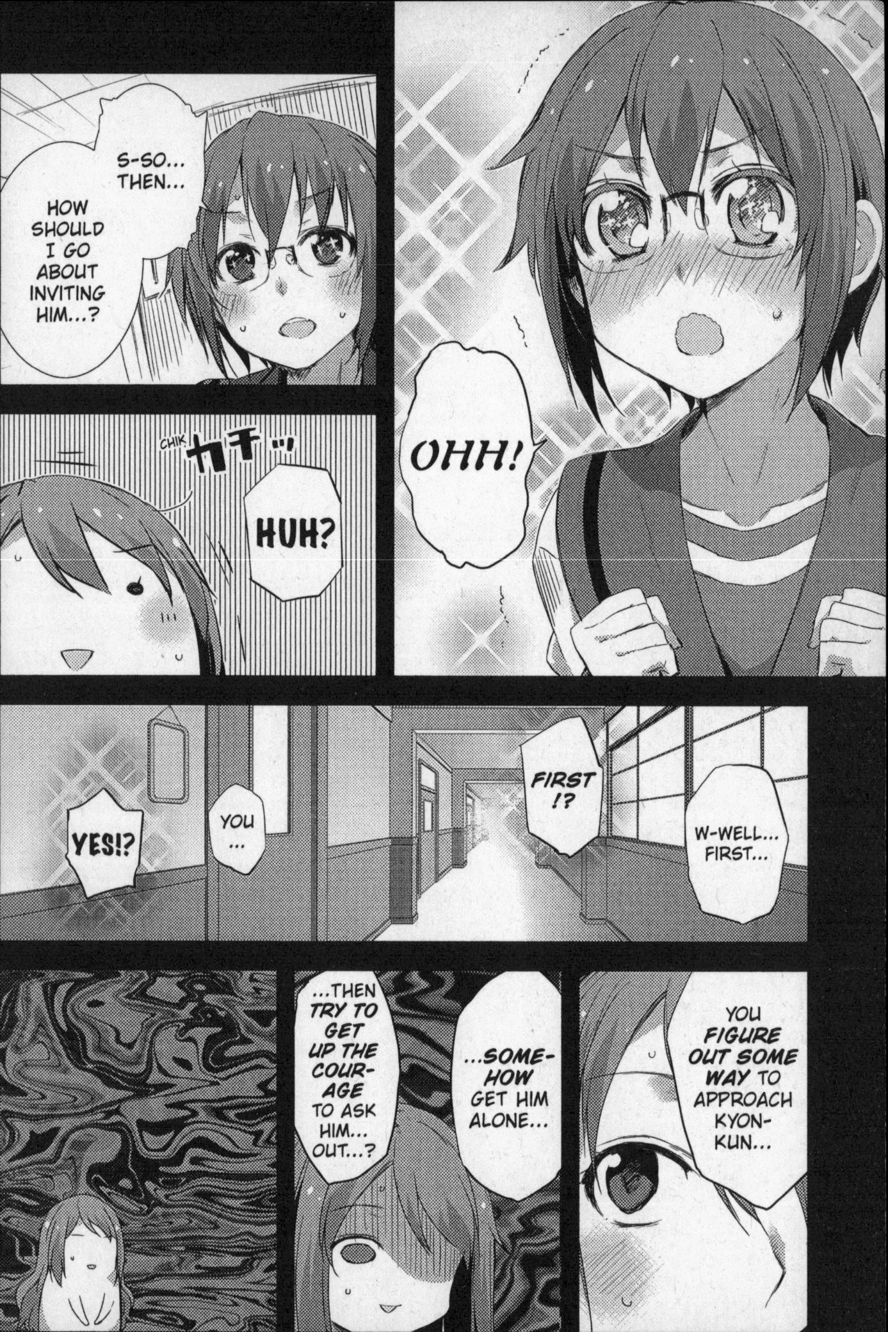
OHH!
S-SO... THEN...
HOW SHOULD I GO ABOUT INVITING HIM...?
CHIK カチッ
HUH?
W-WELL... FIRST...
FIRST!?
YOU...
YES!?
YOU FIGURE OUT SOME WAY TO APPROACH KYON-KUN...
...SOME-HOW GET HIM ALONE...
...THEN TRY TO GET UP THE COUR-AGE TO ASK HIM... OUT...?

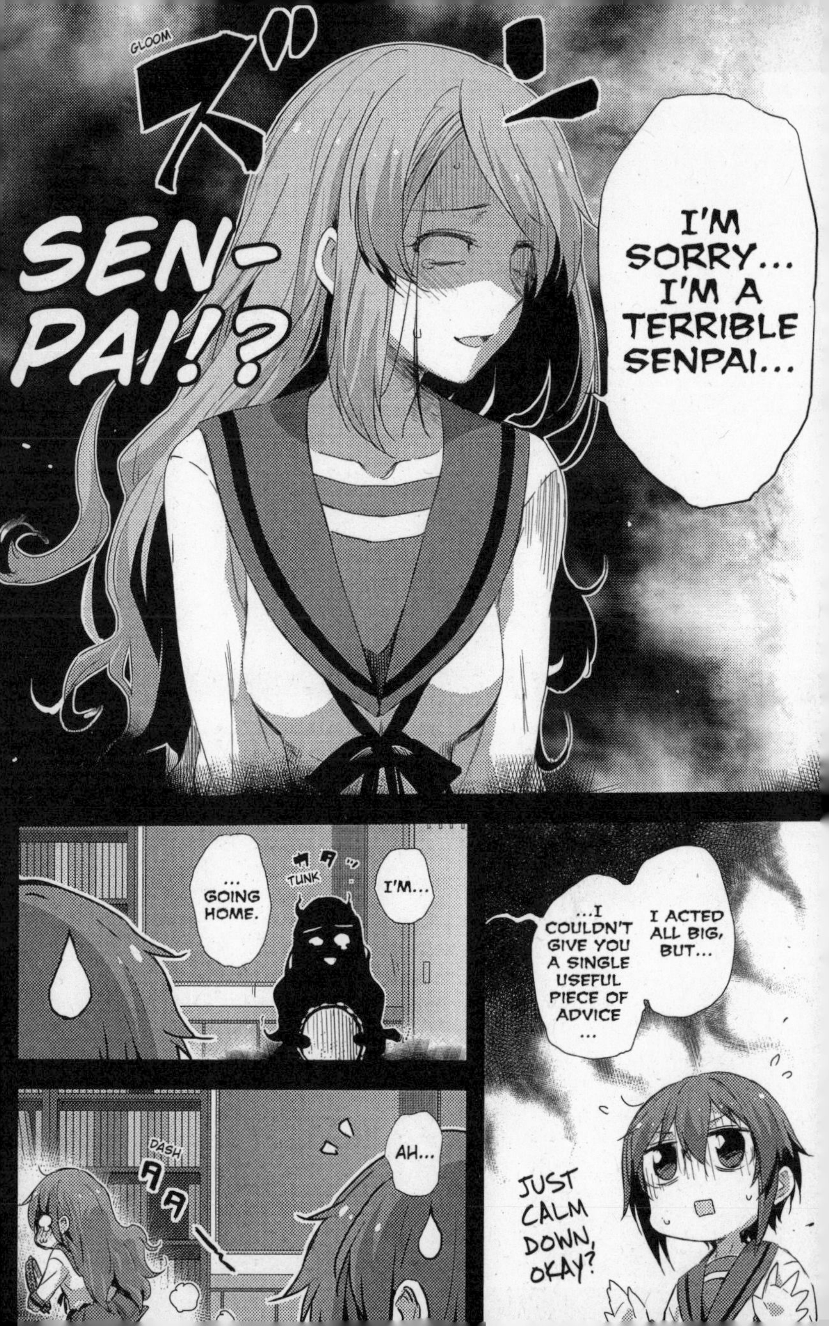
I'M SORRY... I'M A TERRIBLE SENPAI...
GLOOM
SEN-PAI!?
I ACTED ALL BIG, BUT...
...I COULDN'T GIVE YOU A SINGLE USEFUL PIECE OF ADVICE...
JUST CALM DOWN, OKAY?
I'M...
TUNK
...GOING HOME.
AH...
DASH

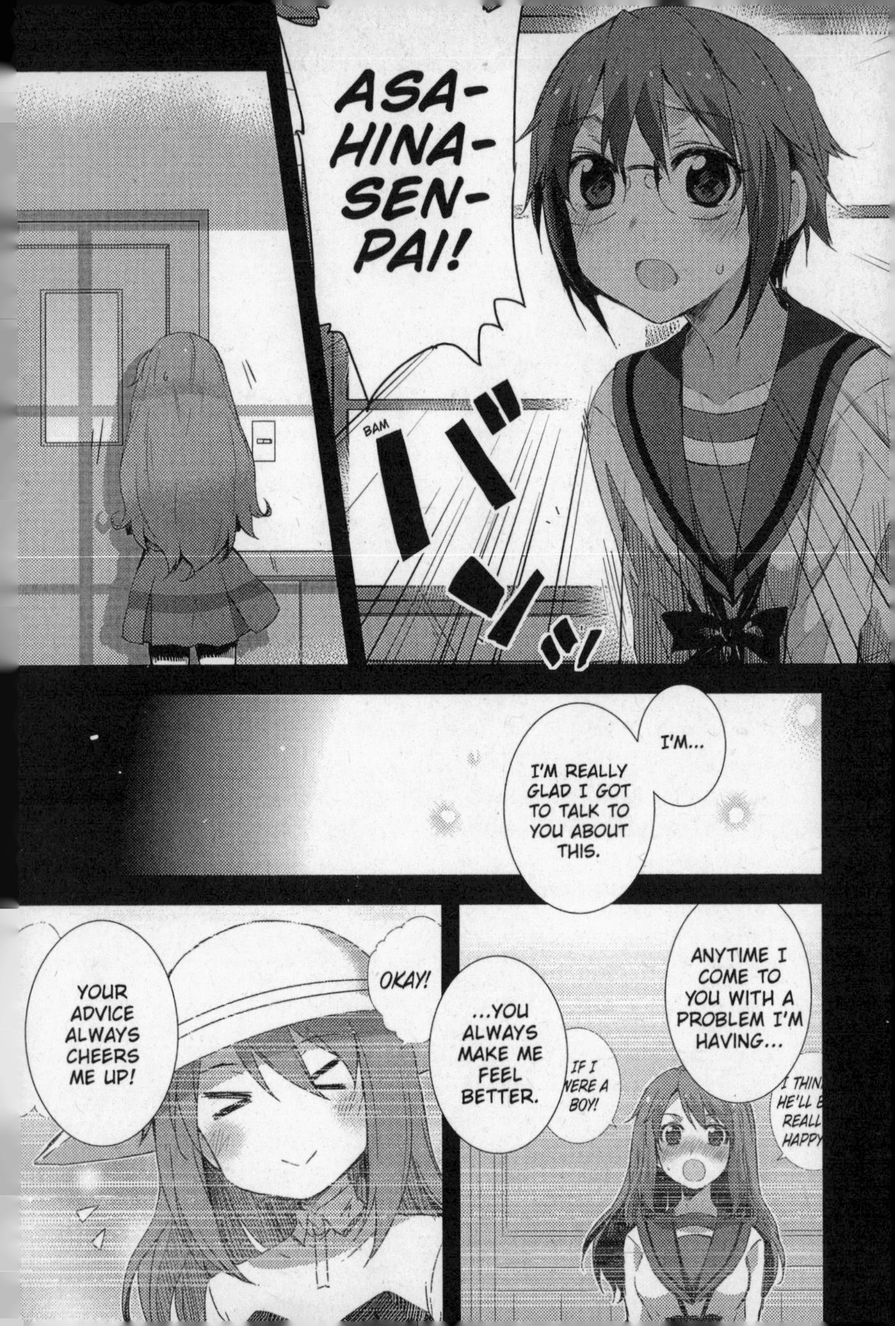
ASA-HINA-SEN-PAI!
BAM
I'M...
I'M REALLY GLAD I GOT TO TALK TO YOU ABOUT THIS.
ANYTIME I COME TO YOU WITH A PROBLEM I'M HAVING...
...YOU ALWAYS MAKE ME FEEL BETTER.
IF I WERE A BOY!
I THIN HE'LL B REALL HAPPY
OKAY!
YOUR ADVICE ALWAYS CHEERS ME UP!

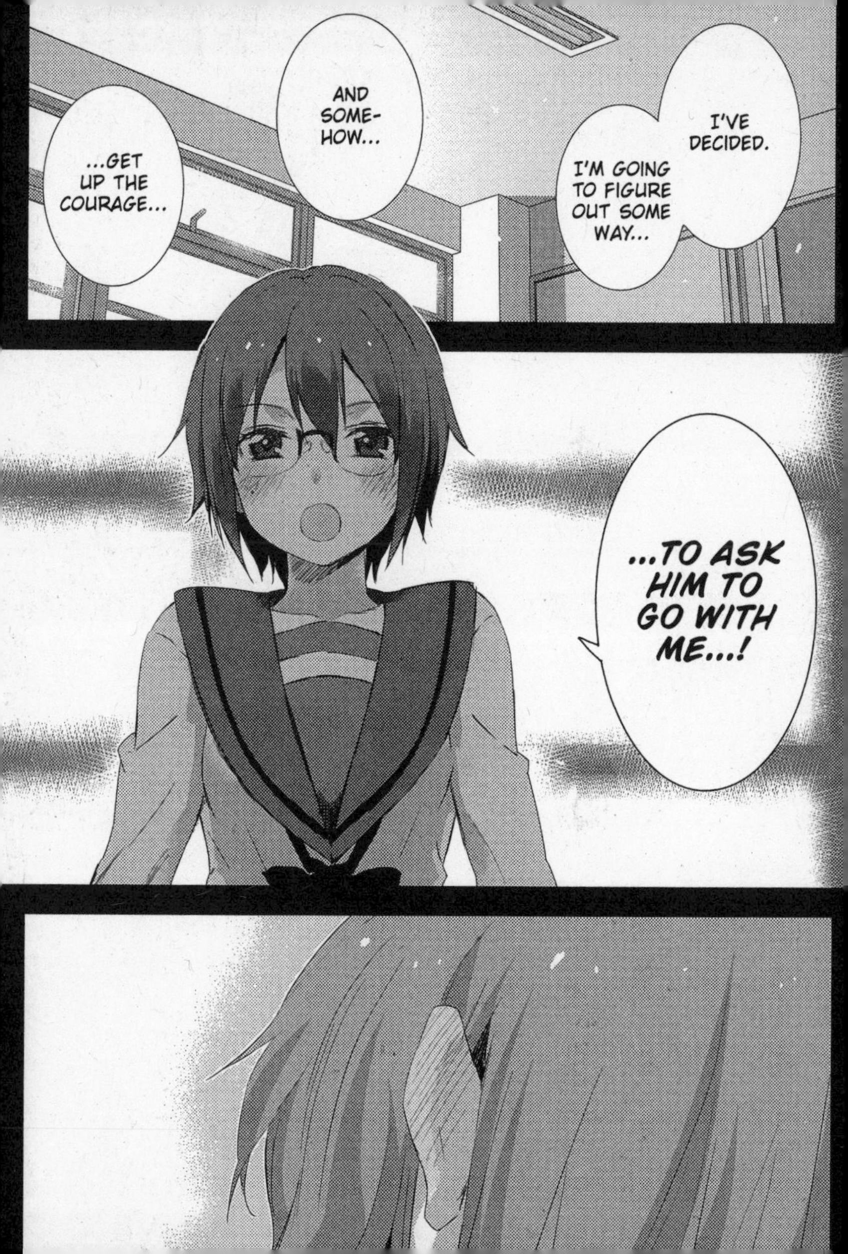
I'VE DECIDED.
I'M GOING TO FIGURE OUT SOME WAY...
AND SOME-HOW...
...GET UP THE COURAGE...
...TO ASK HIM TO GO WITH ME...!

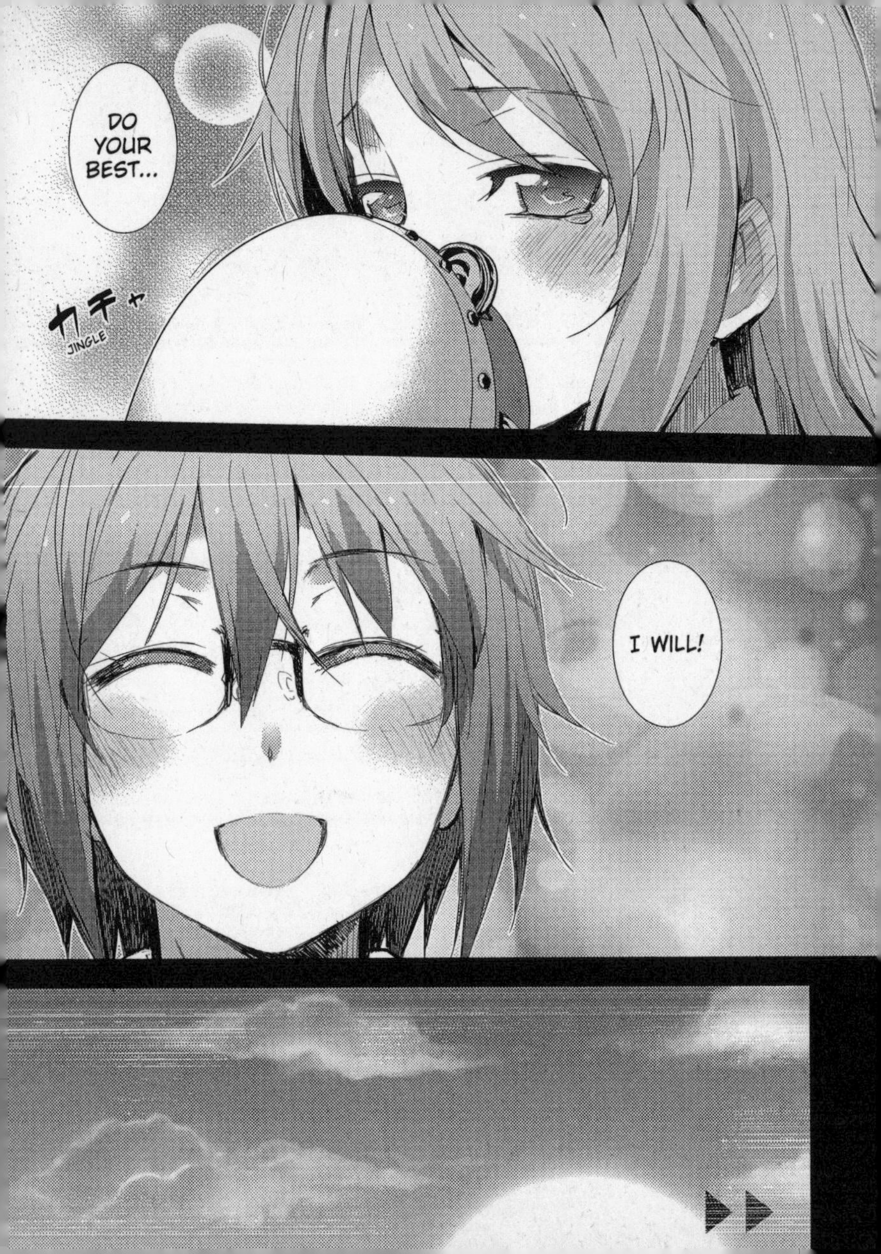
DO YOUR BEST...
カチャ
JINGLE
I WILL!

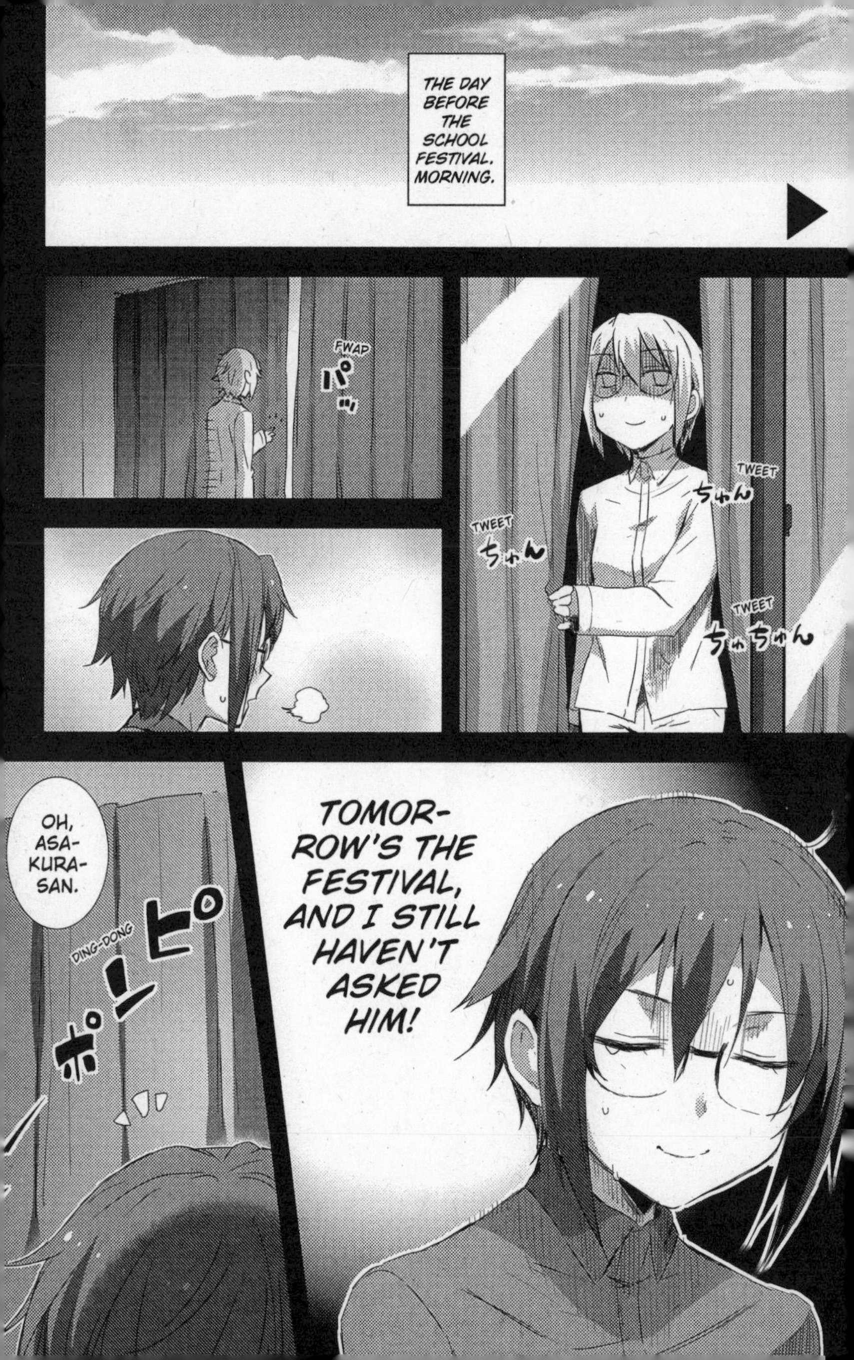
THE DAY BEFORE THE SCHOOL FESTIVAL. MORNING.
TWEET
ちゅん
TWEET
ちゅん
TWEET
ちゅちゅん
FWAP
パッ
TOMORROW'S THE FESTIVAL, AND I STILL HAVEN'T ASKED HIM!
DING-DONG
ピンポン
OH, ASAKURA-SAN.

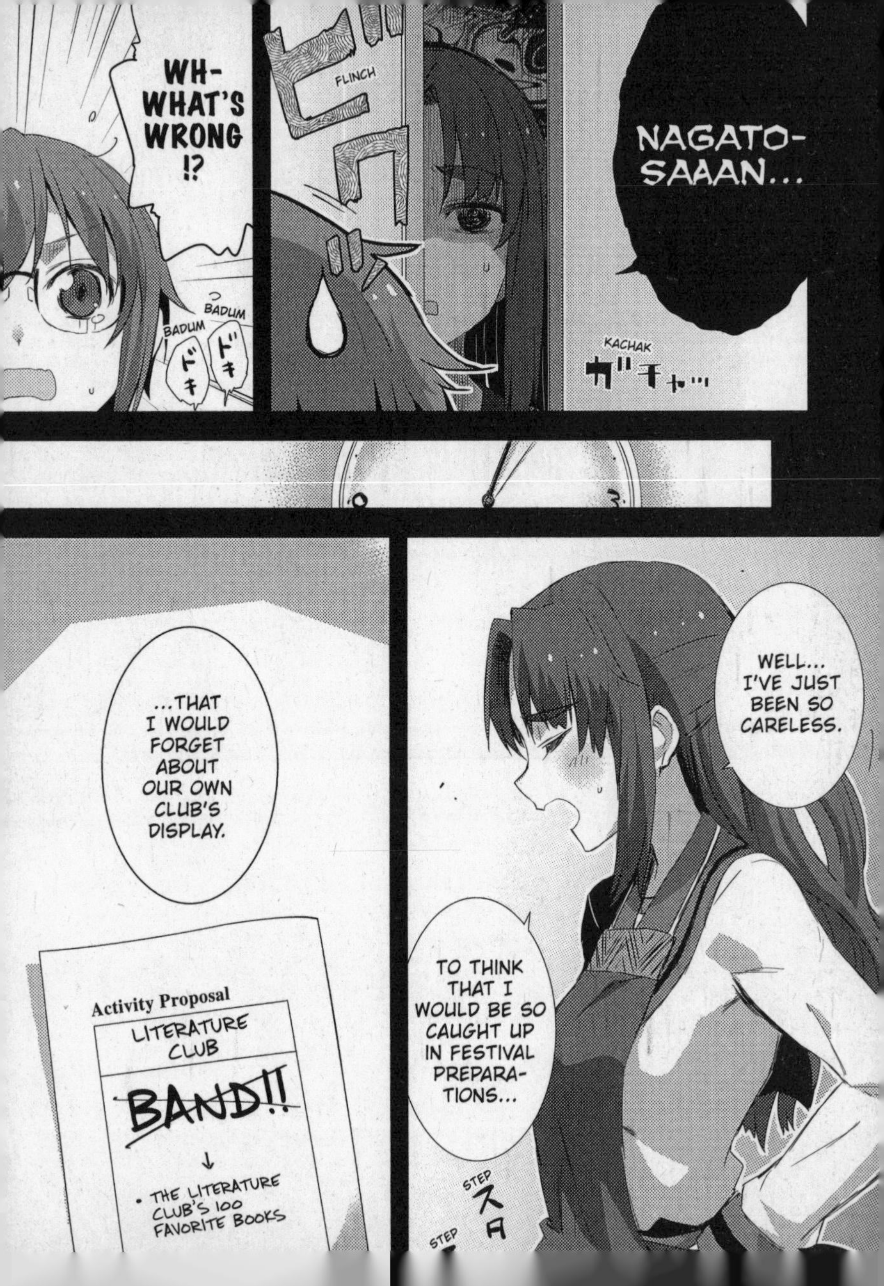
NAGATO-SAAAN...
KACHAK
ガチャッ
FLINCH
WH-WHAT'S WRONG !?
BADUM
BADUM
ドキ
ドキ
WELL... I'VE JUST BEEN SO CARELESS.
TO THINK THAT I WOULD BE SO CAUGHT UP IN FESTIVAL PREPARA-TIONS...
STEP
STEP
スタ
...THAT I WOULD FORGET ABOUT OUR OWN CLUB'S DISPLAY.
Activity Proposal
LITERATURE CLUB
BAND!!
↓
• THE LITERATURE CLUB'S 100 FAVORITE BOOKS

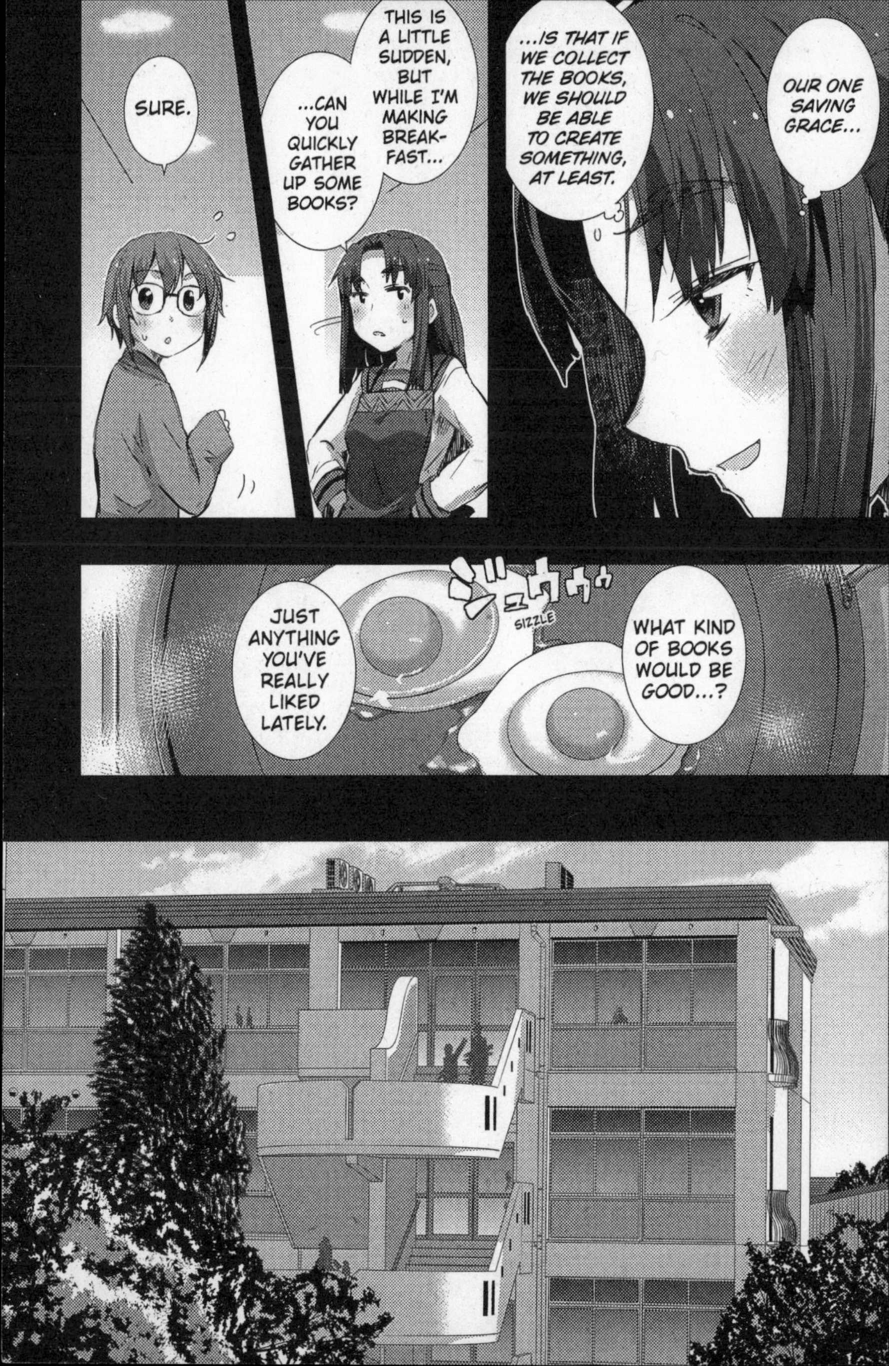
OUR ONE SAVING GRACE...
...IS THAT IF WE COLLECT THE BOOKS, WE SHOULD BE ABLE TO CREATE SOMETHING, AT LEAST.
THIS IS A LITTLE SUDDEN, BUT WHILE I'M MAKING BREAK-FAST...
...CAN YOU QUICKLY GATHER UP SOME BOOKS?
SURE.
WHAT KIND OF BOOKS WOULD BE GOOD...?
SIZZLE
JUST ANYTHING YOU'VE REALLY LIKED LATELY.

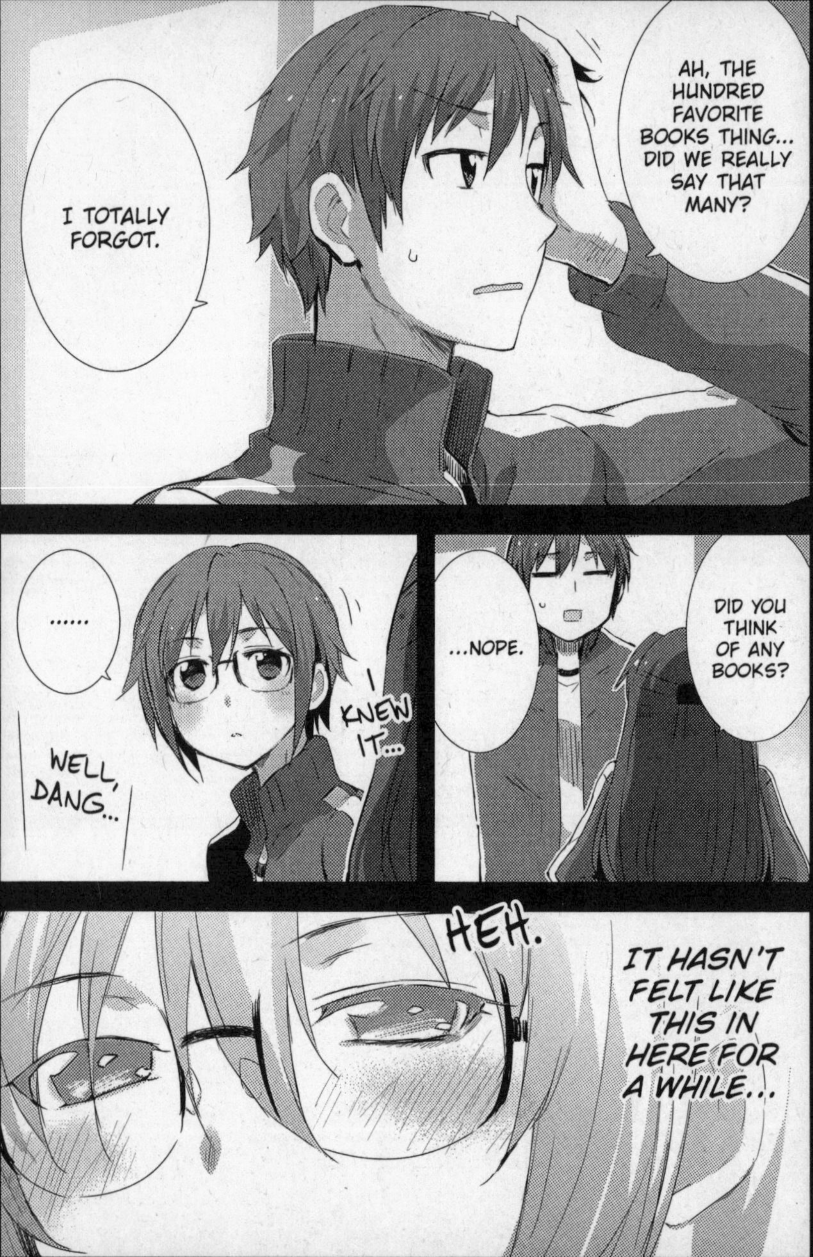
AH, THE HUNDRED FAVORITE BOOKS THING... DID WE REALLY SAY THAT MANY?
I TOTALLY FORGOT.
DID YOU THINK OF ANY BOOKS?
...NOPE.
......
I KNEW IT...
WELL, DANG...
HEH.
IT HASN'T FELT LIKE THIS IN HERE FOR A WHILE...

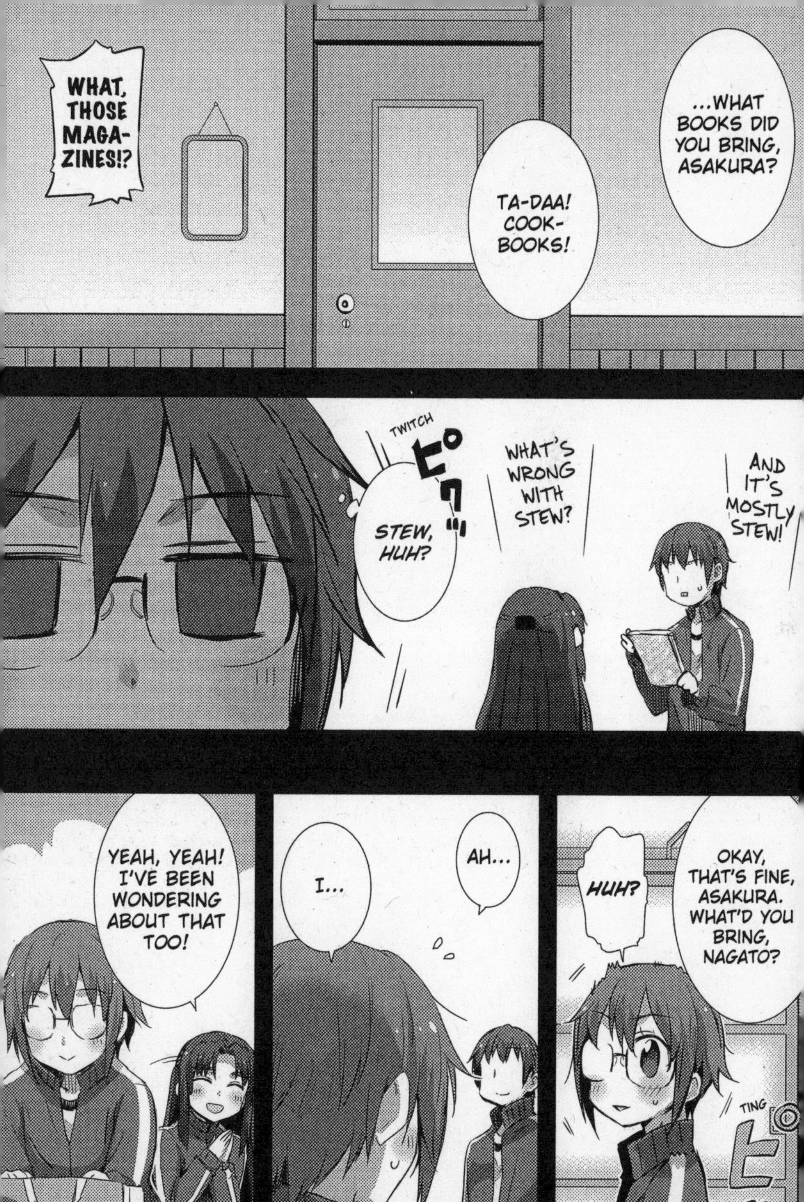
...WHAT BOOKS DID YOU BRING, ASAKURA?
TA-DAA! COOK-BOOKS!
WHAT, THOSE MAGA-ZINES!?
AND IT'S MOSTLY STEW!
WHAT'S WRONG WITH STEW?
TWITCH
STEW, HUH?
OKAY, THAT'S FINE, ASAKURA. WHAT'D YOU BRING, NAGATO?
HUH?
TING
AH...
I...
YEAH, YEAH! I'VE BEEN WONDERING ABOUT THAT TOO!

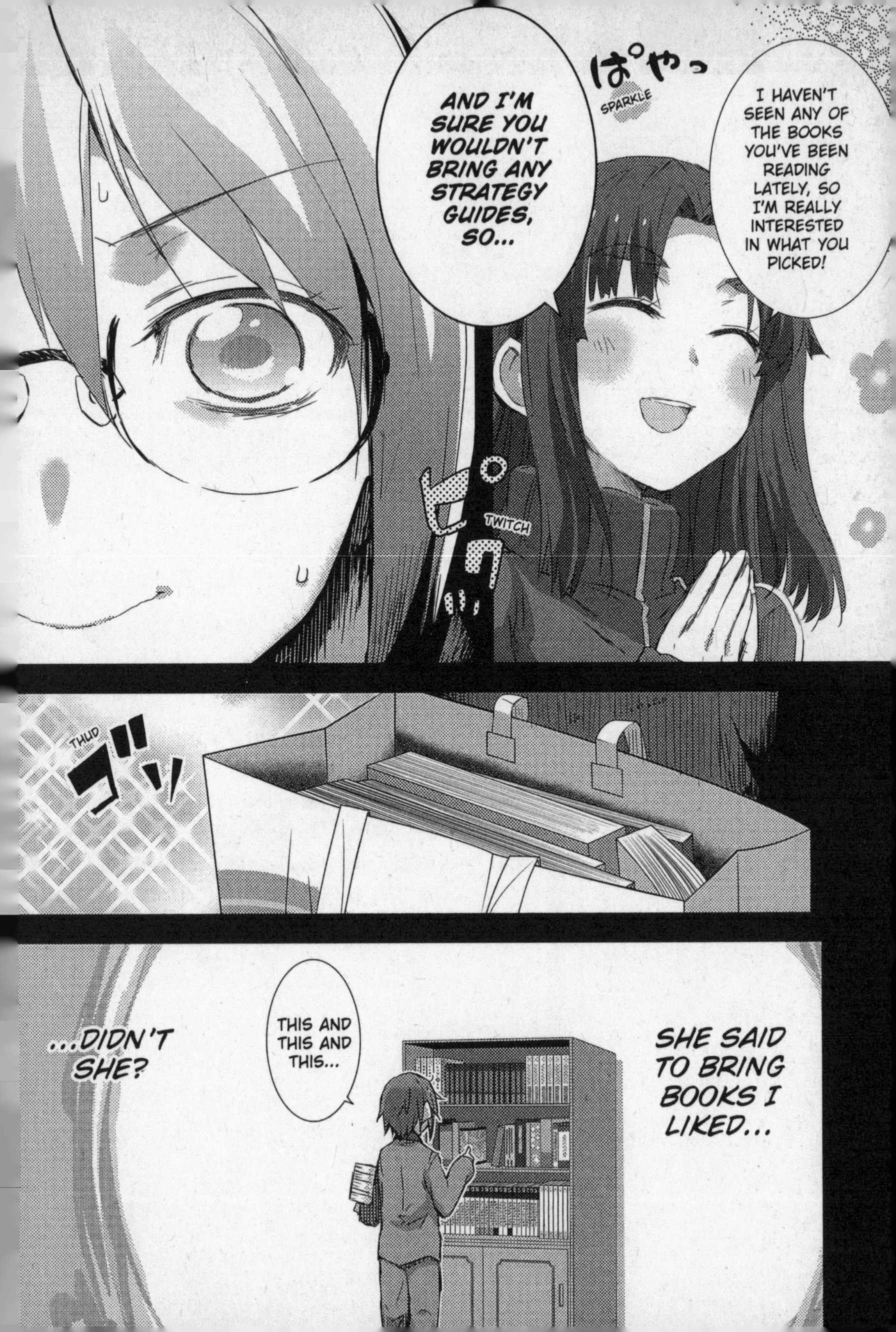
I HAVEN'T SEEN ANY OF THE BOOKS YOU'VE BEEN READING LATELY, SO I'M REALLY INTERESTED IN WHAT YOU PICKED!
ぱやっ
SPARKLE
AND I'M SURE YOU WOULDN'T BRING ANY STRATEGY GUIDES, SO...
TWITCH
THUD
ゴッ
SHE SAID TO BRING BOOKS I LIKED...
THIS AND THIS AND THIS...
...DIDN'T SHE?

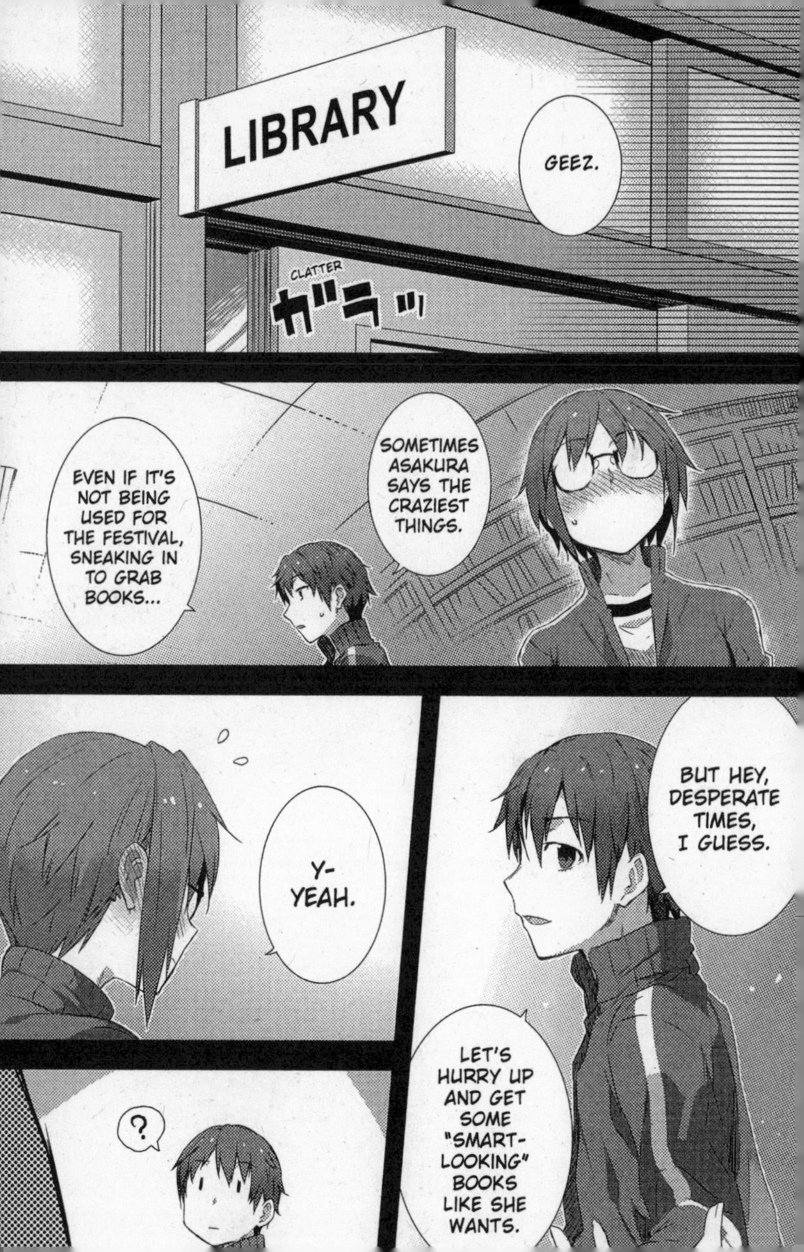
LIBRARY
GEEZ.
CLATTER
ガラッ
SOMETIMES ASAKURA SAYS THE CRAZIEST THINGS.
EVEN IF IT'S NOT BEING USED FOR THE FESTIVAL, SNEAKING IN TO GRAB BOOKS...
BUT HEY, DESPERATE TIMES, I GUESS.
LET'S HURRY UP AND GET SOME "SMART-LOOKING" BOOKS LIKE SHE WANTS.
Y- YEAH.
?

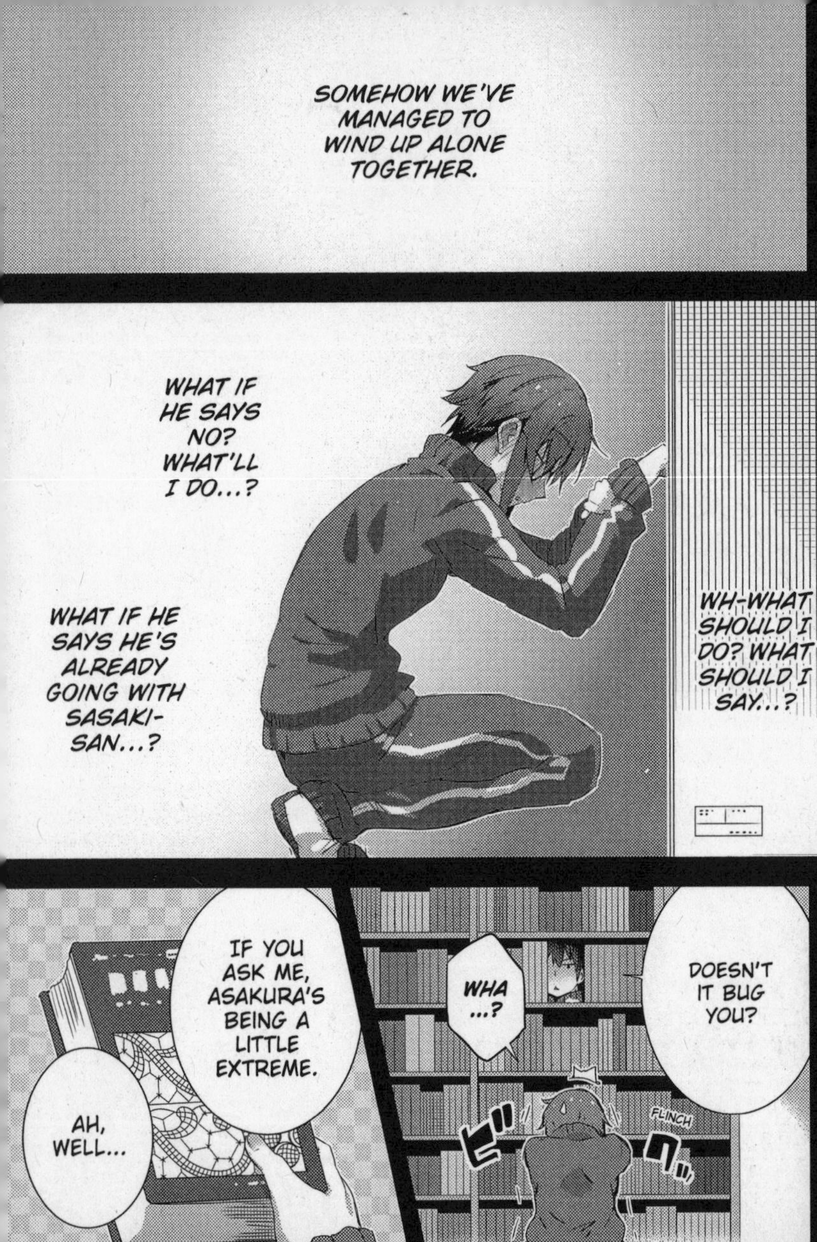
SOMEHOW WE'VE MANAGED TO WIND UP ALONE TOGETHER.
WH-WHAT SHOULD I DO? WHAT SHOULD I SAY...?
WHAT IF HE SAYS NO? WHAT'LL I DO...?
WHAT IF HE SAYS HE'S ALREADY GOING WITH SASAKI-SAN...?
DOESN'T IT BUG YOU?
WHA ...?
FLINCH
IF YOU ASK ME, ASAKURA'S BEING A LITTLE EXTREME.
AH, WELL...

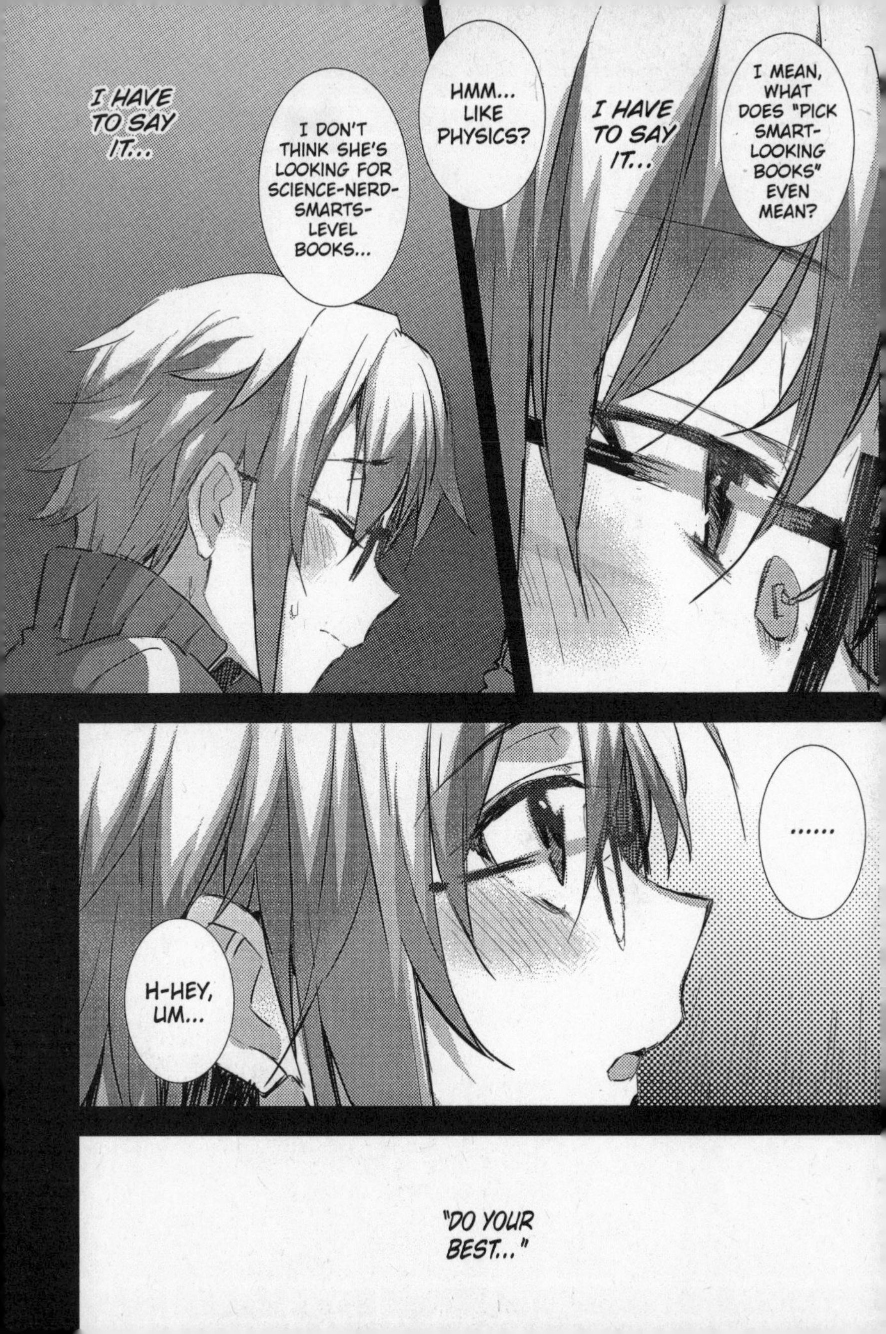
I MEAN, WHAT DOES "PICK SMART-LOOKING BOOKS" EVEN MEAN?
I HAVE TO SAY IT...
HMM... LIKE PHYSICS?
I DON'T THINK SHE'S LOOKING FOR SCIENCE-NERD-SMARTS-LEVEL BOOKS...
I HAVE TO SAY IT...
......
H-HEY, UM...
"DO YOUR BEST..."

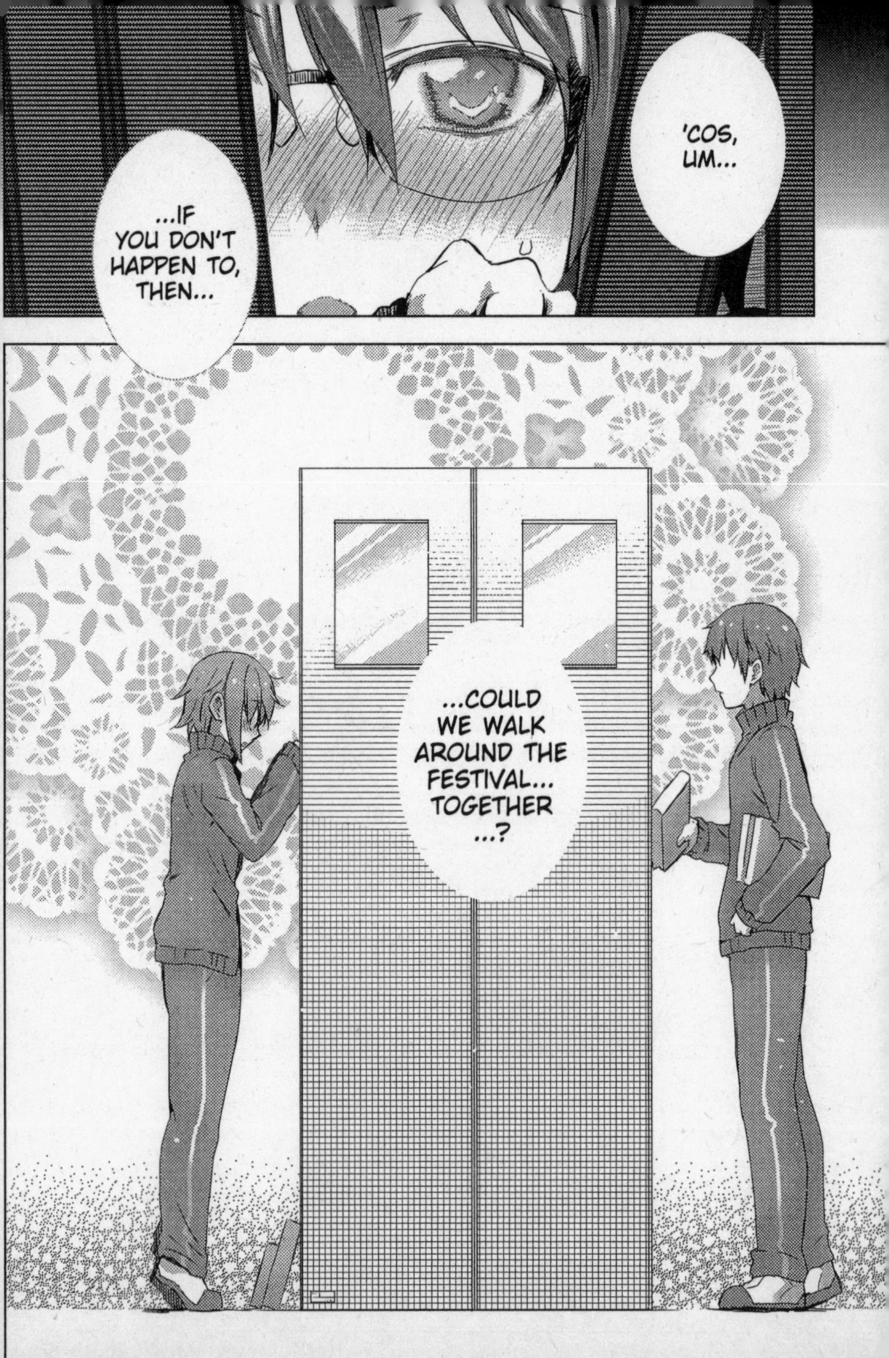
'COS, UM...
...IF YOU DON'T HAPPEN TO, THEN...
...COULD WE WALK AROUND THE FESTIVAL... TOGETHER ...?

HOORAY!

HURRAH!

北高祭

NORTH HIGH FESTIVAL

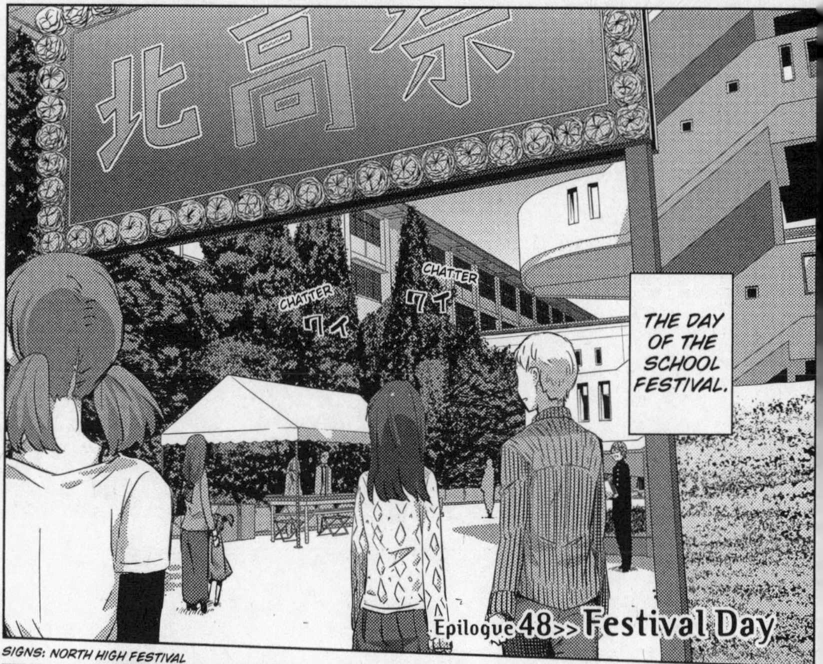
北高祭
THE DAY OF THE SCHOOL FESTIVAL.
CHATTER
ワイ
CHATTER
ワイ
Epilogue 48>> Festival Day

SIGNS: NORTH HIGH FESTIVAL

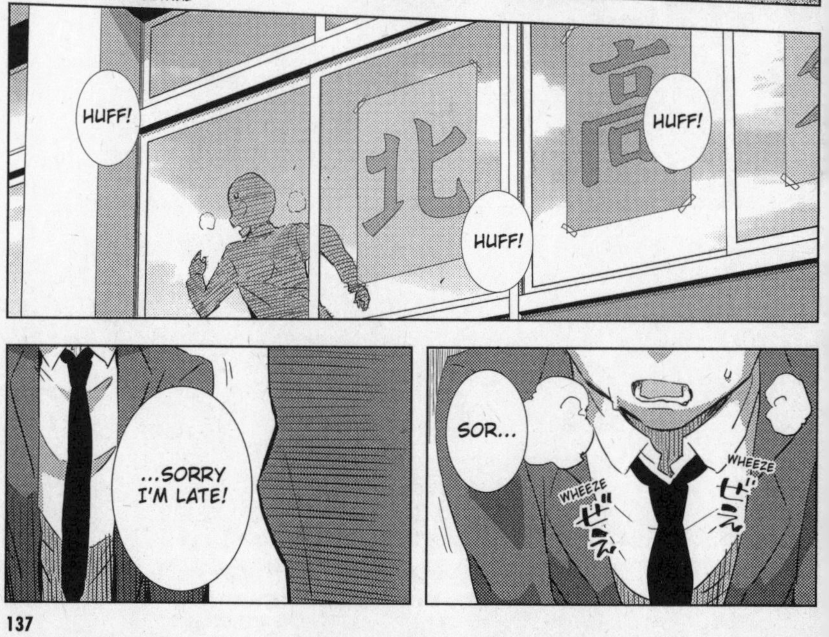
HUFF!
HUFF!
HUFF!
北
高
SOR...
WHEEZE
ゼェ
WHEEZE
ゼェ
...SORRY I'M LATE!

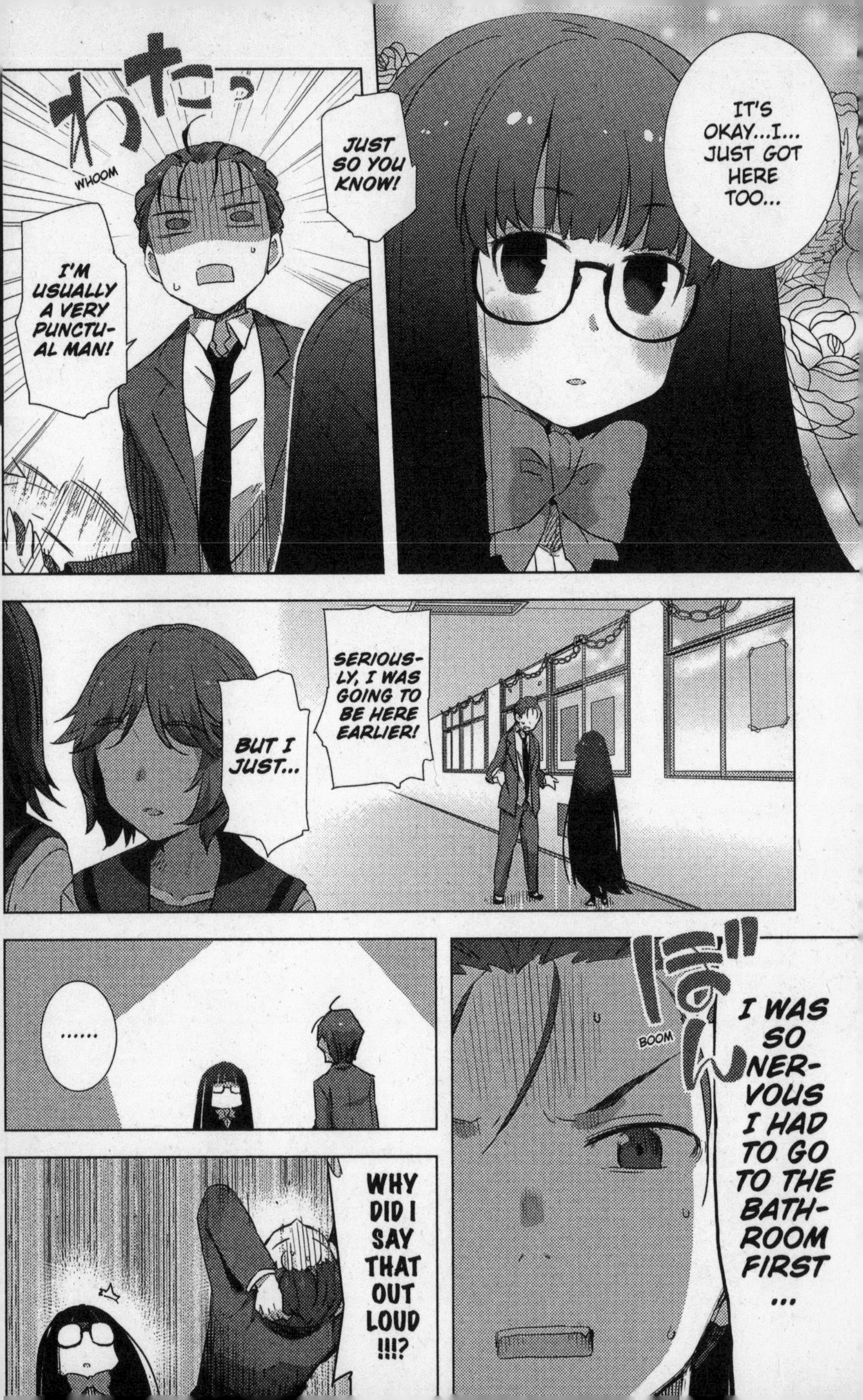

IT'S OKAY...I... JUST GOT HERE TOO...
わたっ
WHOOM
JUST SO YOU KNOW!
I'M USUALLY A VERY PUNCTU-AL MAN!
SERIOUS-LY, I WAS GOING TO BE HERE EARLIER!
BUT I JUST...
どん
BOOM
I WAS SO NER-VOUS I HAD TO GO TO THE BATH-ROOM FIRST...
......
WHY DID I SAY THAT OUT LOUD!!!?

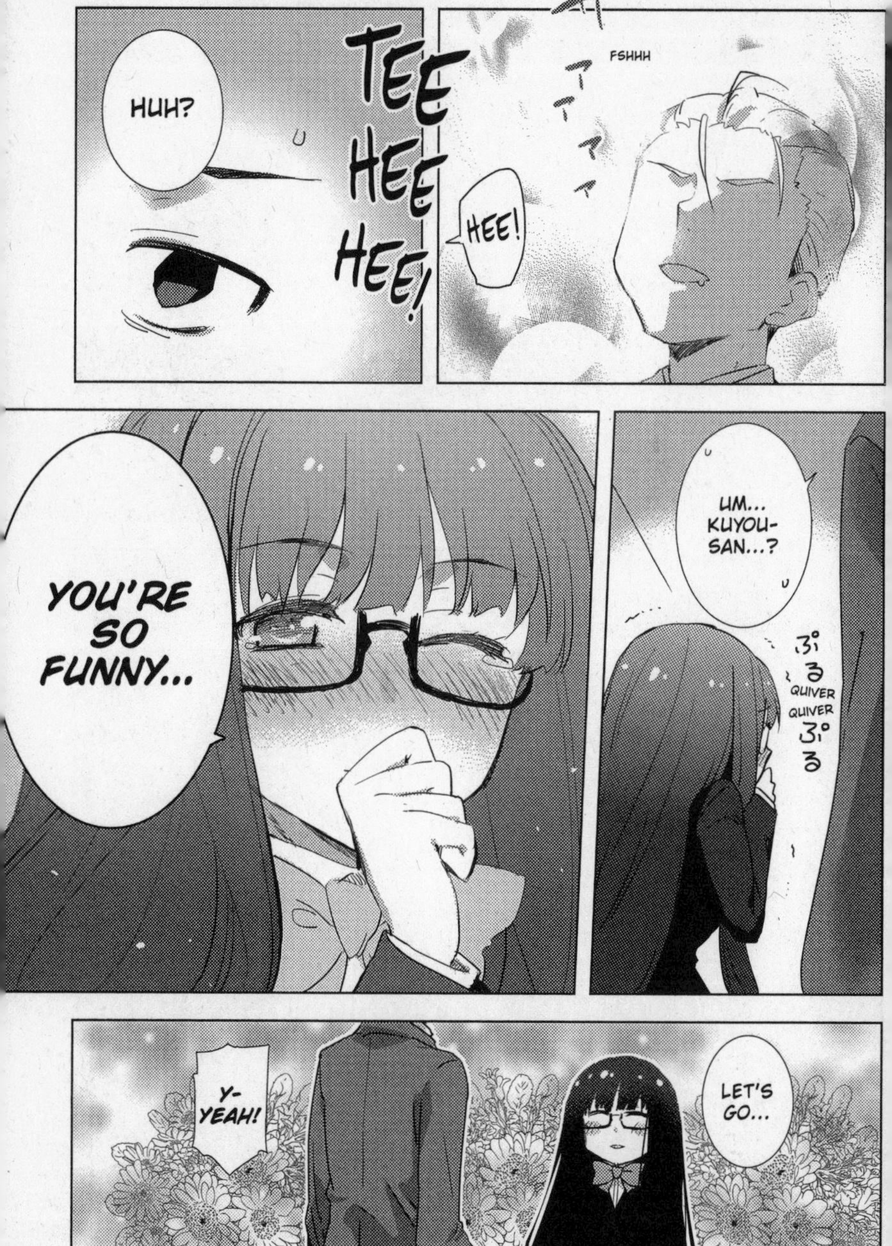
FSHHH
HEE!
TEE HEE HEE!
HUH?
UM... KUYOU-SAN...?
ぷる QUIVER QUIVER ぷる
YOU'RE SO FUNNY...
LET'S GO...
Y-YEAH!

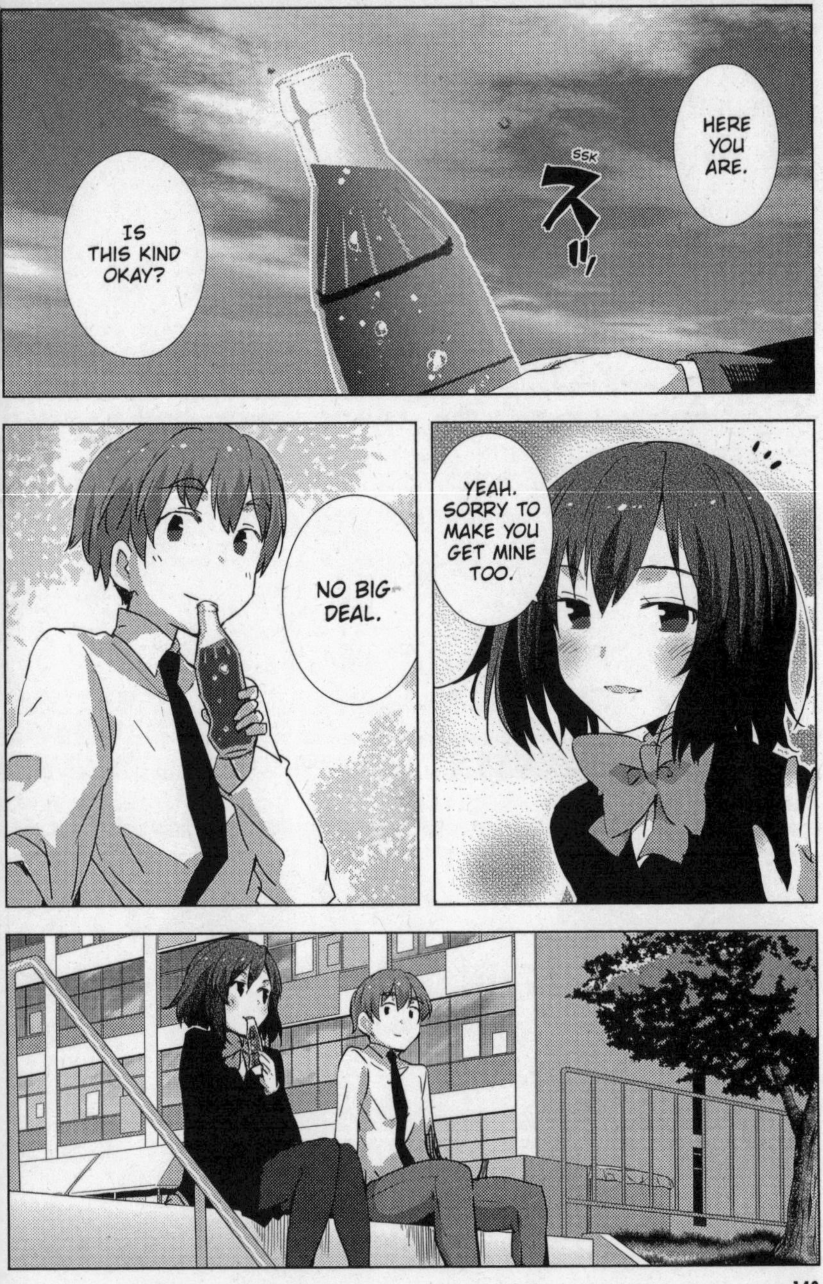
HERE YOU ARE.
SSK
IS THIS KIND OKAY?
YEAH. SORRY TO MAKE YOU GET MINE TOO.
NO BIG DEAL.

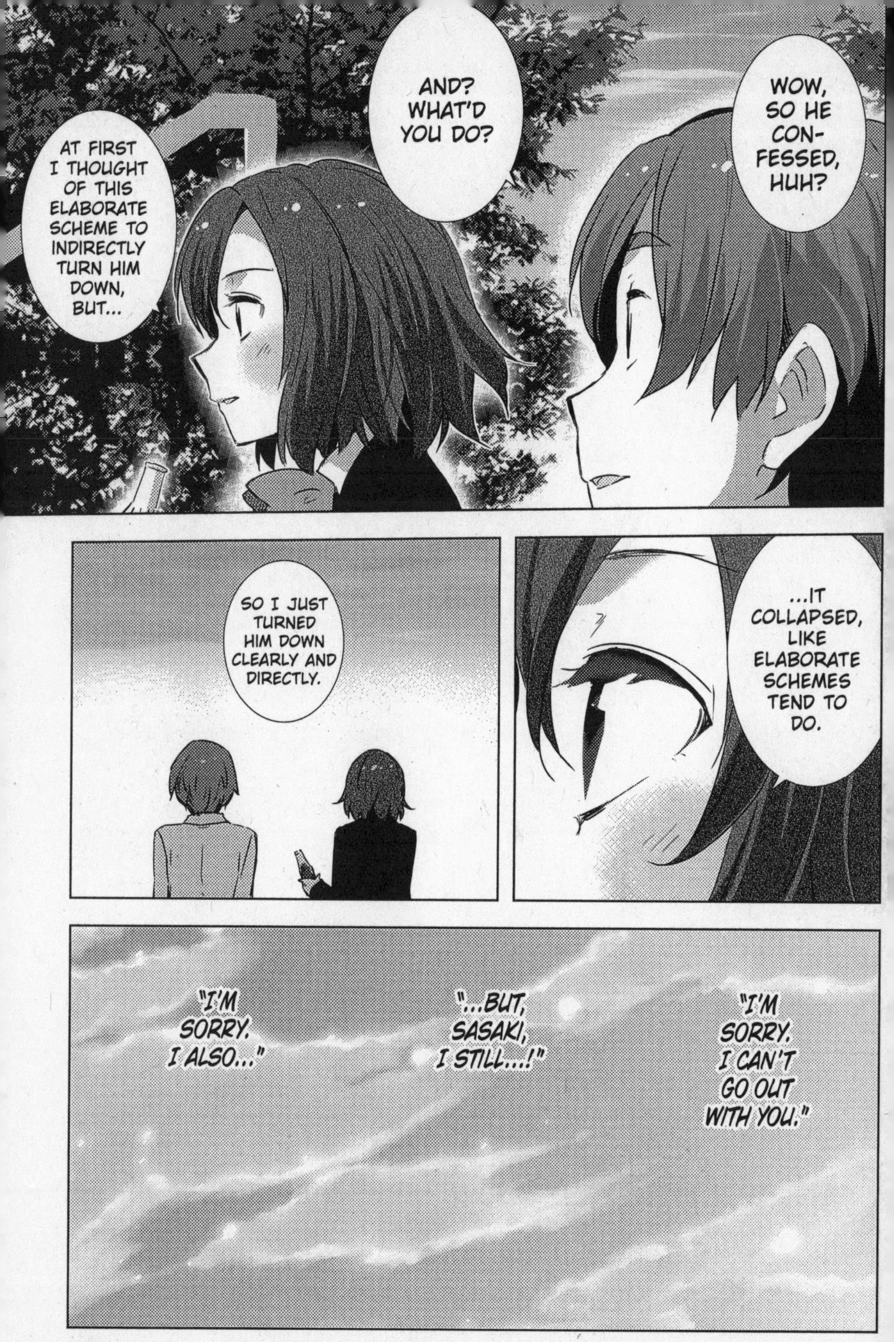
WOW, SO HE CON-FESSED, HUH?
AND? WHAT'D YOU DO?
AT FIRST I THOUGHT OF THIS ELABORATE SCHEME TO INDIRECTLY TURN HIM DOWN, BUT...
...IT COLLAPSED, LIKE ELABORATE SCHEMES TEND TO DO.
SO I JUST TURNED HIM DOWN CLEARLY AND DIRECTLY.
"I'M SORRY. I CAN'T GO OUT WITH YOU."
"...BUT, SASAKI, I STILL...!"
"I'M SORRY. I ALSO..."

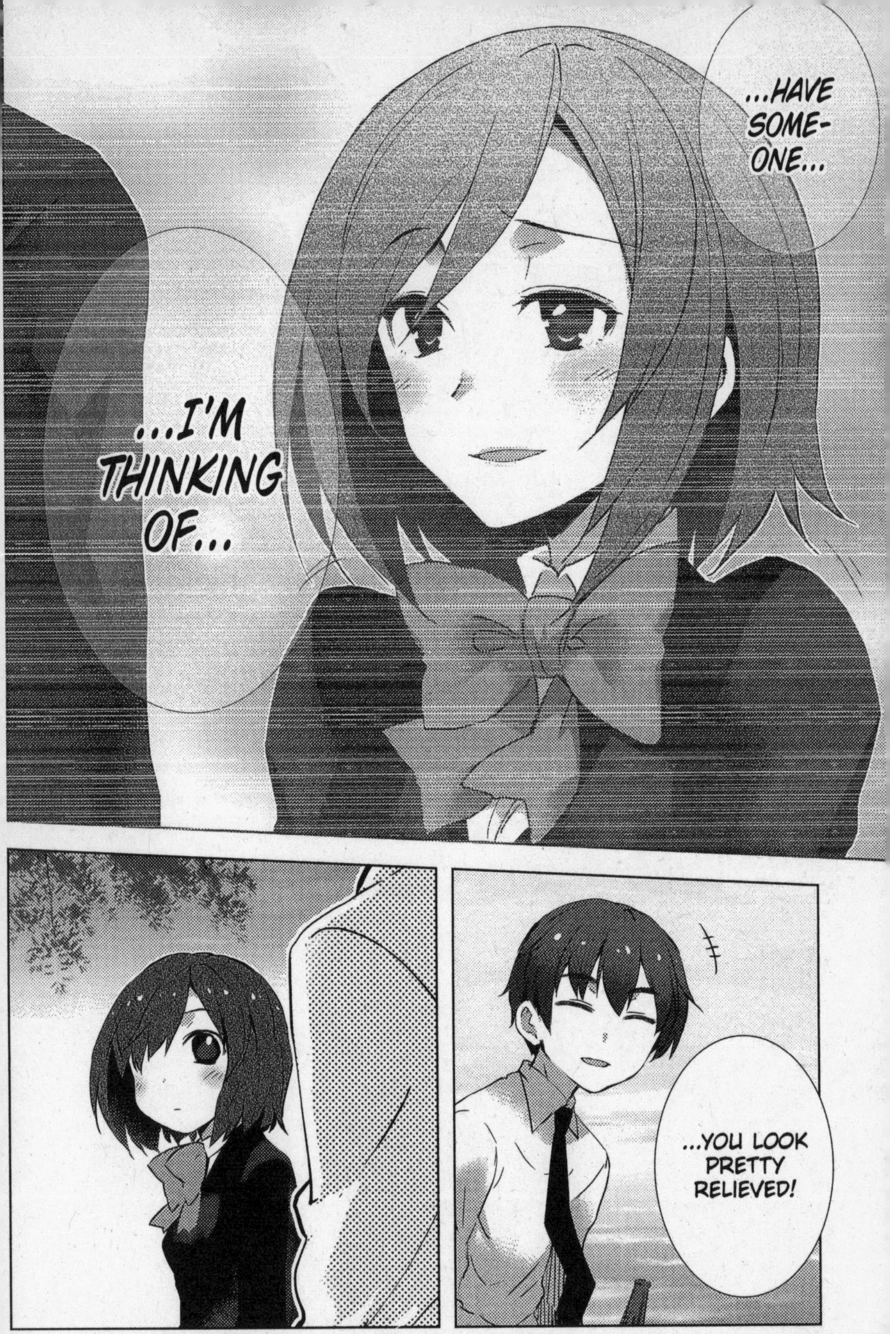
...HAVE SOME-ONE...
...I'M THINKING OF...
...YOU LOOK PRETTY RELIEVED!

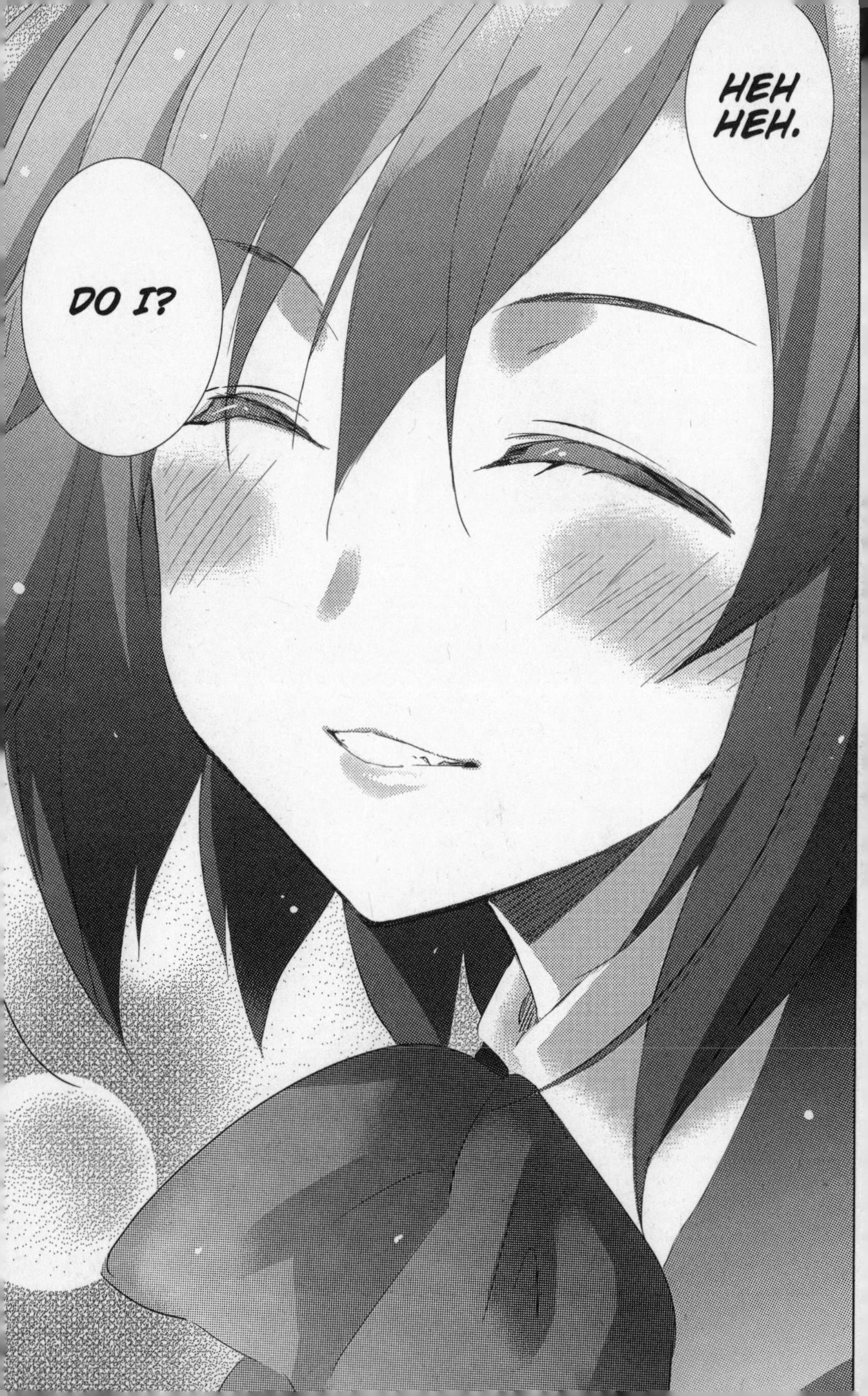
HEH HEH.
DO I?

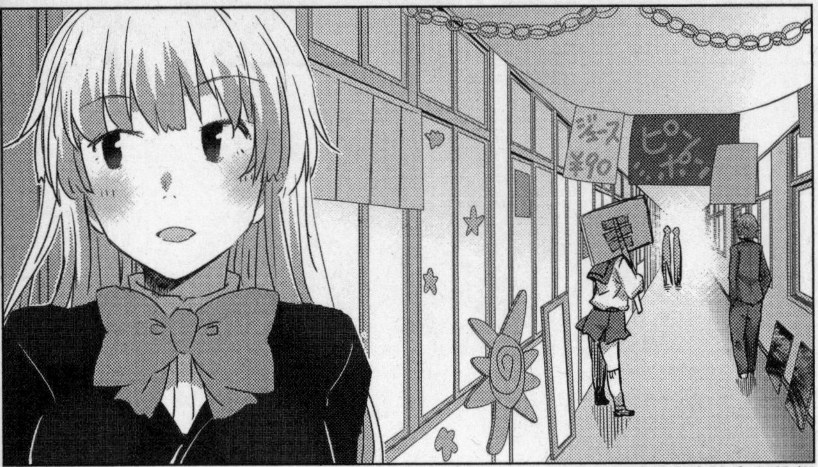
ジュース ¥90
SIGNS: PING-PONG, JUICE ¥90

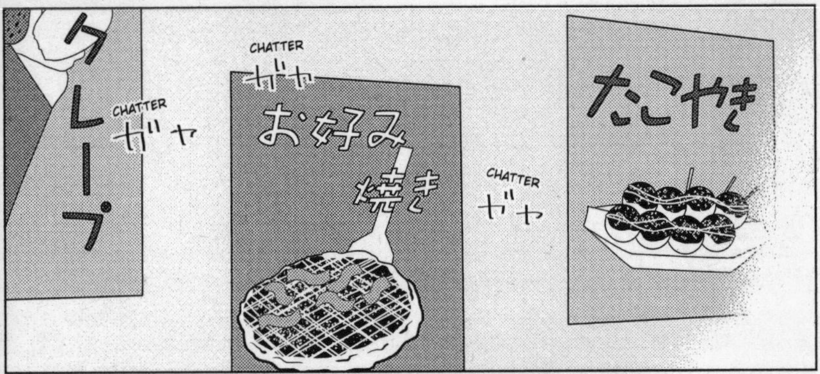
たこやき
CHATTER
ガヤ
CHATTER
ガヤ
お好み焼き
CHATTER
ガヤ
クレープ
SIGNS: CREPES, OKONOMIYAKI, TAKOYAKI

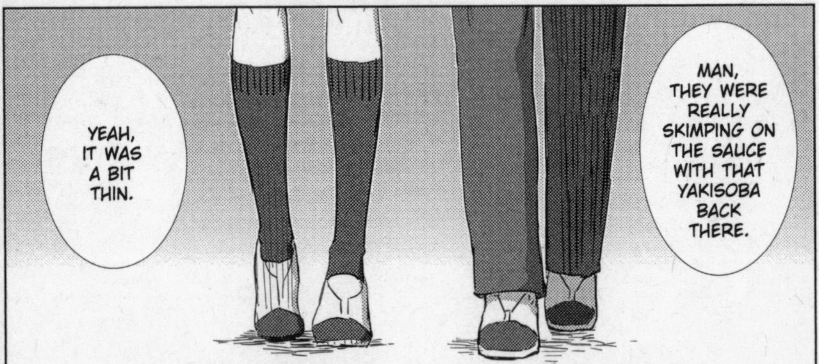
MAN, THEY WERE REALLY SKIMPING ON THE SAUCE WITH THAT YAKISOBA BACK THERE.
YEAH, IT WAS A BIT THIN.

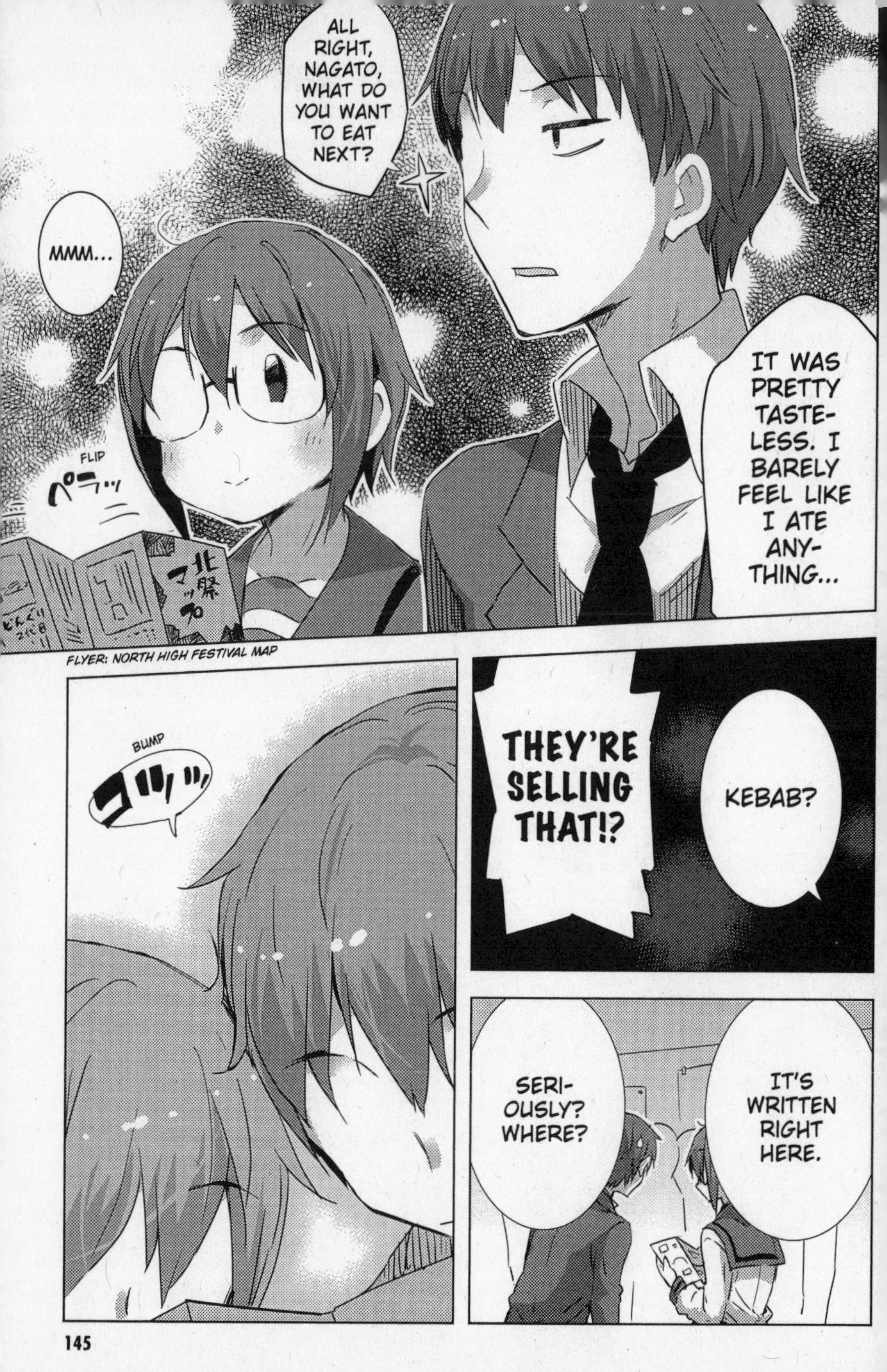
IT WAS PRETTY TASTE-LESS. I BARELY FEEL LIKE I ATE ANY-THING...
ALL RIGHT, NAGATO, WHAT DO YOU WANT TO EAT NEXT?
MMM...
FLIP
パラッ
FLYER: NORTH HIGH FESTIVAL MAP
KEBAB?
THEY'RE SELLING THAT!?
IT'S WRITTEN RIGHT HERE.
SERI-OUSLY? WHERE?
BUMP
ゴツッ

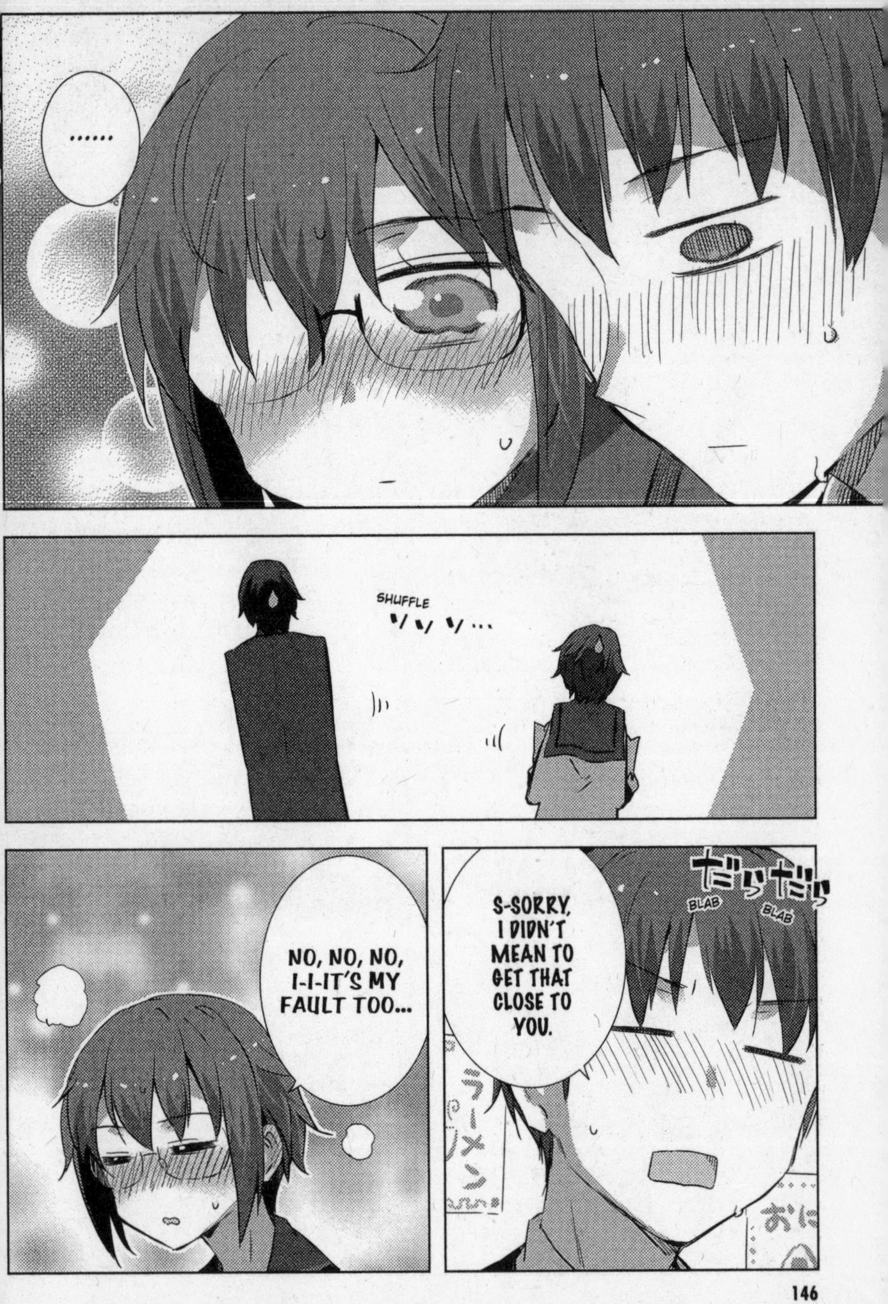
......
SHUFFLE
ソソソ...
だらだら
BLAB BLAB
S-SORRY, I DIDN'T MEAN TO GET THAT CLOSE TO YOU.
ラーメン
NO, NO, NO, I-I-IT'S MY FAULT TOO...

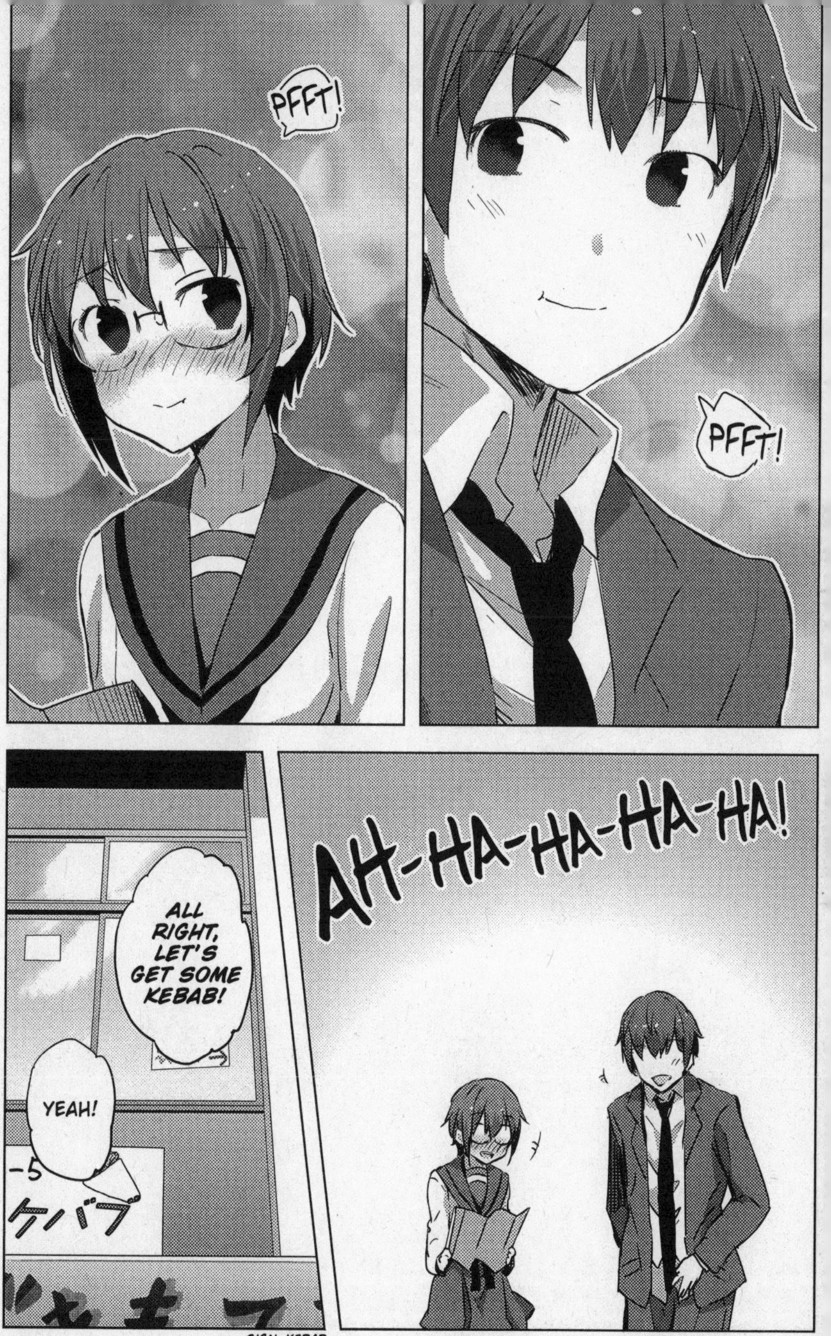
PFFT!
PFFT!
AH-HA-HA-HA-HA!
ALL RIGHT, LET'S GET SOME KEBAB!
YEAH!
ケバブ

SIGN: KEBAB

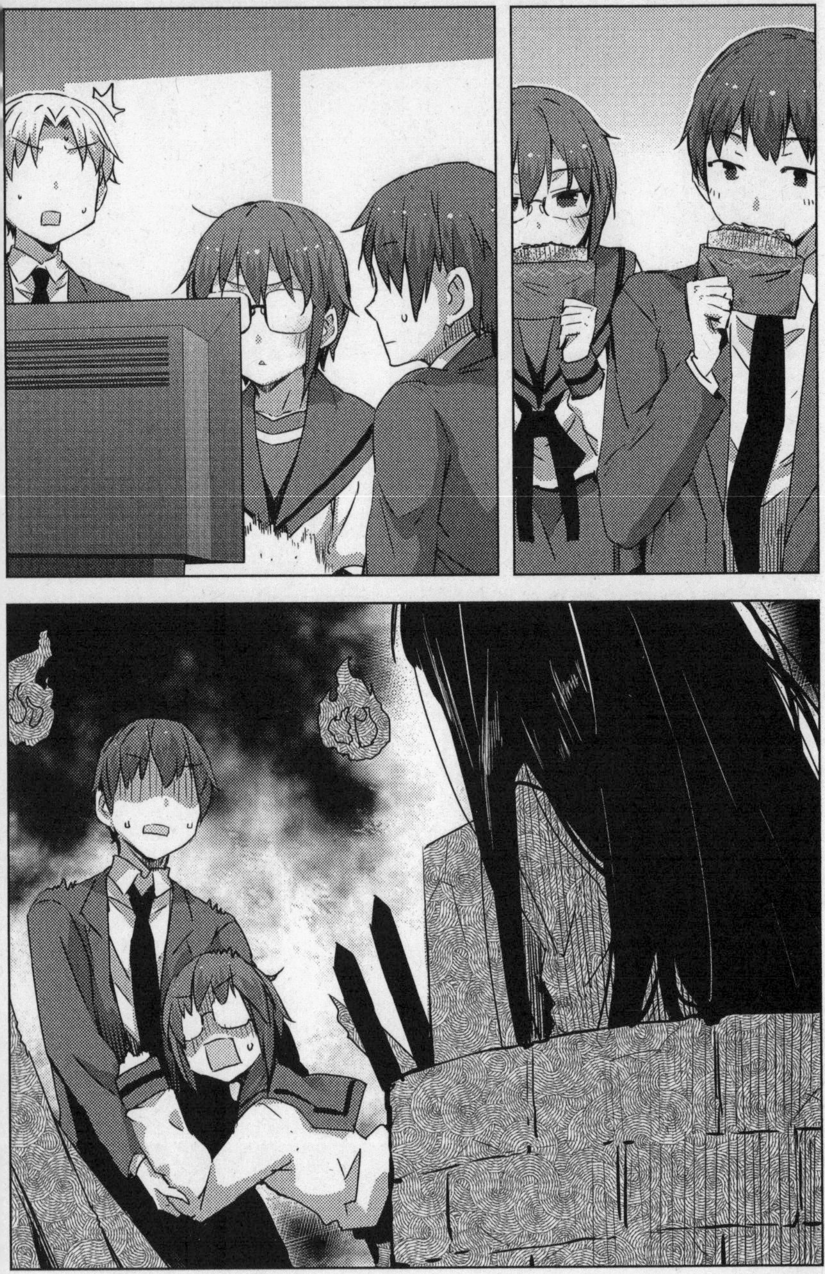

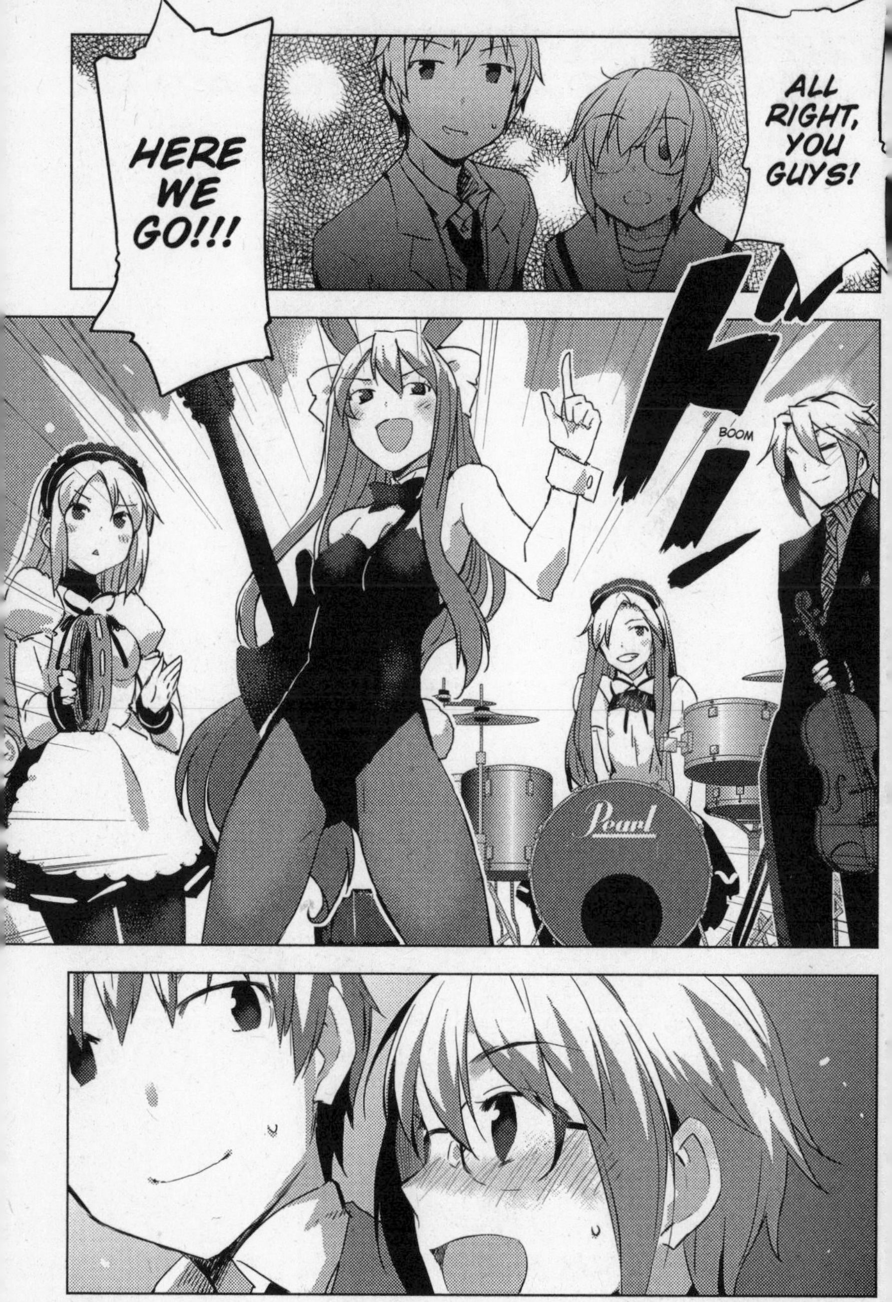
ALL RIGHT, YOU GUYS!
HERE WE GO!!!
BOOM

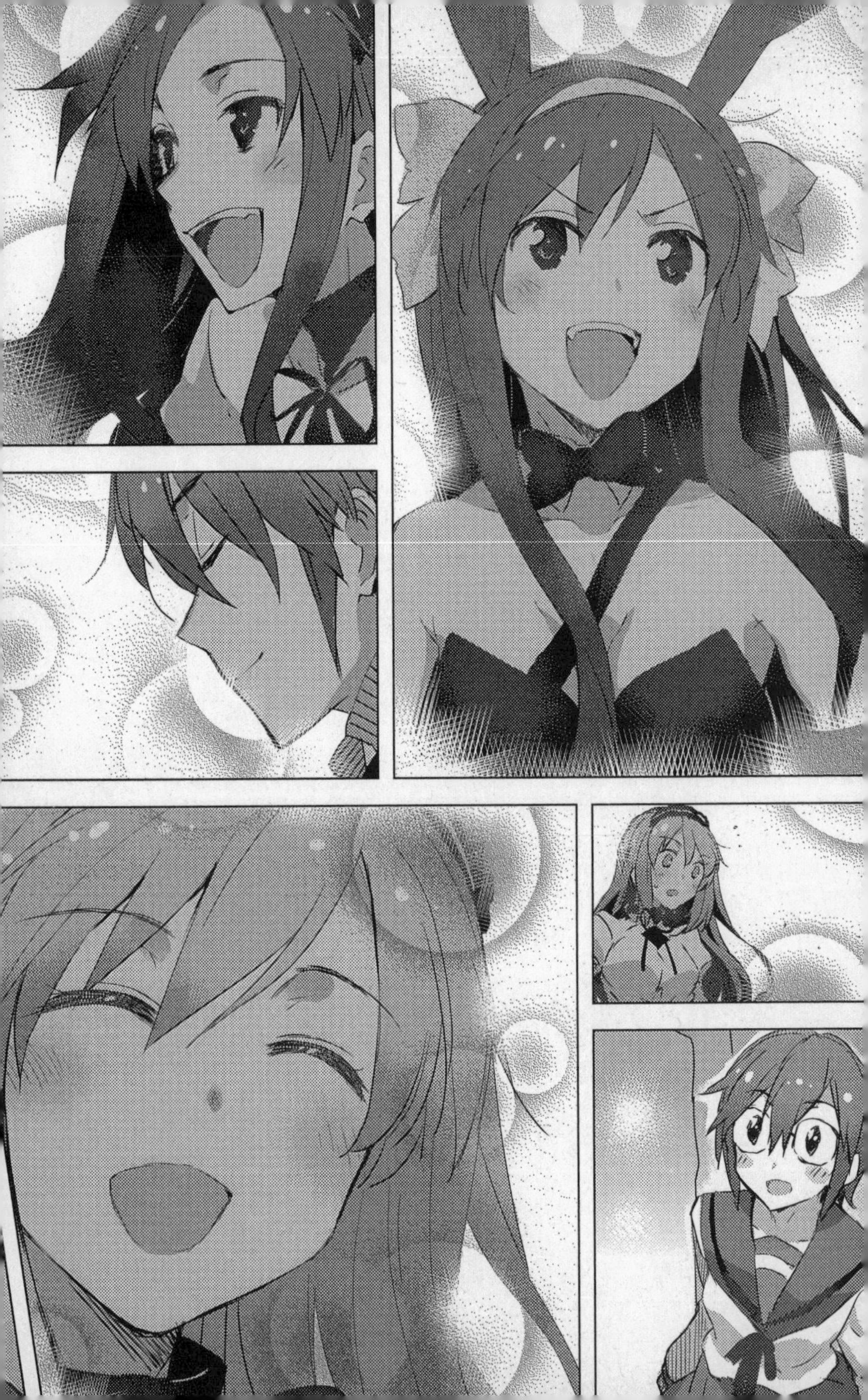

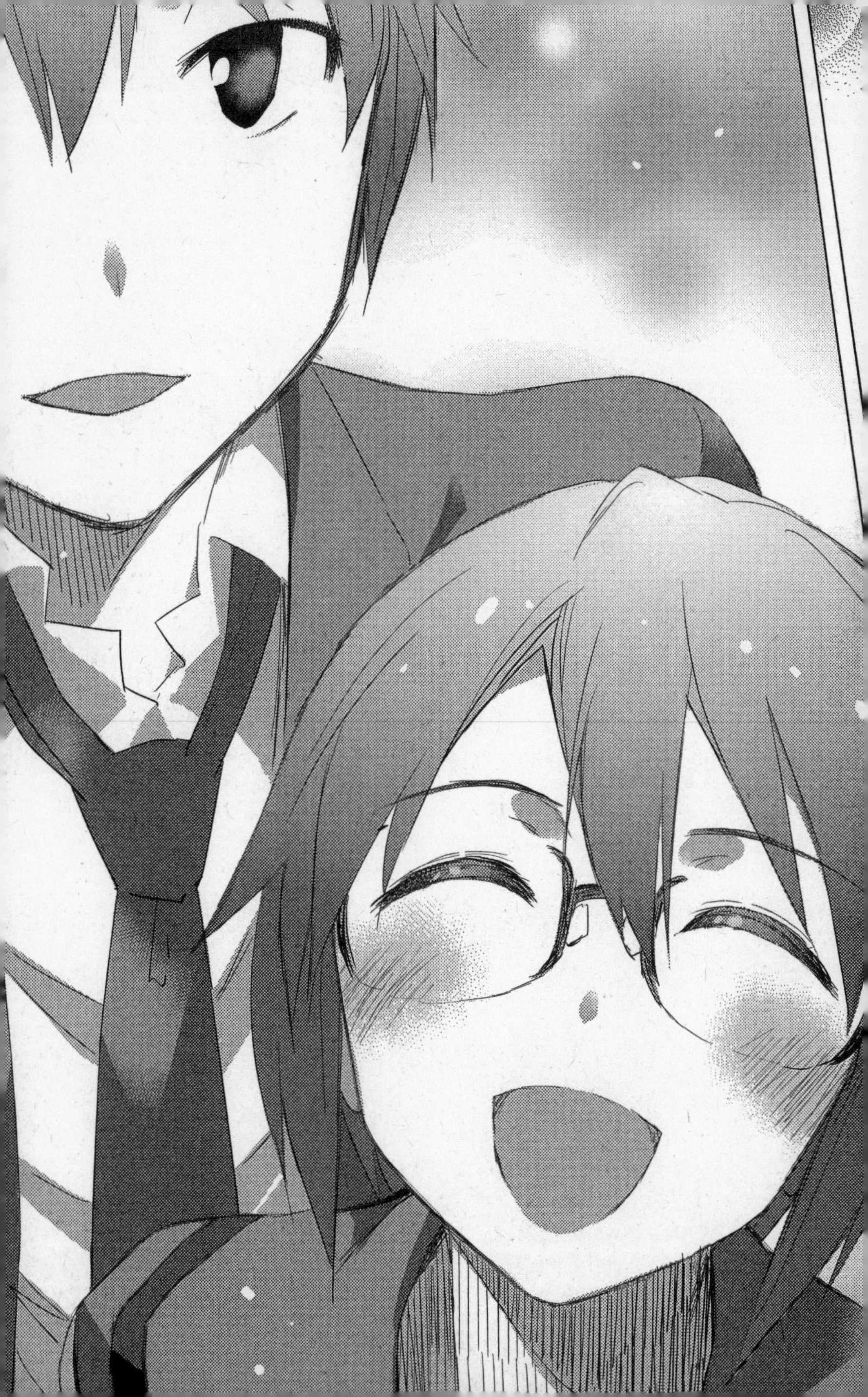

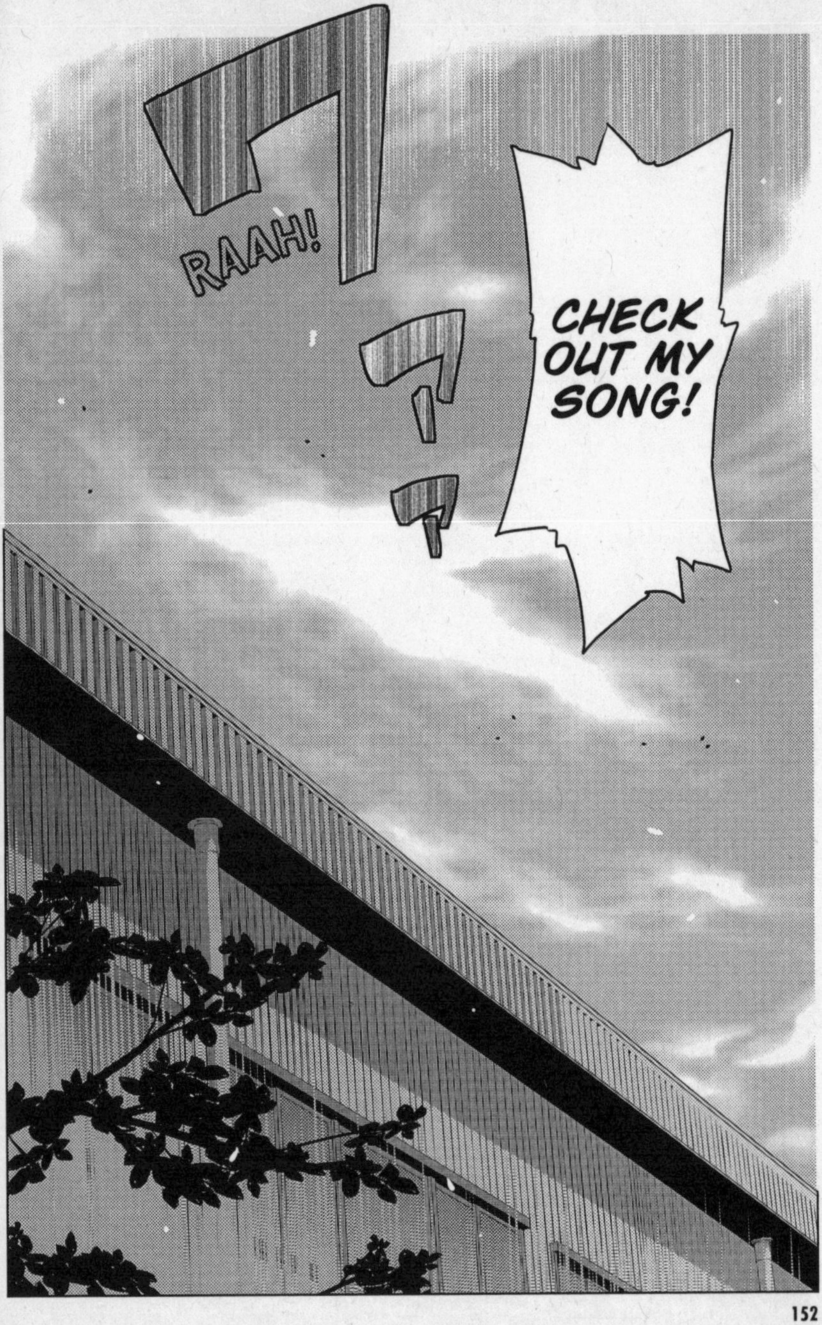
CHECK OUT MY SONG!
RAAH!

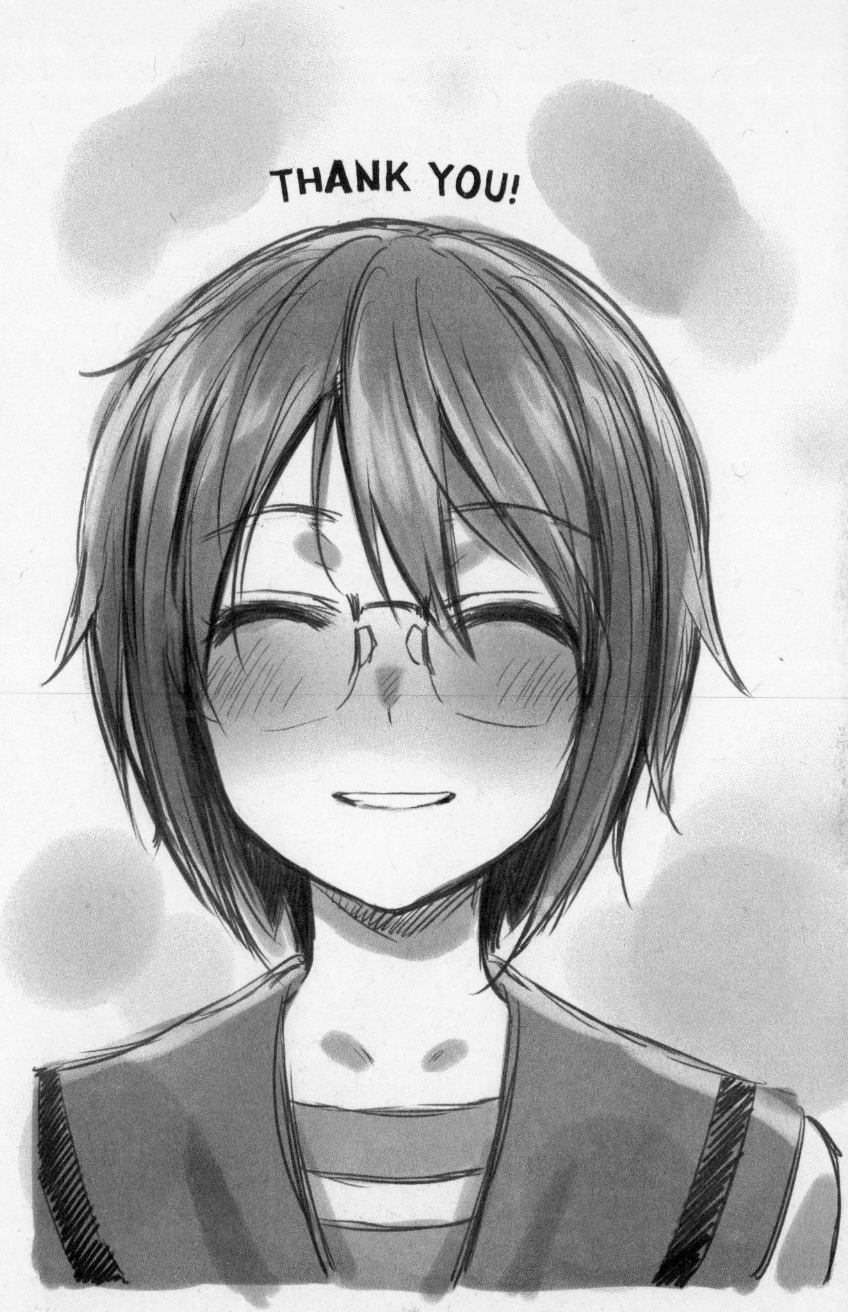
THANK YOU!

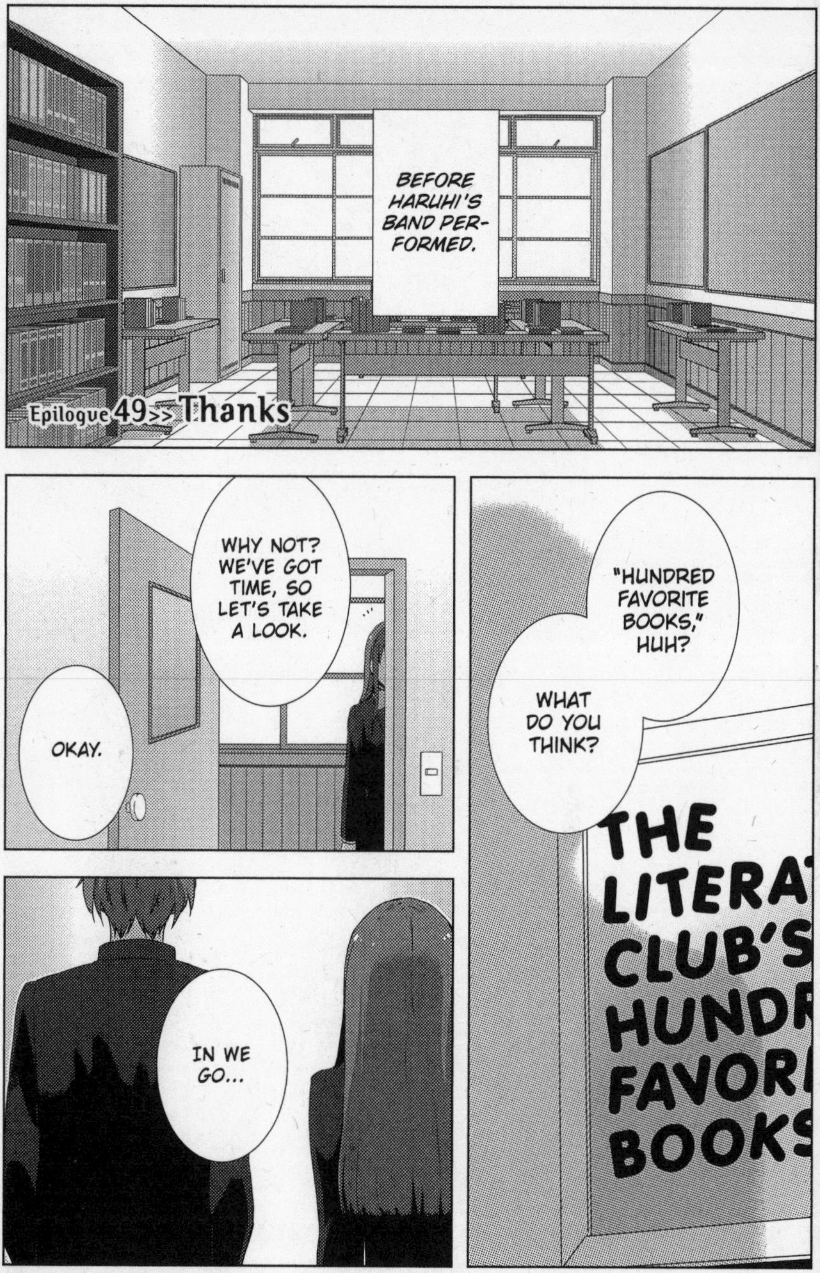
BEFORE HARUHI'S BAND PER-FORMED.
Epilogue 49>> Thanks
"HUNDRED FAVORITE BOOKS," HUH?
WHAT DO YOU THINK?
THE LITERAT CLUB'S HUNDR FAVORI BOOKS
WHY NOT? WE'VE GOT TIME, SO LET'S TAKE A LOOK.
OKAY.
IN WE GO...

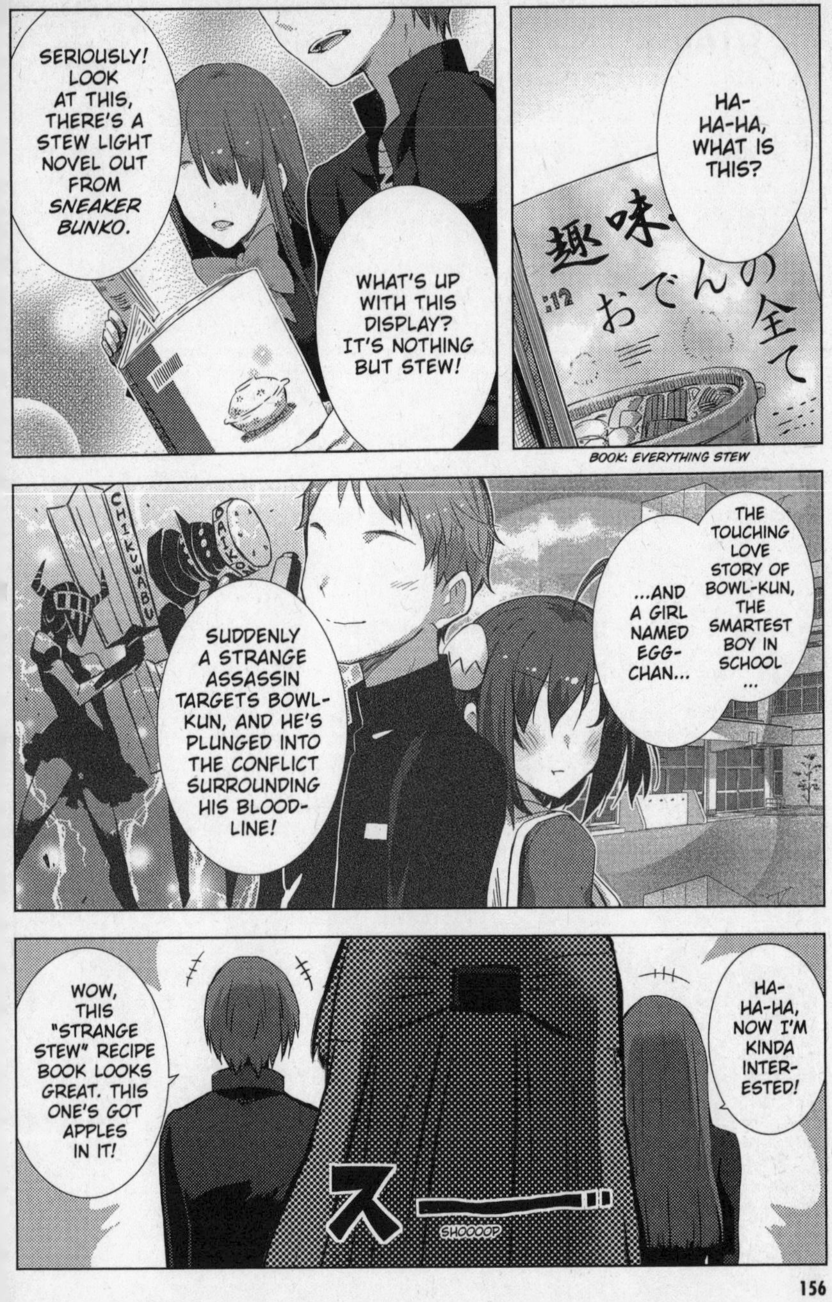
HA-HA-HA, WHAT IS THIS?
趣味・おでんの全て
BOOK: EVERYTHING STEW
WHAT'S UP WITH THIS DISPLAY? IT'S NOTHING BUT STEW!
SERIOUSLY! LOOK AT THIS, THERE'S A STEW LIGHT NOVEL OUT FROM SNEAKER BUNKO.
THE TOUCHING LOVE STORY OF BOWL-KUN, THE SMARTEST BOY IN SCHOOL ...
...AND A GIRL NAMED EGG-CHAN...
DAIKO
CHIKUWABU
SUDDENLY A STRANGE ASSASSIN TARGETS BOWL-KUN, AND HE'S PLUNGED INTO THE CONFLICT SURROUNDING HIS BLOODLINE!
HA-HA-HA, NOW I'M KINDA INTERESTED!
WOW, THIS "STRANGE STEW" RECIPE BOOK LOOKS GREAT. THIS ONE'S GOT APPLES IN IT!
ス―――
SHOOOOP

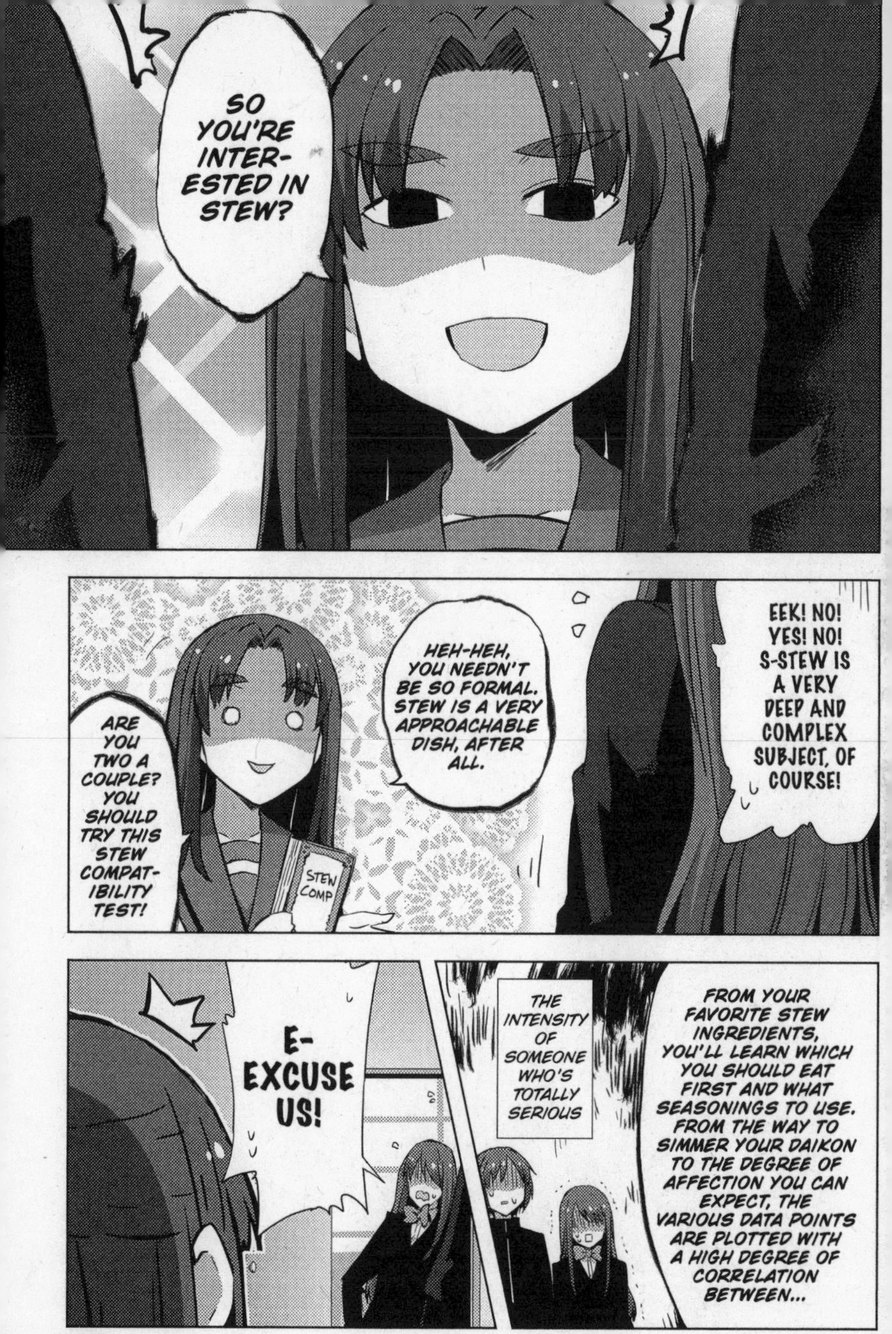
SO YOU'RE INTER-ESTED IN STEW?
EEK! NO! YES! NO! S-STEW IS A VERY DEEP AND COMPLEX SUBJECT, OF COURSE!
HEH-HEH, YOU NEEDN'T BE SO FORMAL. STEW IS A VERY APPROACHABLE DISH, AFTER ALL.
ARE YOU TWO A COUPLE? YOU SHOULD TRY THIS STEW COMPAT-IBILITY TEST!
STEW COMP
FROM YOUR FAVORITE STEW INGREDIENTS, YOU'LL LEARN WHICH YOU SHOULD EAT FIRST AND WHAT SEASONINGS TO USE. FROM THE WAY TO SIMMER YOUR DAIKON TO THE DEGREE OF AFFECTION YOU CAN EXPECT, THE VARIOUS DATA POINTS ARE PLOTTED WITH A HIGH DEGREE OF CORRELATION BETWEEN...
THE INTENSITY OF SOMEONE WHO'S TOTALLY SERIOUS
E-EXCUSE US!

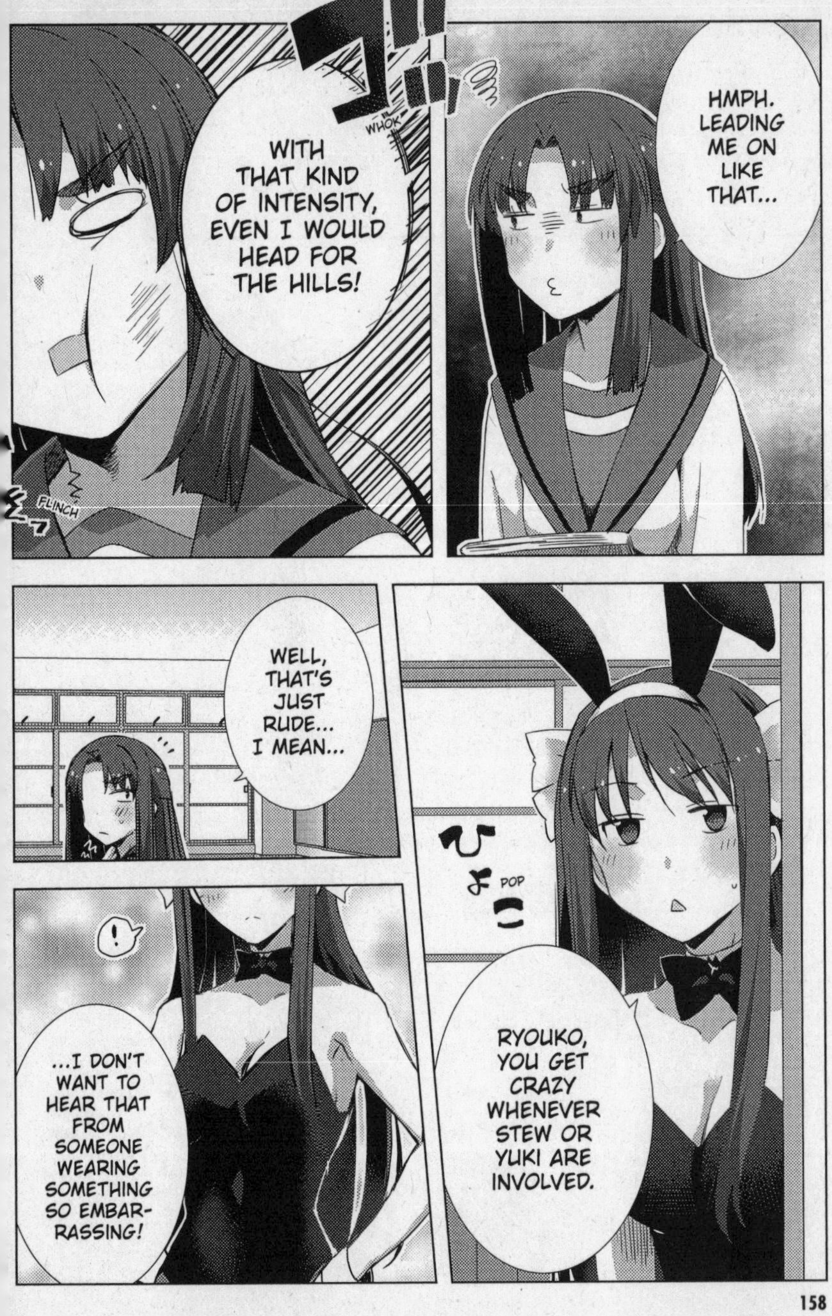
HMPH. LEADING ME ON LIKE THAT...
WHOK
WITH THAT KIND OF INTENSITY, EVEN I WOULD HEAD FOR THE HILLS!
FLINCH
POP
RYOUKO, YOU GET CRAZY WHENEVER STEW OR YUKI ARE INVOLVED.
WELL, THAT'S JUST RUDE... I MEAN...
...I DON'T WANT TO HEAR THAT FROM SOMEONE WEARING SOMETHING SO EMBAR-RASSING!

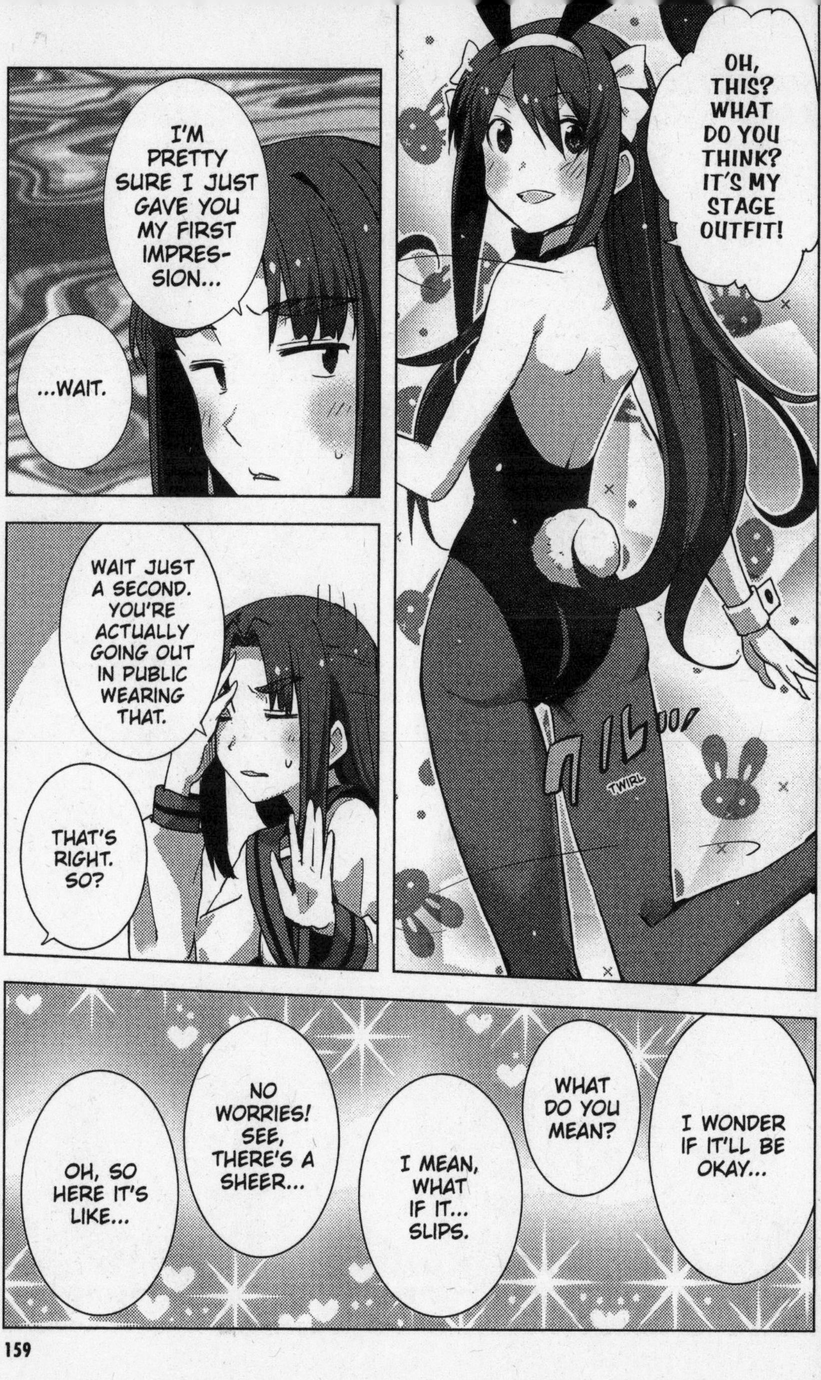
OH, THIS? WHAT DO YOU THINK? IT'S MY STAGE OUTFIT!
TWIRL
I'M PRETTY SURE I JUST GAVE YOU MY FIRST IMPRES-SION...
...WAIT.
WAIT JUST A SECOND. YOU'RE ACTUALLY GOING OUT IN PUBLIC WEARING THAT.
THAT'S RIGHT. SO?
I WONDER IF IT'LL BE OKAY...
WHAT DO YOU MEAN?
I MEAN, WHAT IF IT... SLIPS.
NO WORRIES! SEE, THERE'S A SHEER...
OH, SO HERE IT'S LIKE...

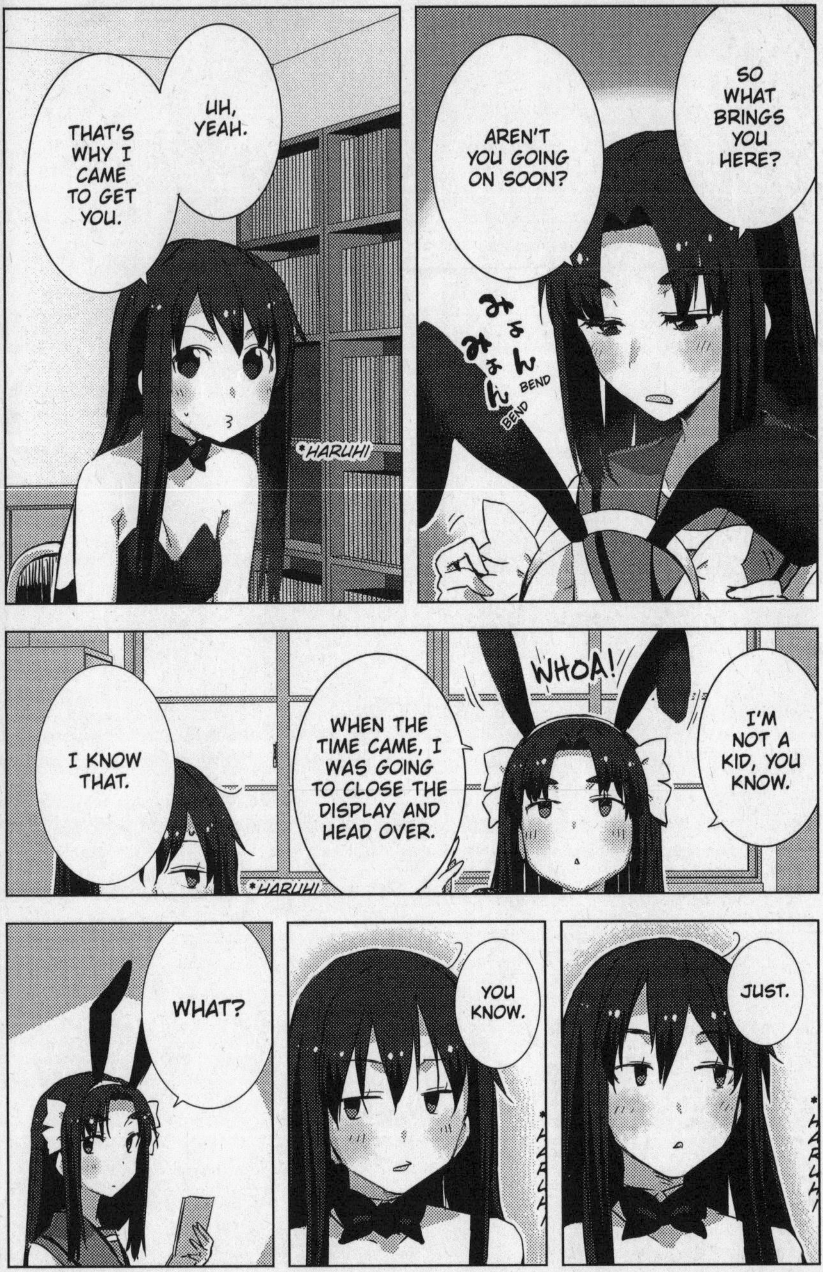
SO WHAT BRINGS YOU HERE?
AREN'T YOU GOING ON SOON?
みょんみょん
BEND
BEND
UH, YEAH.
THAT'S WHY I CAME TO GET YOU.
*HARUHI
WHOA!
I'M NOT A KID, YOU KNOW.
WHEN THE TIME CAME, I WAS GOING TO CLOSE THE DISPLAY AND HEAD OVER.
I KNOW THAT.
*HARUHI
JUST.
*HARUHI
YOU KNOW.
*HARUHI
WHAT?

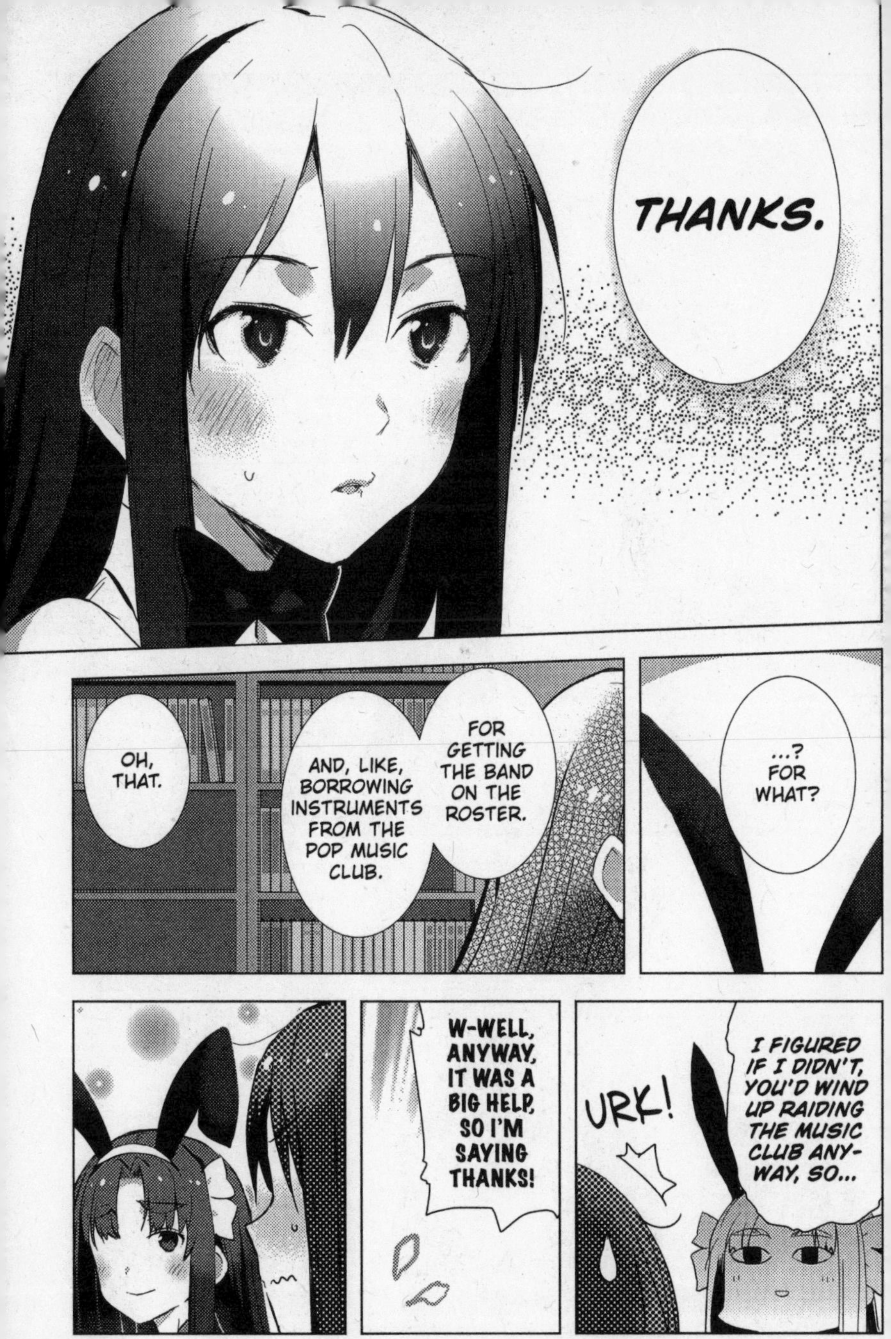
THANKS.
...? FOR WHAT?
FOR GETTING THE BAND ON THE ROSTER.
AND, LIKE, BORROWING INSTRUMENTS FROM THE POP MUSIC CLUB.
OH, THAT.
I FIGURED IF I DIDN'T, YOU'D WIND UP RAIDING THE MUSIC CLUB ANY-WAY, SO...
URK!
W-WELL, ANYWAY, IT WAS A BIG HELP, SO I'M SAYING THANKS!

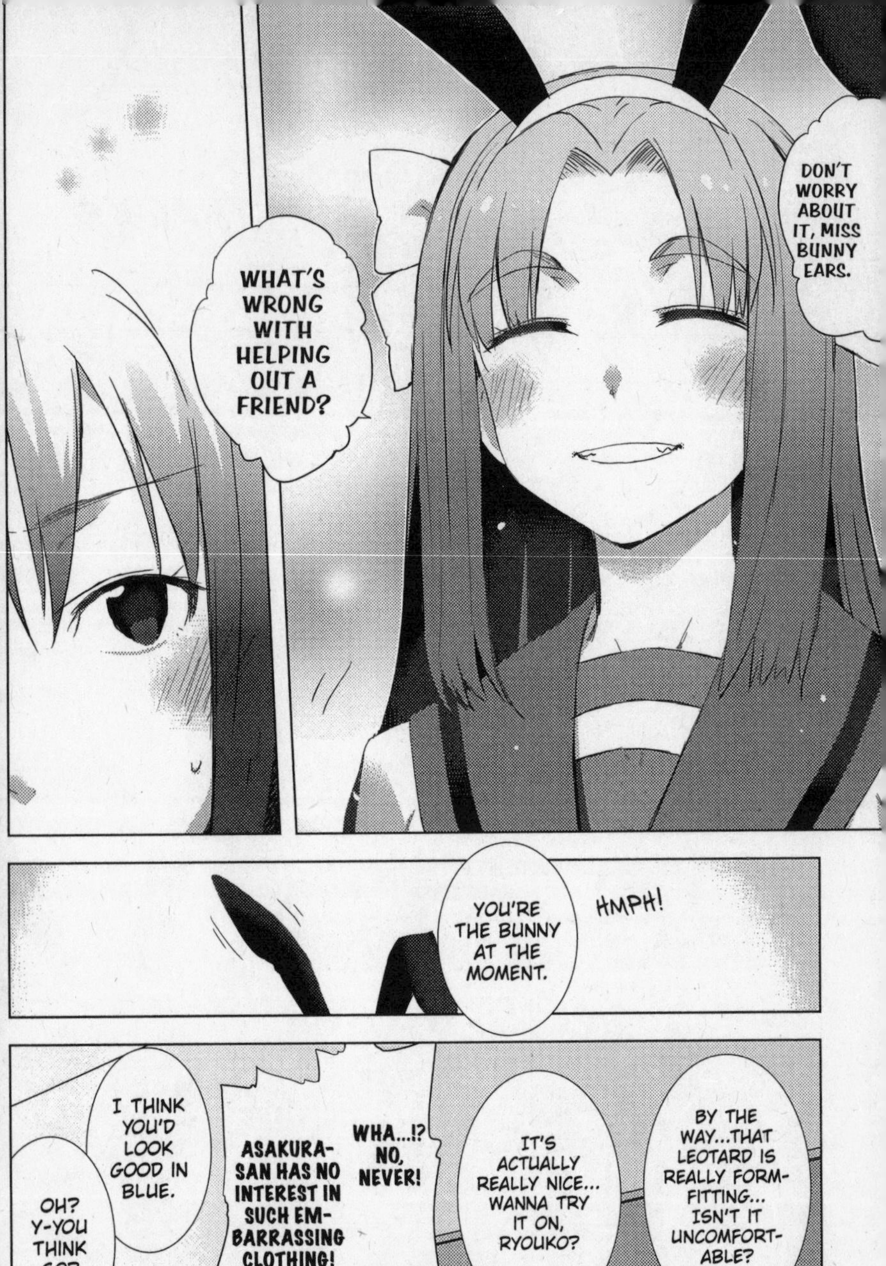
DON'T WORRY ABOUT IT, MISS BUNNY EARS.
WHAT'S WRONG WITH HELPING OUT A FRIEND?
HMPH!
YOU'RE THE BUNNY AT THE MOMENT.
BY THE WAY...THAT LEOTARD IS REALLY FORM-FITTING... ISN'T IT UNCOMFORT-ABLE?
IT'S ACTUALLY REALLY NICE... WANNA TRY IT ON, RYOUKO?
WHA...!? NO, NEVER!
ASAKURA-SAN HAS NO INTEREST IN SUCH EM-BARRASSING CLOTHING!
I THINK YOU'D LOOK GOOD IN BLUE.
OH? Y-YOU THINK SO?

THE NEXT VOLUME IS
THE CHRISTMAS ARC!

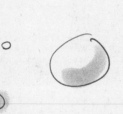

THE DISAPPEARANCE OF NAGATO
YUKI-CHAN
❻

Original Story: Nagaru Tanigawa
Manga: PUYO
Character Design: Noizi Ito

Translation: Paul Starr
Lettering: Abigail Blackman

NAGATO YUKI CHAN NO SHOSHITSU Volume 6 © Nagaru TANIGAWA • Noizi ITO 2013 © PUYO 2013. Edited by KADOKAWA SHOTEN. First published in Japan in 2013 by KADOKAWA CORPORATION, Tokyo. English translation rights arranged with KADOKAWA CORPORATION, Tokyo, through TUTTLE-MORI AGENCY, INC., Tokyo.

English translation © 2014 by Hachette Book Group, Inc.

Yen Press
Hachette Book Group
237 Park Avenue, New York, NY 10017

www.HachetteBookGroup.com
www.YenPress.com

Yen Press is an imprint of Hachette Book Group, Inc.
The Yen Press name and logo are trademarks of Hachette Book Group, Inc.

First Yen Press Edition: September 2014

ISBN: 978-0-316-33607-9

10 9 8 7 6 5 4 3 2 1

BVG

Printed in the United States of America